THE BANQUET BUSINESS

Third Edition

Arno Schmidt

CHIPS BOOKS

THE BANQUET BUSINESS
Third Edition
by Arno Schmidt

Cover photograph courtesy
Chair Covers & Linens, Inc.
25914 John R Road
Madison Heights, Michigan 48071
U.S.A.

Printed in the United States of America
by Integrated Book Technology, Inc.

CHIPS BOOKS
10777 Mazoch Road
Weimar, Texas 78962
U.S.A.

www.chipsbooks.com

Cataloguing Data:

Author: Schmidt, Arno

Title: The Banquet Business
           Third Edition

Subject: Banquets and Catering:
           Planning, Operations, and Management
           Menu Writing
           Menu Planning and Design

ISBN: 0-9669712-5-6

TABLE OF CONTENTS

Chapter Seven
BEVERAGE SALES AND SERVICE   **139**

Chapter Eight
SERVICE   **161**

Chapter Nine

THE CHEF AND THE STEWARD: Two Vital Roles 185

Chapter Ten

BASIC RULES OF MENU CONSTRUCTION 213

Preface

The second edition of *The Banquet Business* was published 1990 and I made already numerous references to computers. Today practically all banquet offices are fully computerized and booking banquets is to a large extent handled by computers. Communicating with clients as well as within the hotel is often by e-mail.

Proprietary software used by hotel companies link the sleeping room inventory with catering space, creating a comprehensive guest portfolio from the moment of the first telephone call or inquiry. There are also many generic catering programs available off the shelf, priced from hundreds to thousands of Dollars. All programs require perseverance, and time consuming learning. Every upgrade or switch to a different program necessitates tedious unlearning.

The computer industry is still in its infancy; it took the railroad industry a number of decades to settle on a standard track gauge and to agree on time zones. Unfortunately computers still crash with frightening frequency. Programs inform without apology *"The program has performed an illegal operation and will be shut down"*.

Virtual Reality in the catering business still means putting the right food on the table at the time when ordered even under challenging circumstances. We cannot go to the bride during a wedding and declare, " *A fatal exception occurred in module 000387692 and your program will be shut down"*. Most catering places wisely have paper records to guard against these unpleasant surprises.

During the last decade many new ingredients have become available. Who would have thought that *Lemongrass* and *Chanterelle Mushrooms, Soba Noodles* and fresh *Foie Gras* would be universally accessible? Along with different ingredients came imagination. There are many young women and men in the catering field brimming with new ideas. Fortunately along with the new generation of chefs came customers willing to try *Gnocchi* and *Sesame Oil, Skate Wings,* and *Ostrich Meat.*

Years ago most banquet menus in fine hotels were custom made, tailored to the budget and anticipation of the specific group. Customizing menus also provided an opportunity to upgrade the menu and hence the check. Today most operations create a list of menu choices, store them in the computer and deviations are not encouraged. Apparently computerization made customizing menus no longer practical.

Just about all menus in the third edition are new. They come from many parts of the country and from a wide range of hotels and catering places. I had to sort through many menus to find interesting ones for this edition. It does not require much knowledge to hand customers a folder with menu choices and, once selected the software will handle the rest. One of my colleagues in a luxury hotel told me that custom menus are a problem and management actively discourages them. It is obviously much easier strike a key and the menu will be printed and a few more keystrokes will print the quantities, recipes, and the order list.

Granted, there are only few animals and meat cuts acceptable at banquets but at a time when restaurants experiment with exciting new food, banquet menus overall have become rather boring. Much credit goes to the people who created the occasionally daring and attractive menus included in this edition. I still stubbornly elaborate in this book how to evaluate customers' expectations and create menus that are exiting, practical, satisfactory and perhaps generate better revenue. Conceivably customers will demand in the future more exciting menus than the bland all-purpose banquet menus.

Just about all menus had to be edited for spelling, style, and choice of words. Apparently the industry does not care enough. Even menus printed on expensive stock and intended to be sent to corporate clients had to be corrected. The misuse of menu terms and indiscriminate sprinkling of the menu with French words to make it more impressive are still going on.

There is a spelling program available called **Menuspell**© with 27,000 menu terms on a disk.

Ten years ago the Internet was created and it provides amazing access to information and dazzling marketing opportunities. Much information can be accessed through chat rooms and there is no limit to the ideas and knowledge the Internet will provide in the future. E-mail makes communicating with clients and within the organization instantaneous.

The hospitality industry still offers unlimited opportunities and specifically the catering market is bound to expand. As more people work away from home, meetings and workshops will become more frequent all requiring food service. The size of private homes is growing leading to increased opportunities for social catering. The profitability of many hotels is contingent on group meetings and conventions necessitating upgrading meeting rooms and function space.

The future is promising and I hope this book will prepare the readers to meet the challenges ahead.

Good luck!

Arno Schmidt, New York, January 2001

Acknowledgments

When the second edition of *The Banquet Business* reached the market I started planning the third edition. Again I had the input from many colleagues and friends who shared banquet menus and kept me updated on the technological advances taking place. I am indebted to all of them.

I was asked by New York University to teach a series of certificate courses about banquet management and I gained a new perspective on the business from the mostly young people in my class. We used the second edition of *The Banquet Business* as the textbook and their comments helped me to revise this edition.

My consulting practice gives me insight into many operations ranging from hotels to conference centers. Semi retirement allows me to travel to conventions overseas and within the United States. I also have more time than previously to attend dinners given by gourmet societies and by the Culinary Institute of America in Hyde Park, New York and in St. Helena, California.

My publisher for many years, Van Nostrand Reinhold, part of Thompson Publishing Company discontinued hospitality books and merged the division with John Wiley and Sons. I found myself without a publisher after a long relationship and I am indebted to Janet and Harry Noe of CHIPS BOOKS who encouraged me to publish this edition with them.

I must give credit to the computer industry. The second edition was already written on a word processor and I was able to coax my present machine to read the material. Although I spent an exorbitant amount of time re-formatting the material I still saved myself much typing.

Last but not least I thank my wife Margaret for her patience allowing me to bring menus home after every dinner and to spend much time updating this book.

****

CHIPS BOOKS would like to thank Todd Lloyd of Chair Covers & Linens, Inc. for providing us with a fabulous cover photo of one of their banquet events.

Chapter One

INTRODUCTION TO THE BANQUET BUSINESS

All American Dinner

Assorted Appetizers:

**Cheeses and Vegetarian Spreads with Toasted Flatbread
Artisan Breads**
(Wisconsin/Vermont)
Chateau Elan Viognier 1997 – Georgia
Mirabelle Brut NV – California

****

Deviled Crab
(Maryland)
Fortis Pinot Gris 1997 – Oregon
Fortis Pinot Blanc Rogue Valley 1997 – Oregon

****

Grilled Tomato Soup with Avocado, Okra, Corn & Roe
(Florida/New York)
Bookwalter Chardonnay Columbia Valley 1997 – Washington

****

Grilled Venison in Cabernet Sauce (Ohio)
Grilled Pork Loin Medallions (Arkansas)
Pistachio Pesto Pasta (California)
Asparagus and Zucchini Wraps (Michigan)
Terra Rosa Laurel Glen Cabernet Sauvignon 1992 and 1994 – California
Marietta Zinfandel Sonoma Valley 1996 – California

****

Bananas Foster (Louisiana)
Linden Late Harvest Vidal 1997 – Virginia
Quady Orange Muscat 1997 – California

****

Red Wine Sampling

Dry Creek Meritage Dry Creek Valley 1987 – California
Dry Creek Meritage Dry Creek Valley 1991 – California
Stag's Leap Cabernet Napa Valley 1992 – California
Silverado Sangiovese Napa Valley 1995 – California

Chapter One
INTRODUCTION TO THE BANQUET BUSINESS

Objectives

- To provide a short overview of the banquet business and its importance today.

- To understand the various segments of the banquet business, from hotel catering to off-premise catering. To know the challenges and opportunities available from different types of catering.

Introduction

Since antiquity people have celebrated feasts by eating and drinking together. Almost all religions have a special reference for food, and history books mention famous feasts held over the centuries. The roman era was famous for bacchanalian parties, and during the medieval ages coronations and royal weddings were often celebrated by huge feasts, in which the population of whole towns participated.

Large parties are also held today which command plenty of attention and publicity. Eating together with friends or strangers for social or other reasons is part of our life. Taking care of this endeavor has become big business.

The Scope of the Business

The banquet business is often referred to as catering business, and it is difficult to make a precise distinction between the two. The traditional meaning of the banquet business is providing food and beverages to a group of people, who will eat together at the same time. The catering business has a wider scope, and means providing food and beverages to people who do not necessarily eat at the same time, and in many cases not at the location where the caterer is located. In this book, the terms banquet business and catering business are used interchangeably.

Banquet business can be lucrative business. In some large convention hotels, banquet food and beverage revenue represents 70% and more of the combined food and beverage revenue from all other outlets such as restaurants, room service and bars. The banquet business can be a relatively risk free business. When a group of guests is attending an event with a prearranged menu in a specific banquet room, when the number of people attending is guaranteed, and the bill paid in advance, the banquet business is good business; providing the rates charged are adequate to pay for the services provided.

Banquet revenues can be huge. A single dinner party of 500 guests, in a medium sized ballroom can produce more revenue than can be generated in several days by a restaurant with 80 seats. For example, if the charge per guest attending the banquet is $80.00, the gross revenue generated by a single party in one night is $40,000.00. Most successful white tablecloth restaurants can accommodate only 1½ seat turnover per night, and in many cases less. If the average check per person is the same as in the ballroom, the maximum restaurant revenue for one evening is only $9,600.00. It would take the restaurant more than four days to produce the revenue generated in one evening in a ballroom. In addition, the direct costs of material and labor per attending guest are lower in the banquet room than in a corresponding restaurant situation.

Because of the potentially huge profits, the banquet business has become very competitive. Hotels are competing for banquet business not only against other hotels, but also against caterers. Off-premise caterers provide full service for parties at other locations, such as private homes, public areas, in museums and corporate buildings. Often, hotel banquet rooms can only be filled with convention business and trade shows. Country clubs and city clubs also compete for social business. Many social functions also take place in church auditoriums and temples.

Banquets held on premise must be profitable to warrant the investment in space that is valuable real estate. It is unfair to compare banquet space occupancy to sleeping room occupancy, but the relatively low occupancy rate of banquet space is the main reason why meals served in banquet rooms cost more than comparable meals served in restaurants. Even in busy banquet operations, the space is idle much of the time. If banquet space does not render a reasonable return, it could be converted into other uses such as office, retail or apartment space.

Available banquet space is vital when booking conventions and business meetings. It is a huge business and even outstanding luxury properties book conventions as long as there are space and room revenues. It is therefore not fair to judge banquet space as a freestanding investment but rather as an integral part of attracting room revenue.

Off-premise catering carries other expenses and risks, such as staffing problems, transportation, low equipment utilization and down time.

Types of Banquet Business

The banquet business can be classified as:

- In-house catering, both social and commercial.
  This includes conventions, trade show and meeting business.

- Off-premise catering.

In-House Catering

Functions that take place in hotels, conference centers, clubs, banquet halls or restaurants are classified as in-house. The space in which banquets take place is not always a designated banquet room, it can be any other suitable area, such as lobbies, patios or gardens, penthouse roofs, dining rooms, meeting rooms, guest suites and even kitchens. The Waldorf-Astoria Hotel in New York City has a private railroad siding and once a cocktail reception was held there.

In hotels and conference centers with sleeping rooms, catering can be grouped into commercial business and social business. Commercial business is business that directly supports sleeping room occupancy. Hotels are in the business of renting sleeping rooms. Any group renting sleeping rooms and banquet space for meetings or food functions can be classified as commercial business. Some examples of commercial business are conventions, trade shows, meetings, incentive business and tours.

This classification does not address the type of functions or the elaborateness of food and beverage service. Commercial business should always be given preference, because it has a greater impact on the total profitability of the hotel than most social business. The reason is that renting sleeping rooms requires less labor and material than providing food and beverage. In many hotels, the Gross Operating Profit (GOP) in the rooms division is between 65% to 75% of revenues, while in the banquet department the GOP is normally between 35% to 45%. The GOP is not a direct indication of the profitability of a hotel, but rather an internal accounting yardstick by which the various departments are measured. Very much depends on the expenses charged to each department.

In hotels, social business is any other business not connected with guest rooms' occupancy. Some of the social business could generate sleeping room business, such as a wedding party needing sleeping rooms to accommodate out of town guests. Changing rooms and a bridal suite are normally provided free of charge, and are an expense. The type of food served and the elegance of the function has no bearing on the classification. In restaurants and clubs, all banquet business can be classified as social business. Some examples of social business are weddings, bar and bat mitzvahs, anniversaries, birthdays, charity events, trade shows, meetings, speeches, seminars, balls and dances. It is important to note that some of these functions are commercial in nature, but are still classified as social business, because they do not generate any sleeping rooms. Social business can also be very profitable, and in some operations is equally as important as commercial business.

Off-Premise Catering

Any kind of catering outside the premises not occupied by the caterer is classified as off-premise catering. Off-premise catering is potentially more profitable than in house catering, because the caterer does not own and maintain the space in which the function is held. If there are rental charges for that space, they are usually passed on to the client. However, the caterer has higher expenses because it must operate away from the commissary, where the food is prepared. Off-premise catering has become so popular that even many operations with large banquet halls, such as hotels and clubs, are also offering this service.

Conversely, some off premise caterers have purchased catering halls to expand the services they are able to offer. The off-premise catering business has become very competitive. Caterers can range from single operators, who work from their homes or apartments to large operators. The facilities of the single operators are in most cases not inspected by the health department, carry little insurance, and operate with a very low overhead. Large operators maintain commissaries, must carry high product liability insurance, must conform to all governmental health regulations and employ a permanent staff. In defense of the small operators it must be said that off-premise catering is a relatively inexpensive way of starting a business, and some major companies have started this way.

Summary

Banquets have been popular throughout history and continue to be so today. Contemporary banquet business is a large and profitable part of the food service industry, and can be broken down into two major parts: in-house catering and off-premise catering. In-house catering takes place in large hotels and consists of commercial business (catering directly related to sleeping room rental) and social business (catering not tied to room rental). Off premise catering can take place almost anywhere that people can gather, and has certain financial advantages and disadvantages when compared to in-house catering.

Discussion questions

- Explain the types of banquet business found in hotels. Give examples.

- What spaces can be used for catered functions in hotels and clubs?

- Describe the impact of banquet revenues on the overall food and beverage revenues.

- Explain examples of commercial banquet business.

- Why is off-premise catering potentially more profitable than on premise catering?

- Explain the competitive advantage of small off-premise caterers over large caterers.

Chapter Two

STAFFING

CALIFORNIA DINNER MENU

RECEPTION

1998 Robert Mondavi Winery Napa Valley Fumé Blanc

DINNER

Asparagus Soup with Salmon Cream and Caviar
1997 Mondavi Winery Stags Leap District Sauvignon Blanc

****

Seared Day Boat Scallops with sweet Pea Purée
Grilled Leeks and Potatoes
1997 Robert Mondavi Winery Caneros District Chardonnay

****

Grilled Veal Chop with Herb Jus and wild Mushrooms
Truffled Risotto Cake and Baby Spring Vegetables
1996 Robert Mondavi Winery Napa Valley Cabernet Sauvignon Reserve

****

Strawberry and Meyer Lemon Semi-Freddo
1996 Robert Mondavi Winery Napa Valley Moscato d'Oro

Chapter Two
STAFFING

Objectives

- To detail the personnel structure in a large catering organization.

- To explain the four major staff groups.

- To be familiar with the titles, responsibilities and qualifications of the employees in each group.

- To show the career paths to positions in the catering industry.

Introduction

The most important ingredient for success in the catering field is the dedication, professionalism and friendliness of the staff. No matter how dazzling the premises are or how beautiful the music is, unless the staff is well trained, patient, knowledgeable and friendly, the business will fail. In the catering field, the staff can be generally classified into four groups:

1. **Selling Staff**

2. **Executing Staff**

3. **Support Staff**

4. **Outside Contractors**

The Selling Staff: Titles, Responsibilities and Qualifications

The selling staff typically consists of:

- Director of Catering

- Banquet Selling Staff

- Banquet Office Staff

- Meeting Planners

- Convention Coordinators

The Director of Catering

This individual is responsible for selling banquets in the most profitable manner possible. In large convention hotels, the *Director of Catering* works for, or in close collaboration with the *Director of Sales*, who is responsible for selling all the services the hotel offers, with emphasis on sleeping room sales. Since group sleeping room sales are often connected with renting meeting rooms and other function space, the *Director of Catering* works closely with the Sales Department and supports the efforts of the *Director of Sales*.

In hotels with less emphasis on group room sales, the *Director of Catering* works directly for the *Director of Food and Beverage*. In conference centers, the *Director of Sales* books sleeping rooms, conference space and reports to the *General Manager*. Food functions are usually routine and do not need to be handled by a *Director of Catering* unless the conference center books substantial outside business on weekends. In restaurants, clubs, catering operations without sleeping rooms, or off-premise caterers, the *Director of Catering* reports to either the food and beverage management or to the owners.

New:
In many convention properties the Catering Office is combined with the Convention Service Office.

Qualifications

The *Director of Catering* should have strong selling skills, a solid background in all phases of food and beverage operations and be a good administrator and a good organizer. This person must have a good grasp of profit potentials, and be able to work long hours.

The best preparation for the position is a college education with a food and beverage management major, and hands-on training after college in hotels, clubs, or restaurants with emphasis on dining room service and public contact. Sales training in hotels or in related fields is also valuable. Ideally, the *Director of Catering* knows the local market and has a good grasp of the local banquet business requirements. The individual has good contacts with potential clients but does not need a "following", which some maitre d's possess. Booking decisions are based on many more aspects than the personality of the *Director of Catering*.

Duties and Responsibilities

The *Director of Catering* has one prime responsibility: Sell, sell and sell banquets, develop a banquet-marketing plan and implement it. He or she also supervises the sales activities of the catering *Banquet Sales Associates* and monitors the revenues and costs of the department. The *Directors* must check the credit rating of every function and make sure all bills are sent out correctly. He or she must develop 5 year, yearly and monthly forecasts.

The *Director* makes sure all information is properly and precisely transmitted to all other departments; he or she works closely with the *Executive Chef* to update menus and with the beverage manager to ensure wine availability. The *Director* energetically supervises the banquet activities, especially service, as much as possible and works closely with the banquet service *Director*. The *Director* monitors the physical condition of the banquet space and initiates repair requests and rehabilitation budgets. He or she makes sure that all government regulations concerning safety are strictly followed.

Dinner Given at a New York hotel
June 1998

RECEPTION

Assortment of hot and cold Hors d'Oeuvres
Selection of Champagnes

DINNER

Ravioli of Seasonal Mushrooms
Summer Vegetables in their Broth
1996 Meursault Grand Charrons Mons. Bouzereau
****

Pan seared Hudson Valley Goose Liver
Sweet Corn
Sauternes Essence
1992 Olivette Lane Pinot Noir
****

Loin of Lamb wrapped in Watercress Mousse
Natural Juice
Glazed Garlic
1981 Château Palmer
1990 Cabernet Sauvignon Firestone (Magnum)
****

Valhorna Chocolate and Hazelnut Surprise
Mignardises
1991 Johannesberg Riesling Firestone
****

Coffee and International Teas

Compensation

The position is salaried. Some companies pay straight salaries to the *Banquet Sales Associates*. In many cases, the portion of the banquet gratuity not paid to hourly employees is used to defray part of or all of the banquet staff salaries. In addition to salary, many companies pay the banquet staff a sales commission. For gratuity breakdown and allocation see **Chapter 8.**

The compelling point for paying a sales commission is very simple. When employees benefit directly from their sales, they will make greater efforts to sell.

The argument against paying commission to the *Banquet Sales Associates* is subtle and can be very convincing. Profitability, not sheer volume of business, determines the value of a banquet booking. A *Banquet Sales Associate* oriented to volume, without regard to overall profitability, is of little value. Since banquet pricing is by necessity flexible (pricing and profitability will be discussed in detail in **Chapter 4**), there is a strong temptation for *Banquet Sales Associates* working on commission to book business regardless of profitability. Computer programs can determine the profit margin when the business is booked, but they are not flexible enough to take into consideration intangible aspects such as the value of sleeping room nights, the season, the advertising value, the political value, the potential good will which can lead to more business, and the volume of business already booked. Whether it is more profitable to turn business down requires human judgment.

Another valid, but seldom admitted, reason for not paying commissions are the large sums paid in big banquet operations, which can be higher than the salaries paid to other executives, including the *General Manager* and *Executive Chef*. Sometimes the *Banquet Sales Associate* will oppose any increase in staff size, to the detriment of the operation, because the gratuity would have to be divided among more employees.

It is not unusual for the *Director of Catering* and the *Banquet Sales Associates* to receive cash gratuities or lavish gifts from guests. This is an accepted way of doing business, but it raises some very thorny ethical questions. If a client offers a cash gratuity or gift in exchange for a reduction in price or some other extra consideration, and the employee accepts it, criminal bribery is involved. The employee should be dismissed immediately and prosecuted to the full extent of the law. It is extremely difficult to document proof that will hold up in court when an employee is accused of accepting bribes, and the employee involved might fight back by claiming discrimination or defamation of character.

Almost all banquet prices are negotiated individually. It is essential for management to monitor the pricing decisions made in the banquet office. It is crucial that the prices charged are the best that can be achieved in a given situation. The temptations for giving in a little for some personal gain are very real. It takes a strong ethical commitment by the *Banquet Sales Associates* to resist these pressures and effective monitoring by management to achieve the best possible prices.

New:

> **Many hotels discourage flexible banquet pricing but savvy clients know that all prices are negotiable.**

Banquet Sales Associates

The *Banquet Sales Associates* report to the *Director of Catering*. In large operations, the staff would be divided among outside people who make cold sales calls, the telephone solicitation staff, and the in house staff.

Qualifications

As with the *Director of Catering*, the foremost quality is the ability to sell. A strong hospitality industry background is necessary. Junior salespeople in a large staff are often used to make routine arrangements for meetings with simple food and beverage requirements, which can be taken from standard menus (also referred to as canned menus in the trade).

A strong profit orientation and good follow up for details are important. Verbal and written communication skills are crucial, as well as the ability to project competence and command trust. Friendliness, willingness to learn and listen, unending patience, diplomacy with guests and staff, and good telephone manners are also vital attributes. Computer literacy and the willingness to learn the software in use are expected.

Banquet Sales Associates are expected to show function rooms which involves a good deal of walking. In off-premise catering *Sales Associates* are expected to tour the facilities where the event will be held.

Duties and Responsibilities

The *Banquet Sales Associate* follows up on banquet leads developed in the catering office and sells to the client. Sales people make sure that all policies regarding paper work and information flow are followed religiously. The *Associate* should be at the disposal of the client before and during the event, and they must be dependable. Within the organization they offer suggestions at the weekly banquet meetings. They report all unusual occurrences to the *Director of Catering*. *Banquet Sales Associates* must be able to work evenings, weekends and holidays.

Compensation

The position is salaried. A sales commission may be part of the salary package.

The comments earlier about ethical questions regarding gratuities also apply to the *Banquet Sales Associates.*

Banquet Office Staff

Executive Assistants often staff the banquet office in large operations. Management trainees may be assigned to the banquet office and given this title. In some operations, the *Executive Assistants* are long-time employees who, for whatever reason, never become part of the *Banquet Sales Associates* team. Secretaries are being phased out of catering offices and their duties divided between *Executive Assistants* and word processing staff.

New:
In most operations the office is automated and all employees selling banquets are required to enter information into the computer themselves. The word processing staff is being phased out.

Most correspondence, and many contracts and *Banquet Event Orders* (BEOs) carry routine information that can be disseminated efficiently through word processing. Catering software can replace routine typing tasks and provide templates for most paperwork and correspondence. The employees must be accurate, be able to work the equipment competently, and be willing to work flexible hours, because some work may have to be done in the evenings or on weekends.

Note:
There are many comprehensive catering software packages on the market and many include the capability of making room reservations and handling billing. All require training, which is provided by the software company and is charged extra.

Qualifications

The *Executive Assistants* must have strong clerical skills, a friendly, polite disposition and good telephone manners. A good memory and excellent organizing abilities are definite assets.

Duties and Responsibilities

The *Executive Assistants* are crucial to the smooth functioning of the catering office. Every event, whether it is a meeting, a trade show, a simple luncheon or an elaborate ball, generates many details that are constantly subject to change. If the *Banquet Sales Associate* were to take care of all these small but important details and changes, their time would not be used effectively. It is good business practice to introduce the *Executive Assistant* to the client after the party has been booked, and delegate to the assistant the handling of some of the details.

Some clients will insist that their arrangements be handled by the *Banquet Sales Associate* or the *Director of Catering* personally, but in most cases an appropriate confidence level can be established between the client and the executive assistant.

The *Executive Assistant's* primary responsibility is to see that every change or detail, no matter how trivial, is properly recorded and followed up. Every function, no matter how routine it seems to be, is a unique event and must be treated accordingly. No detail is too small to be overlooked, and every call and question from a client must be answered with patience and understanding.

Compensation

The *Executive Assistant's* position is salaried and is normally based on a 40 hour week. Evening and weekend work is normally not expected, unless the person is training for a sales position.

Meeting Planners

The position of the *Meeting Planner* is relatively new and is most often found in conference centers and in hotels with many meeting rooms.

Important:
Meeting planners are also working for clients and are either self employed or employed by companies. Their responsibilities are to book the meetings, make sure the meetings run smoothly, and to negotiate the best possible price package.

Qualifications

Meeting Planners should have good interpersonal skills and be able to establish good rapport with clients. Attention to detail and follow through are important assets. They must be able to get things done, and get along with the support staff.

Duties and Responsibilities

Meeting Planners book and set up meetings with clients and arrange for all the services required, such as room set up, audio visual (AV) and other equipment needs, distribution of printed material, food requirements, and in some cases sleeping rooms. The meeting planner is the co-ordinator and liaison between the client and the service providers.

Compensation

The position is normally salaried. Gratuities are not common.

Convention Co-ordinators

Large convention hotels, conference centers, and convention centers require *Convention Co-ordinators* to coordinate all activities. The *Convention Co-ordinator's* qualifications and responsibilities are basically the same as those of *Meeting Planners*, and the position is also usually salaried.

Duties and Responsibilities

These staff members co-ordinate all convention activities, including transportation, room assignments, room welcome gifts, scheduling of events, booth assignments in the case of trade shows, co-ordination of exhibits, credit checks, and billing. One major responsibility is to make sure that the arrival and departure of the groups are smooth and as pleasant as possible and that the convention material is efficiently distributed. The *Convention Co-ordinator* is expected to meet the speakers and make them feel comfortable; demonstrate the audio visual equipment and all other technical paraphernalia.

The Executing Staff

The Executing Staff consists of:

- *Director of Service*
  Banquet Captains
  Banquet Service Staff
  Meeting Room Attendants
  Ushers
  House Men

- *Executive Chef*
  Kitchen Manager
  Banquet Chefs
  Cooks
  Pantry Workers and Other Kitchen Personnel

- *Banquet Steward and Staff*

- *Beverage Manager*
  Liquor Storeroom Staff
  Bartenders
  Bar Backs.

Director of Service

The old title for *Director of Service* was *Banquet Headwaiter* or *Head Waitress*.

The new title better reflects the responsibilities of this position. The *Director of Service* is in charge of all service personnel, which can include captains, servers, ushers, bartenders, bar backs, housemen (setup personnel), and service office staff.

Qualifications

The *Director of Service* should have a multitude of quality characteristics. This person should be friendly, trustworthy, truly service-oriented and unflappable under pressure. Every party, no matter how routine, is special. Some parties are once in a lifetime occurrences. The host/hostess and party givers will turn to the *Director of Service* with concerns, anxieties, demands, requests, and questions. He or she must be patient, supportive, able to listen, and able to take action when needed.

These requirements make up the public image of the *Director of Service*. Grace under pressure determines to a large extent the success of this professional. The *Director of Service* should be likeable and should command the confidence and trust of the guests.

The other requirement of the position is strong management skills. Given the nature of the catering business, banquet service demands fluctuate wildly, and scheduling the proper amount of *Servers* and other staff members is a demanding task. Supervising *Banquet Servers*, especially in large operations with many different functions taking place at the same time, can be difficult. Supervision is equally difficult in an off-premise situation, because the working conditions are often makeshift. So besides being friendly and service-oriented, the *Director of Service* must be an effective, strong disciplinarian and supervisor.

The job of *Director of Service* is also very time consuming. Long hours are required and the work takes great physical stamina. There should be no consumption of alcoholic beverages while on duty. The *Director of Service* should be well groomed and elegant, with a good general appearance.

Duties and Responsibilities

- Making seating diagrams.

- Scheduling *Housemen* and service staff.

- Recording the *Servers'* payroll.

- Supervising setup and breakdown of banquet rooms.

- Making sure all fire regulations are observed.

- Checking all tableware and equipment prior to service for condition and count.

- Checking menus with the *Banquet Chef* prior to the party.

- Confirming the latest count and menu changes with the *Banquet Chef*.

- Coordinating the services of outside contractors, such as AV personnel, florists, decorators, and musicians.

- Carrying out any wishes and changes the client might have.

- Supervising service.

- Keeping track of all counts and extra charges, and making the final bill.

- The duties outlined above are discussed in more detail in **Chapter 8**, **Service**.

Recording the *Server* payroll can be a very complicated process, especially in hotels with a collective bargaining agreement. In large operations, the *Director of Service* has a payroll clerk to handle payroll. Last minute attendance changes and banquet service requests must be recorded, documented and filed.

Compensation

The position is salaried, and the individual participates in the gratuity pool. In addition, cash gratuities are often paid. The income can be substantial.

Banquet Captains

Larger organizations employ *Banquet Captains*. In some houses, these duties are performed by *Assistant Banquet Service Directors*. *Banquet Captains* are in charge of smaller banquets, or supervise one section of the banquet room. In large operations, a *Banquet Charge Captain* is assigned to every function, and this person is responsible for the overall smooth operation of that function.

New:
In many operations *Banquet Captains* are phased out and replaced by salaried employees with titles such as *Service Assistants*. This move obviously saves payroll and reduces the number of union employees.

Qualifications

Banquet Captains must have a strong service orientation and supervisory capabilities, the stamina and ability to work long and late hours and a good appearance. Managerial skill is important because minor disciplinary problems must be handled on the spot.

Duties and Responsibilities

Banquet Captains assist the *Director of Service* in the execution of the duties outlined above and work closely with the *Banquet Chef* with regard to cover counts and timing. When a function takes place, the *Charge Captain* is in full command and co-ordinates all aspects of service, such as timing the orchestra, speaker, liquor service, food pick-up and bussing. The *Charge Captain* is usually in the kitchen when the food is picked up. *Captains* assigned to stations supervise the *Servers*, take care of special requests, and often handle wine service.

Compensation

Banquet Captains are hourly employees and participate in the gratuity pool. In hotels with a collective bargaining agreement they are union members. Cash gratuities are common.

Banquet Service Staff

Banquet Servers can be classified as steady and as extra employees. Even steady employees seldom work a full week every week; they are on call and work only when banquets take place. Steady employees are given preference for work schedules, and it is possible for them to get enough work from one banquet house to make a living. The number of steady *Banquet Servers* employed in hotels with a collective bargaining agreement is a contested issue, because banquet business is seasonal and even in the busy season can vary greatly from week to week. The existing work is spread evenly between the steady *Servers*; more employees potentially reduce the income. In many hotels there is a long list of employees waiting to be promoted to steady *Banquet Server*.

Extra Banquet Servers often work in a number of different banquet places. Their loyalty is determined by working conditions and income.

The situation varies greatly between different operations. Some places have a list of *Steady Extras*, approved employees who are willing to work only a limited number of shifts. Some union locals maintain a list of *Roll Call Servers*, who are available to work as *extras* in any banquet house covered by the union contract. Some operations use restaurant *Servers* on their days off or shifts off to work banquets. The same situation also applies to *Banquet Bartenders*.

Qualifications

Dependability is probably the most important qualification; next is willingness to work flexible hours, often at short notice. Friendliness, helpfulness, and willingness to serve are important qualities, as well as physical stamina, honesty and good appearance. In large cities such as New York City, many *Extra Banquet Servers* are aspiring actresses, actors and models. An audition could be more important to their life than a banquet job.

Duties and Responsibilities

Banquet Servers set up tables and serve food and drink, and they buss and clear tables after the function. They follow orders. The work can be hard and demanding at odd hours followed by long stretches of boredom.

Compensation

Compensation varies greatly. *Banquet Servers* are normally paid by the function (referred to as the job) plus a share of the gratuity. In hotels with a collective bargaining agreement the duties are clearly defined such as setup, breakdown, split tables and so forth. Compensation is given according to the duty.

The salary of steady *Banquet Servers* in New York City hotels can reach six figures.

Steady *Banquet Servers* are on the house payroll and receive vacation and insurance benefits. Extra employees normally do not receive benefits unless they belong to a union. *Banquet Servers* are often college students, homemakers and perhaps aspiring actors or actresses. Working banquets is often a method to subsidize income from other sources. Smaller facilities sometimes pay *Banquet Servers* in cash and do not report this to the Internal Revenue Service. This is obviously illegal.

Meeting Room Attendants and Ushers

Operations with large meeting facilities often employ individuals to take care of meeting needs. In some places, the work is assigned to busboys, officially referred to as *Dining Room Attentants*. As meetings have become more complicated, and more important to the facility, it has become necessary to assign trained *Meeting Room Attendants*.

Qualifications

Meeting Room Attendants must be dependable, friendly and willing to take care of guests' needs. They must be able to follow written instructions and to work with little supervision. Good knowledge of English is expected. *Meeting Room Attendants* should be discreet and trustworthy; during meetings sensitive topics can be discussed and the *Attendants* should not eavesdrop or gossip.

Duties and Responsibilities

Duties include setup of water service, simple breakfast and snack meal service, replacement of candies and writing pads, distribution of printed materials and other related duties.

Compensation

The position is paid by the hour. The employees share in the gratuity pool, but the food revenues generated by meetings are small. The position is steady in many operations and when there is not enough meeting room activity to keep all employees occupied, they can be used as *Banquet Servers* or perform banquet housekeeping duties. *Meeting Room Attendants* are sometimes considered *Banquet Servers* in training, and wait for a position to open up.

Housemen

This title is still masculine, and men perform the work in most places. No other non-sexist title has come into use to describe the position. *Banquet Housemen* normally report to a *Head Houseman*, who in turn reports either to the *Director of Service*, *Meeting Panner* or *Convention Co-ordinator*.

Qualifications

Strength, physical stamina, honesty, willingness to work all hours, and dependability are important, as is the ability to follow written and verbal instructions.

Duties and Responsibilities

Banquet Housemen move furniture in banquet rooms. They follow the room diagram issued by the *Director of Banquet Service* and set up the necessary number of chairs and tables. The work is heavy and can involve removing carpets, setting up platforms, lecterns, podiums, music stands, pianos, and other heavy items. The work has to be done quickly, because room utilization often depends on the speed with which the room can be reset for a new function, or one segment prepared while a function is still going on.

As a general rule, banquet rooms are cleaned and reset after every function, regardless of how late the function ends. When there are no functions scheduled, *Housemen* perform general cleaning duties. In off-premise catering, tables and chairs are normally rented and set up by the rental company. The caterer employs porters to transport food and other equipment.

Compensation

The position is paid by the hour, and is steady in most operations.

Festive Dinner Menu

Pheasant Consommé
Parmesan Cheese and Anise Straws
****

Lobster Ravioli on Purée of Wild Mushrooms
Haricots Verts
Suggested wines:
Dry Riesling or Pinot Grigio
****

Poire William Sorbet
****

Roast Loin of Lamb and Foie Gras Medallions
Braised Fennel
Toasted Almond Cous Cous
Suggested wines:
Cabernet Sauvignon
****

Arugula and Lamb's Lettuce Salad
Stilton Cheese
Walnut Galette
Port Wine Vinaigrette
Suggested wines:
Old Chianti
****

Mocha Vacherin Glacé
Sauternes or Tokaji
****

Demi Tasse
Cordials, Armangnac
****

Petits Fours, Chocolates and Pralines

The Executive Chef

Chapter 9 discusses qualifications, responsibilities and compensation.

Kitchen Manager

The job of *Kitchen Manager* is not clearly defined. In some operations the *Kitchen Manager* handles the duties of the *Kitchen Steward*, which are primarily support responsibilities. In other cases, especially when there are multiple kitchens, the

Kitchen Manager handles the administrative aspects of kitchen management, and the *Executive Chef* handles the culinary responsibilities. Lately the title *Chef de Cuisine* is used in large organizations. *The Chef de Cuisine* handles the culinary responsibilities and the *Executive Chef* is the overall administrator.

Duties and Responsibilities

When the *Kitchen Manager* is the back of the house administrator, this professional will handle the proper distribution of all *BEOs*, follow up on all banquet changes and requests, and be responsible for the availability and cleanliness of all equipment.

Compensation

The position is salaried.

The Banquet Chef

Large operations employ a *Banquet Chef*, who is responsible for all food production. The *Banquet Chef* often supervises a number of *Banquet Cooks* and *Banquet Pantry Workers*.

Qualifications

The *Banquet Chef* needs good cooking skills, and should be especially skilled in quantity cooking. Strength, stamina and the ability to work long and late hours are required when necessary. This employee should be even-tempered, resourceful and have good organizing skills, the ability to follow instructions, and to calculate quantities and maintain consistency in portion control. Characteristics should also include flexibility and a willingness to take orders and direction from the *Charge Captain*. One major aspect is strict adherence to sanitation and food safety procedures. Banquet food is often prepared ahead of time and on busy days under adverse conditions. The *Banquet Chef* is responsible for the wholesomeness and safety of all food items.

New:
Some hotel companies are experimenting with decentralizing the kitchen administration and are promoting the *Banquet Chef* to a department head position on the same level as the *Executive Chef*. This new position reports directly to the *Catering Director*.

Duties and Responsibilities

Preparation and dishing out of cold and hot banquet food, under the overall direction of the *Executive Chef*. The *Banquet Chef* must follow the established timetable and have the proper number of portions available, along with special requests. He or she must work closely with the service and *Steward* staff.

The position can be hourly or salaried.

Example of a poorly written menu. See comments below.

Menu
Sautéed Hudson Valley Foie Gras
With tart green apples, shallot puree
onion caramel and sherry vinegar

****

Canadian Guinea hen
with potato puree, braised thigh meat,
red wine fig puree and vidalia onion jus

****

Herb crusted domestic rack of lamb
with potato confit, provencale vegetable tian
oil cured tomatoes and ligurian olives

****

Selection of cheese
Mimolette, Parmesan, Comte

****

Fine apple galette
with Tahitian vanilla bean ice cream
and caramel sauce

****

Coffee, Tea, Petits Fours

Poorly written menu with spelling mistakes and flaunting all rules of menu construction.
Apples, potatoes, and caramel are used twice, potato confit is fabrication,
and the term _"tian"_ is obscure. Cheese should be plural.
Chapters 10 and 11 deal with menu composition and menu language.

Cooks, Pantry Workers

Most large operations employ _Banquet Cooks_ and _Banquet Pantry Workers_ specifically for banquet preparation work. _Banquet Pantry Workers_ customarily prepare light cold food, such as salads, juices, fruit appetizers, and dish out desserts. _Banquet Cooks_ prepare all hot food under the direction of the _Banquet Chef_. _Banquet Cooks_ help prepare elaborate cold food for buffets often referred to as _Garde Manger_ work.

The term *Garde Manger* is French and describes the part of the kitchen where perishable food was stored and cold food prepared. Today, the term is used to describe decorated cold food. Hot hors d'oeuvres and cold canapés are prepared by *Banquet Cooks*.

Desserts are usually prepared by the *Pastry Chef*.

Qualifications

Banquet Cooks and *Banquet Pantry Workers* need good cooking skills. In some operations, artistic skills are needed for *Garde Manger* work and for carving ice pieces. Qualities needed are dependability, willingness to work odd hours, an even temperament, physical strength, ability to work under pressure and to co-operate with others. *Banquet Cooks* and *Banquet Pantry Workers* have less pressure than line cooks. Many of them are part time employees.

Duties and Responsibilities

Banquet Cooks and *Banquet Pantry Workers* prepare and dish out, under supervision, hot and cold banquet food. They must be able to follow instructions and to calculate and measure quantities. They must see that all instructions are carried out and that portions are counted correctly.

Compensation

The position is paid by the hour.

The Banquet Steward and Staff

The duties, responsibilities and the vital contribution of the *Steward's Department* to the success of a catering operation is described in detail in **Chapter 9.**

The Beverage Manager and Liquor Room Staff

The duties, responsibilities, and role of the *Beverage Department* in a banquet operation are described in detail in **Chapter 7.**

The Support Staff

Housekeeping Employees

Banquet operations, especially in hotels and conference centers, interact with the *Housekeeping Department* in many ways:

- Supply of linen, tablecloths, napkins and side towels.

- Supply of uniforms.

- Dry cleaning and maintenance of drapes, carpets and related items.

- General housekeeping of public space.

- Specific housekeeping of public space during a function.

These services are generally not performed by the *Catering Department*, and are not under the direct supervision of the *Director of Catering*. In order to assure smooth execution of housekeeping duties, close co-operation between the *Catering* and the *Housekeeping Departments* is necessary. Duties performed by the *Housekeeping Department* are charged to the *Catering Department*.

Washroom Attendants

Washroom Attendants perform an important duty. They normally work for the *Housekeeping Department*, but it is the responsibility of the *Charge Captain* or *Meeting Planner* to make sure that the facilities are maintained in a spotless condition. *Washroom Attendants* often have the bad habit of displaying a tip bowl. This makes a bad impression on the operation and on the host. The cleanliness of washrooms is also a crucial aspect of off-premise catering.

Coat Room Attendants

In some facilities, the operation of the coat rooms is a concession; in other places housekeeping employees staff the coat room. It is important that the coat room is adequately staffed. It makes a bad impression when it is difficult to deposit or get coats back. It is also annoying when attendants forget to keep track of miscellaneous checked items, such as briefcases, umbrellas, and hats. Sometimes, the host pays for coat room services, in which case a "No Tipping" sign should be displayed and the guests advised that the coat room will be hosted.

Electricians and Carpenters

Electricians work for the *Engineering Department*. Their services are needed for operating spotlights, or to provide extra power. All *Banquet Sales Associates* and *Meeting* and *Convention Planners* must be aware that all extra power requirements for displays, spots, demonstration machinery, and related items, must be co-ordinated and approved by the licensed house *Electrician*.

In off-premise catering, the services of *Electricians* are often required to provide extra power supply for cooking and refrigeration equipment. The charges incurred for these services are passed on to clients. The minimum charge is normally for a time span of four hours. The *Electricians* are also responsible for changing light bulbs in function rooms.

Carpenters report to the *Engineering Department*. They are needed to hang banners, pictures, and screens or to build special platforms or raisers. The charges incurred are passed on to clients. The minimum charge is normally for a time span of four hours. The services of *Carpenters* are also needed to maintain the banquet furniture and moldings. *Painters* and *Carpenters* often work in the same department. Large hotels also employ *Upholsterers*. *Carpenters* also make dummy cakes and special platforms for buffet displays.

Cashiers

Parties occasionally require à la carte beverage sales, and *Cashiers* are needed for this job. *Cashiers* work for the *Cashier Department*. This department is part of the *Accounting Office*. Years ago the *Cashier Department* in large hotels had many employees because every restaurant required a cashier while it was open. With general use of credit cards *Cashiers* are generally no longer needed.

The charges for *Cashier's* services are passed on to the clients. The minimum charge is normally for a time span of four hours. In some instances, the charges for the *Cashier* are correlated with the volume of beverages sold, and adjusted accordingly. This is discussed further in **Chapter 4**.

Cashiers are not normally involved in checking attendance or in controlling admittance.

Outside Contractors

Special services are sometimes required that are best performed by outside contractors.

- Equipment Rental Companies.

- Audio Visual Rental Companies.

- Florists.

- Photographers.

- Decorators.

- Musicians.

- Security Guards.

- Party Planners.

The hotel or caterer is entitled to a commission, which is normally 10% to 15% of the amount charged to the client. The commission is perfectly legal, and compensates the caterer for the expense of letting the outside contractor perform the service. The commission is payable to the caterer and is classified as extra income. It should never be paid to any employee.

Outside contractors always bill the clients directly. In the case of a dispute about the services performed by them, the caterers billing will not be adversely affected. The bills of outside contractors can be substantial. Decorations in a large ballroom can run into six figures; music costs can exceed $10,000.00 and elaborate audio visual (AV) presentations can also be very expensive. The caterer should not finance these expenses.

Outside contractors must provide proof of insurance and sign a *Hold Harmless Certificate*.

Equipment Rental Companies

Off-premise caterers usually own very little equipment, besides what is installed in the commissary and what is needed to transport the food. The reason is that the demands are so varied that it would seldom be economical to purchase and store all the equipment. It is customary for off-premise caterers to rent most equipment, such as furniture, tableware, linens, and service appointments. Equipment rental companies can also supply tents, carpets, and dance floors, as well as portable kitchen equipment, heating and cooling devices, and portable generators.

Some caterers occasionally own an equipment rental subsidiary company, but generally they concentrate on providing only the food and services. The caterer usually works closely with a limited number of rental companies and receives a referral fee, or commission for the business booked with them. Occasionally, hotels, restaurants, and clubs rent special furniture, linen, and other equipment. The charges are normally passed on the client.

Audio Visual Rentals

Most hotels, restaurants, clubs, and caterers do not directly supply audio visual equipment, such as projectors, video screens, microphones, and speakers. Keeping pace with changing technology, maintenance, and installation requests are normally too expensive and too complicated for in-house personnel to handle. When requests for AV installations are received, clients are advised to contact a selected supplier, who is dependable and familiar with the house. Large hotels provide the AV rental company in house with office and equipment storage rooms. The client is billed directly.

Conference centers normally own and maintain built-in equipment. The use of this equipment is part of the daily fee.

Florists and Photographers

All operations have a working relationship with florists and photographers, who are dependable and know the house well. In large operations, a house florist rents space and maintains a flower shop on premise. These florists should be recommended because they are on-premise and can work easily in their allocated space. Otherwise there is little room for the florist to set up and work.

Outside photographers may not know the hotel well, will occasionally require ladders or stand on chairs or generally make a nuisance of themselves. The hotel and the customers are best served with a limited number of approved photographers.

Floral decorations are a matter of individual taste however, and hostesses, especially brides, sometimes insist on bringing their own florists as well as their own photographers. In this situation, the caterer should make every effort to accommodate the florist and photographer to make the party a success, even if this does not generate any commission. The client is billed directly by the florist and or photographer.

Decorators

When a decorator is needed, the client normally recommends a specific supplier to carry out a theme. Coordination with the hotel or caterer is always through the *Engineering Department*, and a responsible employee should review all decoration plans and coordinate delivery of materials, installation, and dismantling after the party. A *Catering Department* employee must be present while the decorations are installed to make sure that all applicable building code and fire regulations are observed. It is also important that decorations are installed without undue damage to the banquet room. Billing is direct to the client. The services of the caterer's supervising employee should be charged to the client.

Musicians

Most catering companies work with a number of orchestras, which they recommend. The musicians' union often specifies the minimum number of musicians required to play for dancing in a specific room. Audio visual requirements should be co-ordinated with a competent and knowledgeable person. Noise level can be a major problem; noise can inconvenience guests attending other parties, sleeping room guests, or neighbors. Billing is direct to the client.

A minor but important topic to be discussed with the client is that of providing food and beverages for the musicians. The best solution is to provide staff meals for a small charge. Musicians should not have to pick from food displays or buffets after the guests have moved to another room.

Security Guards

Security guards are sometimes hired to guard certain exhibits, to prevent party crashers from entering, to keep order, or to guard special guests. It is best to recommend to the client a choice of reputable security firms and let the client make all necessary arrangements. All arrangements must be made with the *Director of Security.* Outside security personnel should not be allowed to be armed under any circumstances. Billing is direct to the client.

A minor but important topic to be discussed with the client is that of providing food and beverages for the security guards. The best solution is to provide staff meals for a small charge. Guards should not have to pick from food displays or buffets after the guests have moved to another room.

Party Planners

There are two groups of *Party Planners.* One consists of those who are self-employed and offer party consulting services. The other group consists of employees of large corporations that do a great deal of entertaining. These employees can also perform the functions of convention planners and travel co-ordinators.

The clients pay the *Party Planner* a percentage fee between 4% and 6% of the total cost of the party. Sometimes *Party Planners* also get a commission from the caterer and from outside contractors. Many hotels refuse to pay a commission to *Party Planners*, but are required to work with them. *Party Planners* represent the client; their interest is to get the best possible space, food, and service for the budget.

Although the client will often select the hotel or caterer for the party, a *Party Planner* can have considerable influence over the decision and can steer business to certain operations. Corporate *Party Planners* must work within the framework of an established budget. Since they are experienced buyers, they will negotiate the best possible deals. Their influence in selecting a facility can be very significant.

MENU

Vegetable Terrine
Accompanied by Cold Delicacies
Tarragon Vinaigrette

****

Steamed Pink Scallops
Fennel Sauce
Vineyard Hill Chardonnay

****

Veal Rib Eye Steak Wrapped in Bacon
Sauce Madeira
Sautéed Straw Mushrooms
Snow Peas, Red Peppers and Tomatoes
Sprinkled with Sesame Seeds

****

Assorted Rolls and Butter

****

Coffee, Tea, Decaffeinated Coffee

****

Dessert Buffet in the Ballroom Foyer

Summary:

There are many positions in the catering field, and various career paths lead to employment opportunities on different levels. Most positions require flexible scheduling, and in some cases, long work hours. Some employees share the gratuity pool, others work for straight salaries, and some are hourly employees. There is controversy about paying commissions to sales people. The *Catering Department* needs staff from other departments to stage parties or for maintenance of the facility. All operations use outside contractors to perform specialized duties. *Party Planners* and convention coordinators play an important role in today's catering industry.

Discussion questions

- Explain the four major employee groups.

- Discuss the advantages and disadvantages of paying commissions to *Sales Staff.*

- Describe the duties of the *Director of Services.*

- What other departments interact with the *Catering Department?*

- What are the duties of *Housemen?*

- Describe the role of *Party Planners.*

- Why are outside contractors used?

- Why are the services of outside contractors billed directly to the client?

Chapter Three
MARKETING

Elegant Clambake

Hors d'Oeuvres

Artichoke Leaves Filled with Scallop Ceviche
Miniature Crab and Potato Fritters
Champagne Charies de Fere Tradition

Appetizers

Platters of Oysters and Clams
Platters of Clams baked in Seaweed and
Shrimp Baked with Oregano and Olive Oil

Buffet

Roasted Split Lobsters with Drawn Butter and Two Sauces
Local Corn on the Cob
New Potatoes with Garlic and Sea Salt
Poached Red Snapper Served Cold with Herb Mayonnaise
Cucumber and Dill Salad   String Beans and Onion Salad
Wild Greens with Mustard Vinaigrette

Bridgehampton Estate Reserve Chardonnay

****
Platters of New York Cheeses and Seasonal Fruits

Bedell Cellars North Fork Merlot 1989
****

Lemon Meringue Tarts   Fresh Fruits and Berries
Bowls of Whipped Cream and Sabayon
Miniature Chocolate Velvet Cakes
Ice Bowls of Brandied Cherry Ice Cream
Petits Fours
Coffee   Tea

The Clam Bake had obviously a New York theme, featuring New York State wines, and cheeses. The lobsters were split and the tail meat was loosened to make it easy to remove. The claws were steamed separately and served without shells. At events when people walk around and there is random seating it is important that the food can be eaten without too much fuss. On each table was a basket with a roll of paper towels.

Chapter Three
MARKETING

Objectives

- To understand the selling techniques and logistics of operating the banquet office.

- To be able to develop and evaluate a marketing plan.

- To know how to monitor selling performance.

- To know how to collect the right information.

- To understand the importance, and learn the technique of preparing a forecast.

- To understand how to solicit business and which sales tools are available.

- To learn about banquet staff meetings and the accepted format.

- To know how to maintain banquet files.

- To understand credit policies.

Introduction

No business can succeed without effective marketing. This is especially true of the catering business, which is very competitive. In many cities new hotels with larger and more modern banquet facilities are being built and many off-premise caterers are entering the market, all competing for the same business. Although the market is strong in a vibrant economy it can change quickly. Companies respond to an economic downturn by restricting the number of employees attending conventions, the size and scope of social events are often influenced by the condition of the stock market, and some health and nutrition concerns curtail the lavishness of food events.

In many cities public spaces compete directly with hotels for banquets. These public spaces can be more exciting than tired hotel ballrooms. There is hardly a city that has not built a convention center, refurbished parks, botanical gardens and zoos, opened piers, or created exciting public indoor spaces in office buildings through zoning covenants. Off-premise caterers normally service these spaces, for they are better equipped and more aggressive than many hotel catering departments.

In this competitive climate marketing has assumed a very important role. Today customers no longer come automatically to the hotel; they have many more choices. They want to be sold.

In order to sell effectively the banquet office must be well organized and the *Banquet Sales Associates* well trained. Sales goals must be set and a competitive atmosphere must prevail in the sales office. The competition is strong, and the best organization will get the business.

Getting the Business

It is no easy task to fill banquet space or utilize kitchen capacity with profitable business day after day. In theory, banquet space could be utilized three or even four times a day. Nobody achieves this kind of maximum utilization, but it is disturbing to note that many operations utilize the available space to capacity only 20% to 30% of the time.

There can be many reasons and excuses for this lack of utilization. Obviously, it is a lack of business. There is always new business out there and it requires fresh thinking and an open mind to bring the business into the house. Top management occasionally must make difficult choices about the kind of business that should be booked. Should all business be booked as long as it is profitable, regardless of image? Is upholding the reputation more valuable than an empty ballroom and no revenue? Is it acceptable to have people milling around with nametags in a luxury hotel? Is high level business shifting to smaller boutique hotels because there is more privacy? Can the hotel be accused of discrimination when it refuses to book a convention of a minority group?

Some often quoted reasons for under utilization of banquet space are:

- The catering business is mostly seasonal.

- Specialization can be limiting - a banquet hall concentrating on wedding business is more in demand on weekends than on Monday nights.

- Holidays also cut into the utilization of banquet space. A conference room is harder to sell on Easter Sunday morning than during the week.

- Banquet operations are often too timid in re-selling banquet space again after another function is over.

- The banquet office fails to diversify the market sufficiently in order to book other business when the traditional business is slow.

36

Calculating the Utilization Rates

To understand how effectively the banquet space is utilized, a number of methods can be used singly or in combination. They are:

- Computing the revenue by square foot.

- Number of times times the banquet space has been occupied.

- Number of covers served.

- Average banquet check.

Each method gives an incomplete, and in many cases distorted result. Used together or selectively they could provide some measure of how well space is utilized.

Revenue by square foot

Revenue per square foot is a fair way to measure the profitability of banquet space. The hotel business is real estate business and renting banquet space is no exception. The devil is in the details. Do lobbies, wide staircases, elaborate stages, foyers, or seldom used balconies count in the square foot calculations? A major convention can tie up banquet space with relatively low food revenue but generate excellent sleeping room revenue. This has to be taken into account when utilization of banquet space is analyzed. The basic formula is to divide the total square footage of all banquet rooms by all banquet revenues, including room rentals.

This should be done monthly or yearly to be meaningful. Doing it more often could distort the picture.

Number of times times the banquet space has been occupied

Banquet space has the potential of being occupied at least 3 times a day (once for each meal period, or all day in case of an all day meeting or trade show) 7 days a week. Potentially then, banquet space has 21 time slots per week (3 x 7 days).

Occupancy of hotel sleeping rooms is measured in percentages of rooms sold of the total number of rooms available. If a hotel has 600 available sleeping rooms, and 300 are occupied on a specific day, the occupancy for that day is 50%. Room occupancy varies greatly, but should be at least between 60% and 75% per year for a hotel to be profitable. If the same yardstick is applied to banquet space, and it is assumed that banquet rooms are available 3 times a day, there would be 1,092 time slots (21 slots per week x 52 weeks) to fill. Thus, if a banquet room is used 200 times a year, the occupancy rate is only be 18%. If the calculation of space utilization is based on more realistic two times a day, the occupance would still be only 27 %. These occupancy results will shock most people.

The occupancy rate can be based on the number of times a banquet room is reset, meaning the furniture is changed. If a room is used for an all day meeting, and later for a dinner, the occupancy for the day would be two.

Hotel Dinner Menu

MENU

Coriander Cured Grilled Salmon
Michigan Bean Medley
Lime Dressing

Fortant Chardonnay 1994, Burgundy
****

Broiled Beef Tenderloin
Oyster Mushrooms with roasted Rosemary
Glazed Chestnuts   Autumn Vegetables
Cornmeal Gnocchi
J. Pedroncelli Zinfandel 1994
Sonoma County, California
****

Romaine, Endive and Oak Leaf Lettuce
Balsamic Basil Dressing
Port Salute Cheese
Sliced French Bread
****

Bartlett Pear Tart with Pecans
Caramel Custard Sauce

****

Cookies and Chocolate Truffles
Coffee from Colombia

Number of covers served

Many hotels keep close track of covers. The definition of a cover is one meal served to one person, regardless of time of day or meal period. To calculate covers, the total number of covers are divided by days; to calculate the banquet covers for a year is achieved by dividing them by 365 days. The resulting figure is the average number of covers served per day.

Calculating space utilization by covers only is also misleading. This method does not take into consideration meetings, trade shows, and receptions. Social functions often require a reception area and a dance floor. The revenue might be high, but the cover count low. Often food and beverages are sold in bulk units and therefore no covers can be counted.

Average Banquet Check

Utilization based on the average banquet check is also deceptive. Banquet revenue is divided by the number of covers served. Again details can be misleading. Does the average check include alcoholic beverages? Is the average check divided into meal periods such as breakfast, lunch, dinner, and receptions? *Banquet Sales Associates* like to quote the average banquet check. There is more about this subject later in this chapter.

In many large hotels banquet revenue is by far the major contributor to the profitability of the Food and Beverage Department, but this does not guarantee that the space is utilized to capacity. Banquet spaces have built-in continuing expenses such as rent, maintenance, insurance, utilities and mortgages and must be sold aggressively. A small restaurant may have a back room available for parties. A luncheon club may have rooms that stand empty in the afternoon or evenings. A cafeteria type restaurant in an office building could make space available for meetings in the early evening hours. A dinner restaurant could increase its earnings by renting space not needed during lunch. The space is there to be sold. To maximize profitability, it must be marketed aggressively.

The Marketing Plan

In order to sell effectively, a concept commonly referred to as a marketing plan is developed. Every business needs a marketing plan, and catering businesses are no exception. The size and scope of the marketing plan will vary according to the size of business, the length of time the company has been in business and the expectations of the owners.

The plan is a joint effort of all the employees engaged in selling banquet space. In hotels, the marketing plan is a joint product of the *Catering Department* and the *Sales Department*, which sells sleeping room space. A marketing plan is based on following information:

- Identification of needs.

- Evaluation of existing business sources.

- Evaluation of potential business sources.

- Evaluation of space utilization.

- Evaluation of competition.

- Self assessment of operation.

- Setting financial goals.

- Action plan.

Identification of needs

Following questions should be discussed:

- What type of business is needed, more revenue or more covers or both?

- If more revenue is needed, should it come from a higher average check?

- How can the check average be increased? Should it come from a better mix of business, such as more high check meals?

- Should it come from better-priced menus?

- Should it come from better selling practices, such as selling more beverages?

- If the hotel has a flat package rate for weddings or conferences is the package revenue split properly?

- Should à la carte liquor sales be emphasized over package sales?

- Is the room rental policy aggressive enough?

- Are all clients charged properly, or are there hidden giveaways which should be charged?

- If more covers are needed, when are the covers needed most: breakfasts, luncheons, meetings, receptions, or dinners?

- What days of the week are the covers needed most?

Evaluation of existing business sources

Where is the business coming from?

- Is it commercial or social business?

- Is it local business, or out of state business?

- Is the *Catering Department* relying primarily on convention business booked by the *Sales Department?*

- Is there more weekend or weekday business?

- How well are holidays utilized?

- When evaluating past and present business, is there a trend, and can it be reversed if necessary?

- Is a lost business evaluation performed?

- Are the results of advertising monitored?

- Is the attendance of annual parties shrinking?

Evaluation of potential business sources

- Are new companies emerging as potential customers?

- Are new customer groups emerging as clients?

Evaluation of space utilization

- Is better utilization of space possible?

- Was business lost because space was not available?

- Was business lost because space was not suitable?

- Is the space managed properly?

- Is space released on time?

Evaluation of the competition

Identifying the main competitors. What are their strong points?

- Better location?

- Better parking?

- More elegant facilities?

- Better food and service?

- Better pricing policies?

- More aggressive *Banquet Sales Associates*?

- Better name?

- Better meeting facilities?

- Better marketing of their space on the Internet?

Honest Self Assessment of Operation

What are our strong selling points?

- Image?

- Configuration of space?

- Location?

- Decor?

- Pricing policy?

- Better food and service than the competition?

- Newer equipment?

- Good advertising support?

- Support from *Sales Department* (in hotels)?

Honest identification of deficiencies:

- Is our place getting shabby?

- Are our function rooms up to date in technical requirements such as wiring, AV capabilities, telephone, and Internet access?

- Function rooms too ornate for business meetings?

- Function rooms too bland for social functions?

- Size of function rooms, lack of breakout rooms?

- Quality of food and beverage service?

- Prices too high?

- Quality of tableware?

Setting financial goals

Corporations establish financial goals for each unit. These goals are often dictated by the necessity to maintain the stock price and pay the expected dividends. Amazingly high goals are often achieved because they spur the employees to work smarter and to be more imaginative.

- Are the goals realistic and optimistic?

- Are the goals based only on past history?

- Are the goals set according to potential?

There are a number of ways of setting financial goals. Obviously achieving overall higher revenue for the *Catering Department* is the goal. They can be refined by setting performance goals such as:

- Financial goals for each month often referred to as *Plan, Budget,* or *Forecast.*

- Financial sales goals for each *Banquet Sales Associate.* This is extremely difficult to administer fairly. *Senior Sales Associates* normally get the better business assigned. It is only fair and reasonable that experienced personnel should handle the larger and often more complex parties.

- Financial sales goals for new business. The predictable repeat business should be evaluated separately.

- Sales goals by category identified as most needed.

Setting sales goals in smaller places that do not keep track of banquet revenue separately could be done by calculating how much additional revenue the banquet space could achieve if sold more frequently, for example twice a week. If a function room in a small restaurant can seat 25 guests, it would be fair to calculate that it can be sold additionally every week for one meal function and for one rental without food and beverage. The meal functions, at $35.00 per person would generate $45,500.00 per year; the rental at $200.00 would generate $10,400. The total additional banquet sales goal for the year could be $55,900.00.

Setting sales goals in an off-premise catering operation is more difficult. One method is to set as a goal the additional revenue that could be generated on a slow day. If the revenue on a slow day is $1,600.00, and there are traditionally 2 slow days every week, then the additional revenue goal for the year is $166,400.00.

New:
Catering software easily generates all financial information.

Action Plan

The most important segment of the *Marketing Plan* is the *Action Plan*. It consists of identification of target markets such as:

- Corporate business.

- Financial institutions.

- Tenants in new office buildings.

- New corporations, or newly merged corporations.

- Airlines/cruise lines and other travel related businesses. They often organize incentive meetings.

- Tour business.

- Embassies, consulates (for parties on national holidays), foreign trade missions.

- High schools (proms) and universities.

- College reunions, fraternity meetings.

- Social and ethnic clubs.

- Civic organizations.

- Religious organizations.

- Charities, foundations.

- Fund raising events, testimonial dinners.

- Social parties, weddings, bar/bas mitzvah.

- Fraternal organizations.

- Trade groups, trade shows.

- Political groups.

- Introduction of new products.

- Union groups.

Obviously, not every market is the right market for every operation. The action plan often contains recommendations such as:

- Increasing or re-evaluating the advertising budget.

- Renovations, maintenance projects and updating of facilities.

- Personnel changes.

- Recommendations to solve recurring problems such as parking access.

- Recommendations for equipment purchases.

Often *Marketing Plans* include a price tag for the suggested improvements and a realistic payback period.

The Forecast, Budget or Plan

Forecasting is looking ahead and estimating as precisely as possible how much business will be generated in the future. Every business person should know how much revenue could be expected; this is the only way to allocate resources and estimate expenses. Large corporations often make five-year forecasts and then a yearly forecast that is updated by the monthly forecast. The overall operations forecast is often referred to as the plan or budget. It is the responsibility of the *Director of Catering* to write the catering forecast.

In established operations, the five year plan is based on historical records, and is modified by a number of known factors, such as:

- Anticipated inflation.

- Increase or decrease of available banquet space when space will either be enlarged or taken out of service for rehabilitation.

- Status of competition, additional space becoming available or competitors closing.

- Trend of operations, anticipated guest rooms business.

45

- Demographic trends.

- Industry trends.

- Economic health of the region and the nation.

- Cyclical convention business affecting hotels and conference centers.

- Major events in the region, such as sports events, state visits or the opening of a public facility.

- Business already booked.

Most of the same considerations can be applied when making a business plan for a new operation or for an off-premise catering company.

Both the five-year and the yearly plan detail the overall revenue. The yearly forecast is based on monthly forecasts. The monthly forecast in the *Catering Department* is based on the business booked or pending. To be as accurate as possible, it should be prepared for every day of the month, and should contain estimated revenue, number of covers, average check, and rental income. The base for the monthly forecasts is business definitely booked and realistic estimate of tentative bookings. The figures recorded in the computer are estimated attendance figures, given by the client. When the date of a function draws nearer, these figures can change considerably. Large fluctuations in attendance are common in the catering business.

This is when experience and knowing the market prove their worth. Forecasting cannot safely be based on copying the business listed in the computer; it must be a realistic estimate of how business will materialize. A considerable amount of walk-in business may also exist in certain operations. Walk-in business can be estimated by knowing what is happening in town, how the competition is doing, and having faith in the abilities of the *Banquet Sales Associates*. The rest of the forecast consists of educated guesses.

The monthly forecast, submitted at the beginning of the year, is updated every month. The more information that is used to make the forecast, the more accurate it will be. All items of importance that could affect banquet bookings, from parades and elections to street repairs, and even the weather forecast, are important. Because preparing the forecast is so important, every *Banquet Sales Associate* should be required to submit a monthly progress report showing definite and tentative sales.

Monitoring Performance

Marketing plans fail if they are not constantly evaluated and updated when necessary.

Monitoring the production of each Banquet Sales Associate

New:
Most catering software can generate impressive pie charts showing the production of each *Banquet Sales Associate.*

- The sales volume in dollars divided between new and repeat business.

- The average check for each meal period.

- The food and beverage costs for the month and year to date.

- The rank within the department based on business volume.

Additional information to be considered could be:

- Banquet room rental income.

- Sleeping room nights generated through renting function space.

Fairness when comparing revenues and costs is important. Obviously a well-established sales person might have a following and attract better business than a junior person, who is often delegated to handle low-ticket coffee breaks and breakfast business.

Monitoring the average check

There are different ways to compute the average check. It is important that the method, once established is used consistently by all employees and in hotel chains by all properties.

The basic method consists of dividing the dollar revenue by covers. It is an acceptable method but can be misleading. In many operations food is sold in units such as gallons of coffee, trays of pastries and reception food. The number of customers is often not recorded. When all revenue is included disregarding the number of customers the average check is obviously inflated.

In other cases the number of customers attending a reception is known but the reception food and beverage check could be low and the number of covers could be very large. To include reception covers could give a distorted picture. Some operations exclude breakfast covers from average check calculations because they can also distort the numbers. The fairest method is to calculate the average check by meal period and exclude all reception and miscellaneous revenues. To make the numbers meaningful the same method must be used every month.

Monitoring food cost.

Food cost should be calculated for every function. Catering software can automatically calculate food cost and overall profit contribution for each party if the information is up-to-date. Parties are often booked many months in advance and the material costs could have changed. All costs are approximate unless a rigid recipe card system is used and all leftovers are accounted for. This is rarely the case.

Operations selling many custom menus must calculate the food cost with the help of the chef or the food controller. Beverage costs can also vary, because prices can go up.

Before implementing the *Banquet Marketing Plan* and encouraging the staff to go ahead to sell banquets, it is essential that all salespeople know the *Marketing Plan* and the *Forecast* and support it enthusiastically, in order to sell effectively. All salespeople have to know their product, that is their own operation. It would help if every sales person would spend some time in the kitchen with the *Executive Chef* and with the *Director of Service*. Unfortunately that happens rarely for a number of reasons. Many sales persons are hired with little understanding of the logistics and efforts needed to make a party happen.

Sales Tools

Menus

- Attractively printed and accurate brochures and folders with menu choices.

Precise Floor Plans

- Floor plans and required set-ups can be easily computer generated and e-mailed to the prospective client. It is advisable to take pictures or video tours of the facilities to show the clients the decor, flow, and connection between the function rooms. However the computer does not take into consideration vicinity to kitchens and other banquet rooms, light levels during different times of the day and season, hot and cold spots and drafts in certain sections, obstructed views and other plusses and minuses. The *Banquet Sales Associates* must know each banquet room thoroughly. Many hotels have precisely scaled floor plans, usually in ¼" scale, detailing windows, doors, columns and other architectural features to show the clients the layout of each banquet room.

Possible Setup, Furniture and Room Information:

Banquet rooms can be set up many different ways. The *Banquet Sales Associates* must know the sizes and proper names of all tables, chairs and other moveable equipment owned by the hotel and rentable furniture. It is also helpful to know the number of pieces available. If there are a limited number of oval tables available all rooms cannot be set with oval tables at the same time.

Possible Room Setups and Configurations:

- Theater style meetings, with chairs facing the speaker.

- Classroom style meetings, with tables and chairs facing the speaker.

- Meetings with open or closed horseshoe shaped tables.

- Meetings with one single conference table.

- Meals with round tables of 8 or 10 at each table.

- Meals with buffet.

- Meals with dance floor.

- Receptions with cocktail tables.

- Receptions with passed food and drinks.

- Receptions with buffets.

Each banquet room has a legal occupancy limit but it does not indicate what kind of set-up is used. As a general guideline for seated dinners 10 square feet per customer seated at tables of ten are calculated.

Additional information the *Banquet Sales Associates* must know:

- Exhibit space capacity.

- Size of freight elevators.

- Ceiling heights.

- Size of stage.

- Distance to restrooms.

- Size of dance floor.

- Accessibility for handicapped people for each function room.

- Operating hours and menus of in house restaurants.

- Operating hours and approximate distance to other restaurants in town.

- Location and number of telephone jacks.

- Number of pay phones near function rooms.

- Screens and other AV equipment either in-house or available.

- Microphone outlets.

- Availability of spotlights.

- Stage equipment available.

- Location of electrical outlets and amount of power available.

- Business center facilities.

Simple Luncheon to Compliment the Wines of Domaine Michel

Keen's Chophouse New York City
February 8, 1991

Turban of Sole
1985 Domaine Michel Chardonnay in Magnums
1988 Domaine Michel Chardonnay

****

Roast Loin of Veal with Mushroom Essence
Rosemary Potatoes
Assorted Vegetables
1984 Domaine Michel Cabarenet Sauvignon in Magnums
1987 Domaine Michel Cabernet Sauvignon

****

Selection of Cheeses
1988 Domaine Michel Reserve Cabernet Sauvignon Master Blend

****

New Zealand Berries
1990 Domaine Michel Muscat Blanc

Furniture Sizes and nomenclature and Rental Information:

- Almost anything can be rented, but the *Banquet Sales Associate* should be knowledgeable about costs and sources.

  New:
  The Internet provides worldwide access to rental companies.

- Table sizes and other furniture, called lumber in the trade. To book a meeting and refer to tables as "skinny" is not professional.

- Sizes and shapes of platforms, raisers, podiums.

- Linen and uniforms choices.

- Types and quantities of special china, glassware, and buffet equipment available in house or available for rent.

- Possible flower arrangements and decorations, such as candelabras, vases and decorative displays.

Kitchen Capabilities/Menus

- Stock banquet menus, beverage and wine lists.

- Is there a bakeshop on the premises?

- Is all meat cut in house? This is difficult to answer because it can vary. If fresh fish is used it should be mentioned. To declare that all seafood is fresh is nonsense because most banquet operations buy frozen shrimp, often already cooked.

- Is the *Executive Chef* a prizewinner in culinary competitions or a graduate from a particular culinary school?

- Is the strength of the kitchen in buffet work? Ice carving? Sit down dinners? Desserts? This should encourage the *Banquet Sales Associates* to sell what the operation is best able to produce.

- Are fresh vegetables used? Are soups made from scratch? This is a difficult question because cooking consists of assembling many components.

- Will the chef create special menus and is he/she open minded?

Simple Dinner Menu

Tomato Aspic with Caviar and Smoked Trout
Horseradish Sauce
Maison Louis Jadot Chardonnay 1998
Chicken Curry in Vol en Vent
Basmati Rice
Spalletti Poggio Reale
Chianti Rufina Riserva 1993
****

Hazelnut Vacherin Glacé
Hot Chocolate Sauce
Domaine Carneros Brut 1996
****

This menu is simple and straightforward. It was served before a theater performance and had to be served and eaten quickly and without fuss. Anything with bones attached such, as rack of lamb, chops, or poultry would not have worked. The choice of wines is interesting; the chianti worked well with chicken curry.

Other Sales Tools

Many other sales tools should be available to the *Banquet Sales Associates*. Here are some examples:

- Pictures of function rooms in addition to web pages showing the facility.

- Video tours of all function rooms with different setups. The tapes could be mailed to prospective clients. It is unlikely that a client would like to watch a tape in the sales office.

- China and glass samples.

- Linen samples.

- Pictures of wedding cakes and other cakes.

- Pictures of buffets.

- Sample gourmet menus.

- Ability to offer the client a meal in the restaurant, or in a suitable place if the business is off-premise catering.

- Being able to arrange for sample meals. They should be offered to prospective clients only when the parties are large or when absolutely necessary because they can be time consuming and disruptive.

About the Competition

Salespeople should also know as much as possible about the competition. It is illegal to conspire to set prices, but it is legal find out how much the competition is charging. Sales representatives can find out a lot about the competition by attending functions in other places. This practice is often referred to as competitive shopping, and it gives a good insight into the quality of food and service, state of equipment, cleanliness of the function rooms and the overall efficiency of the operation.

The Sales Operation

Handling inquiries

It is very important that inquiries are handled properly. They often come by telephone, so the telephones should be staffed as long as possible. In large organizations this means six days a week until at least 8 p.m. In smaller places, answering devices should be installed. All inquires should be handled by a pleasant, knowledgeable person who has good telephone manners. Automated telephone systems used by most companies are annoying when the client is forced to listen to advertising, music and to numerous choices given in a chirpy voice before reaching a *Banquet Sales Associate*. A prospective client should not have to listen to numerous menus choices before reaching the *Banquet Sales Office*.

Inquiries are frequently sent by e-mail. The *Director of Catering* has to decide what e-mail address should be used for general inquiries. It is probably better to channel all e-mail to one basic address and have it checked frequently by a competent person who has access to the space availability schedule, rather than to individuals. E-mail inquiries require immediate response, and sales personnel might be busy with other clients, out of the office or attending to other chores and thereby missing urgent messages.

For many years the space was controlled by the *Function Book*, also called the *Diary*. Today the function book is computerized, and date and space availability information are accessible from each sales desk.

The very first step is to check space availability!

When an inquiry is received a printed banquet inquiry form is used to record all pertinent information. The banquet inquiry form is now automatically displayed on the computer screen. The form should be filled out while the caller is still on the phone; it will prompt the *Banquet Sales Associate* to ask the right questions.

However, most banquet operations still use paper forms. It is rare that a major piece of business is actually booked over the telephone; in most cases the *Banquet Sales Associate* makes an appointment either at the banquet office, so the space can be shown, or at a place convenient to the client. The *Director of Catering* evaluates the completed banquet inquiry forms every evening. A letter or telephone call should follow up on inquiries. An inquiry is a hot sales lead, and every effort should be made to book the party. The inquiry sheets form an important database for evaluating the general state of catering demand.

Inquiries also come from walk–in customers. Some are ready to be sold; others are curiosity seekers or comparison shoppers. When possible, the walk in client should be handled by an experienced *Banquet Sales Associate*, no matter how disruptive to the schedule. But of course scheduled appointments should never have to wait because of a walk-in.

Soliciting Business

The business cannot wait until it comes to the door, it must be solicited. There are a number of methods for establishing contact with potential clients. Marketing can be done even while a function is being held. It is an iron rule that the *Banquet Sales Associate* that booked a party be available, properly attired, to greet the party's host. This often gives the *Banquet Sales Associate* an opportunity to mingle with guests, meet potential new clients, and even discreetly solicit new business.

The information boards in lobbies (called reader boards) of competing hotels should be read as often as possible. They will provide good information about what groups are in town, and how many smaller functions are generated by a large convention. One facility is too small to handle a large convention, and smaller parties can be held away from the convention hotel. The convention and visitors bureau in most cities publishes information about conventions coming to town; and these groups should be solicited for additional business or for hosting the convention the next time. In some cases, a convention may be growing (or shrinking) making it unsuitable for the hotel presently being used. Effective marketing could bring this business to your establishment.

A great deal of entertaining takes place when a large convention is in town. This creates an opportunity for creative off-premise catering in offices or other locations being attended or visited by the convention attendees. Trade newspapers are a good source of commercial information.

The *Banquet Sales Associates* should remember to treat a company or group's office staff with respect, for it is often the *Executive Assistants* who make meeting and dinner decisions. And if they are not making the decision directly, they control access to the decision-makers, or at least can exercise some influence.

Telephone solicitations can be productive. Inactive banquet files, information from trade papers, or referrals can be used as information base. Some organizations also make cold calls to find out who books meeting and banquet business in organizations. Ringing doorbells is a time consuming process, and seldom cost effective. However it is done to introduce new banquet facilities. Junior sales personnel are sent to selected companies and try to establish rapport with the department personnel in charge of booking functions. This is often followed by an invitation to a reception to familiarize the potential customers with the facility.

The social market is primarily a referral market. A successful charity ball has a direct influence on the wedding market. Balls are attended by young, eligible women. If a ball takes place in a glamorous, romantic, and beautiful setting, weddings will follow. Successful weddings bring more weddings, because prospective brides and their relatives attend them. A good way to remind customers of your operation is to send anniversary cards or small gifts. If the party was successful, more referrals will result. Weddings are often booked one year or more in advance to secure the space and have time to plan all activities.

The social pages of newspapers provide information about weddings and other social events. Although the business is normally already booked when the information is published, there might be an opportunity to solicit business from the family for another celebration.

Party Planners In larger cities can play an important role in steering business to a hotel or a caterer. There are two types of planners, the independent planning consultant, and the social liaison person who is working for the caterer. The independent consultant is hired by the client and orchestrates the whole event, from selecting the caterer to hiring the decorators, musicians, and other contractors. The independent consultant is paid a percentage fee of the whole cost of the event, normally 5%. The client pays this fee. The social liaison person works for the caterer on a retainer basis. This is usually a person who is well connected socially, and who acts as a discreet ambassador for the caterer. The value of this person is measured by their performance in getting advance notice of social events, creating events, talking about the caterer, and spreading goodwill at parties.

Large corporations maintain a convention travel office employing professional party planners.

Although political dinners have little influence on the social market, they do expose the facility to a large segment of the business community and general public. There may also be media coverage of the event. Although the event is focused on the speaker or candidate it should not be neglected. A bad experience will chase business away. The *Banquet Sales Associates* should be available to make sure the event is handled properly and to make contacts.

Sample Banquet Event Order # 12786 Ca

Menu Instructions: **Guarantee 225**

Reception

Deck set up:

Two (2) double bars on outside deck
Patio tables with umbrellas, casual seating
Control table at entrance
Piano and microphone on lower deck

6:45 PM to 7:15 PM

Hosted Cocktails.
Call Brands
Domestic and Imported Beer
1996 Gallo Chardonnay
1997 Kendall Jackson White Zinfandel
Assorted Soft Drinks and Mineral Waters

Hors d'Oeuvres to be Passed:
300 Smoked Trout Canapés
300 Marinated Artichoke Quarters
300 Scallop Skewers

Staff:

4 *Bartenders* and 4 *Servers*

7:15 PM

Dinner
Preset Salad of Assorted Wild Baby Greens with
Raspberry Vinaigrette
Boneless Free-Range Chicken Breast with
Smoked Apple, Almond and Chive Risotto
Tiny Carrots and Baby Squash
Preset House Rolls and Butter
Note: 15 Vegetable Plates
Local Berries, Sabayon Sauce
Brownies
Ice Tea and Coffee

Wines with dinner:

Louis Latour Chardonnay 1996
Robert Mondavi Cabernet Sauvignon 1997

Note: **Guests will attend the light show at 10:00 PM**

See following information about charges.

Maintaining Banquet Files

New:
Every time an inquiry is received, a banquet file is started automatically by the computer and is given a file number, which could be a combination of a date code and a chronological number. The number will identify the event. See the file number on the menu sample above.

Most operations use physical files in addition to the information stored in the computer. The physical file is much more comprehensive than any possible computer file. It could contain copies of menus, and linen color samples, pictures, business cards and much more information.

Many large hotel chains have centralized banquet file and trace systems at headquarters and send pertinent banquet lead information to branch hotels approximately 8 months before the event. Banquet files contain historical data about past functions, including size of party, attendance, charges, and compliments or complaints and credit information. The file also shows if the party is an annual event, and It should contain all correspondence and suggestions for solicitation of future business.

Banquet trace files contain information about business contacted, events held in the city on a regular basis, functions held by corporations, a record of all inquiries coming into the operation concerning possible future business, and all personal contacts with potential clients.

All files must be reviewed and followed up every month. If the solicitation effort was not successful, a lost business report should be filed. The lost business report must be reviewed and evaluated by the *Director of Catering* to determine why the business was lost.

Smaller operations cannot afford the time for the paperwork large corporations generate, but the small entrepreneur can use some of the same ideas. It is always necessary to solicit business, and it is essential to know why business was lost. Studying lost business reports can reveal trends or patterns that can be corrected. Are the prices too high? Do the banquet rooms meet expectations? Is the food up to date? The service friendly? If the reasons why business was lost are known, solutions can be found.

The Importance of image

The catering business, even at the most utilitarian level, is a glamour business. It is important that a good image is projected at all times.

- *Banquet Sales Associates* should be well groomed, and should exhibit restraint and good taste in clothes.

- Sales personnel must be polite and helpful, show good manners, offer clients a seat right away and escort them to the door after the visit. Informality has become a curse in business dealings. It is always better to err on the side of formality than to address potential clients with their first names right away. First names should be used only after a cordial business relationship has been established.

- All correspondence originating from the catering office should be on attractive stationery and should be impeccably written. With the availability of word processors, there is no excuse for incorrect use of grammar or spelling mistakes.

- The correct spelling of menu terms is important. They are often misspelled. The computer program **Menuspell©** lists 27, 000 menu terms and is easy to use.

- A hand written thank you note to the party giver is a sign of class as long as the note is short and neat.

- All information received by clients should be recorded precisely, and confirmed in writing as soon as possible. Telephone manners are important. Putting a client on hold numerous times during the conversation because the office is understaffed is bad business. Booking banquets is a matter of trust, and the first impression a client gets establishes the foundation of that trust.

- All printed material should be accurate. When outdated or incorrect, printed material should never be corrected with tape or patches. It should be replaced regardless of cost.

- The banquet office should be furnished in good taste and reflect the quality the establishment wishes to project. It should not be too elegant in a commercial place, or too plain in a fine hotel. Off-premise caterers often create a small sales office adjacent to the kitchen, or furnished like a small, cozy kitchen to emphasize the importance of food.

- Gourmet dinners and a fine chef are good sales tools, because they demonstrate that the establishment is capable of performing above normal.

Collecting information

Selling banquets is quite different from selling shoes or automobiles. Selling a banquet is selling a memorable event and often a unique one: a wedding; a bar mitzvah; an anniversary; a jubilee; or perhaps a debutante ball. Even business meetings, commercial luncheons, and other seemingly routine parties are special and unique to the party giver because they will never be repeated.

FITNESS MENU CHOICES

BREAKFAST

Coffee, Tea, Herb Tea, Fresh Fruit Juice, Bottled Water
Fruit Smoothies & Veggie Shakes
Banana with Strawberries, Blueberries on Yogurt topped with Granola
Hot and cold Cereals (Skim and 1% Milk Available)
Low Fat Pastries and Muffins
Yogurt in Assorted Flavors with Fruit Toppings
Chicken, Veggie or Turkey Bacon and Sausage
Eggbeater Omelet
Potatoes, Onions and Scallions and Cracked Pepper Sautéed in Olive Oil

LUNCH

Cold Fruit Soup
Red Lettuce, Goat Cheese and Asparagus Salad
Tossed Salad with Rosemary Vinaigrette and toasted Pine Nuts
Grilled Chicken Salad on Mixed Greens
Oriental Chicken and Vegetables over steamed Brown Rice
Broccoli, Garlic, and Vermicelli sautéed in Olive Oil
Topped with Romano Cheese
Broiled Salmon Fillet marinated with Lime Juice and Basil
Chocolate Sorbet on crisp Wafer and Berries
Low Fat Apple Pie

DINNER

Warm Potato and Smoked Salmon Tart
Mozzarella & Tomato Salad with Basil and Red Onions
Tossed Salad Greens with Savory, Capers, Lemon Juice and Olive Oil
Mahi Mahi with Oyster Mushrooms atop steamed Spinach and Curry Rice
Grilled Chicken Paillard on Greens with Sun-dried Tomato Vinaigrette
Steamed Vegetables and Low Fat mashed Potatoes and Tomato Olive Oil
Low Fat Ricotta Cream Cheese Cake
Low Calorie Mango, Papaya, or Pineapple Sherbet
Coffee, Herb Teas, Green Tea and Mineral Waters
Soho Sodas, Citrus Iced Tea

Advising the client

No party is routine. A good *Banquet Sales Associate* must have an inquiring mind and a good measure of curiosity. The *Banquet Sales Associate* sells not only an event but also belief and confidence that the event will be memorable and successful. He or she must initiate a process of communication that will turn up as much information as possible about the prospective guests. The *Banquet Sales Associate* must ask the right questions about the group to be entertained and give honest answers to questions asked. The *Banquet Sales Associate* must try to think about the party as the prospective client does.

In many cases, the prospective client may not be familiar with all aspects of social etiquette or the catering business. A good sales person will counsel the client and, if necessary, make strong recommendations and give advice if he or she feels some venue suggested by the client is not appropriate or practical. At the same time the *Banquet Sales Associate* must be very careful to entertain all suggestions with an open mind and not appear negative or non-cooperative. In just about every case a compromise can be reached which incorporates most suggestions and fantasies of the client with the realities of logistics of the catering business. The most successful *Banquet Sales Associates* are known for never saying no.

The focus must be on the purpose of the event. If the party is festive and formal, selecting a ballroom with a wide staircase will add to the glamor of the occasion, because people like to show off their evening clothes. Luncheons or business dinners can be elegant or informal. When there are different rooms available, selecting the right room can set the stage for a successful event. The timing is very important, especially when speeches are scheduled. Food that takes too long to eat, or distracts from the purpose of the event is not appropriate. If the event is given to honor someone, the *Banquet Sales Associate* should try to find out the food preferences of the guest of honor. In some cases, this food would not be appropriate to serve to the others attending the function, but a special dish could be provided for the guest of honor. Should the home State of the person honored be reflected on the menu? Small touches like these show that the *Banquet Sales Associate* cares. Is the guest speaker small or short? Perhaps a platform could be placed next to the lectern. The New York Hilton Hotel routinely provided this for Mayor Beame, and to this day the platform is called the *Beame Box*.

The composition of the group is also important. Is the group one sex or mixed? Diet conscious or expecting to eat heartily? Of a specific religious denomination? Jewish groups normally have their meals catered by a kosher caterer or the food prepared under the supervision of a *Mashgia*, a rabbinical supervisor who certifies that the food prepared is kosher. Jewish wedding ceremonies taking place in a hotel ballroom require a *chuppah*: a small baldachin made of greenery for the couple during the ceremony and a glass wrapped in a napkin to be broken by the groom. Other Jewish weddings require access to a balcony to be married under the sky.

If a party is attended by Jewish and Gentile guests, it is important to advise the kitchen to have special meals available. Even non-kosher customers often prefer meat well done, or rather ask for plain fish or a fruit plate. Many customers could be vegetarians and will order vegetable plates. If the *Banquet Sales Associate* forgets to inquire about these possible requests the party can be a disaster.

After the day and date are established and the appropriate room is selected, the *Banquet Sales Associate* must keep in mind the time of year the party will take place. Food eaten at Christmas is different from food eaten in July. Sometimes a holiday theme will fit the occasion.

To make sure that the menu is appropriate, the *Banquet Sales Associate* also needs to know the following: What is the makeup of the group? Are the guests mostly young or elderly? What is the economic background of the group? This is not necessarily a monetary evaluation rather an assessment of expectations. Is the group all male, all female or mixed? A group of women may well like a different meal than a group of men. Will the occasion be festive, formal, or businesslike? Is there dancing between courses? For evening events, it is also important to suggest food that can be eaten easily and gracefully without danger of ruining an evening gown or tuxedo.

The fact that the party giver is willing to spend money is no guarantee that the invited guests will enjoy unfamiliar delicacies, such as caviar, or quails stuffed with truffles and goose liver. People have strong likes and dislikes in food, and what is elegant to some is inedible to others. I have seen elegant food come back to the kitchen hardly touched when the menu chosen for the occasion was just not right for the invited guests. Some customers are fanatical about the quality of bread and others the quality of their coffee.

For wedding parties, successful menu planning must take into consideration the food preferences of the bride, the groom, and their parents. Does the bride or her family have a favorite dish? In some families, a certain type of food brings back memories of happy family times. Perhaps this dish can be incorporated into the menu. What is the color scheme of the bridal party? Should the colors be part of the decor, or of the wedding cake? How big is the bridal party? How many changing rooms are necessary?

What is said about food is also true about beverages. Favorite drinks and wine preference should be ascertained and incorporated in the menu. Even dislikes are important. Any kind of information is useful to make the event a success.

In short, the *Banquet Sales Associate* should make every effort to gather as much information as possible. The more the *Banquet Sales Associate* knows, the better-equipped will she/he be to organize a successful event. The following checklist is comprehensive and is a reminder to ask questions.

Routine questions to ask when booking a party

It is not enough to hand printed menus and a questionnaire to clients. They must be advised and sold.

New:
Most catering software prompts the *Banquet Sales Associate* to ask most of the following routine questions.

- Time. When does the reception start? When does the dinner commence? When will the meal be over?

- Control. Will the *Servers* collect tickets? Who will settle ticket disputes? Are security guards needed? Are any gatecrashers expected?

- Signs. Are any signs necessary or desired? What kind of signs can be put up? The wording on signs. Who will pay if special signs are requested?

- Checkroom. Should the checkroom charge be included in the arrangements, or is individual tipping appropriate?

- Beverages. What kind of beverages will be served? What style of service will be needed? Is the client advised about the legal drinking age and the right to refuse alcoholic beverages to intoxicated guests?

- House policies and government regulations regarding removal of alcoholic beverages to guestrooms or off premise.

- Decorations. What is the client's choice of linen, flowers, and other decorations? Will there be elaborate decorations put up by professional decorators? How long will it take to put up the decorations? Will the room be out of commission for an excessive amount of time? Should rent be charged? Will decorators supply certificates that the decorations are flame proof and sign a hold harmless certificate?

- China. Should special patterns be rented?

- Furniture. Should special chairs and chair covers be rented?

- Gifts and Door Prizes. Will gifts and door prizes be given? Who will receive, control, and distribute them? Will there be a raffle drawing or door prize?

- Music. Who will hire the orchestra? Will there be dancing between courses? Amplification needs and concerns about noise. Is rehearsal time needed?

- National anthem. When will it be played and by whom?

- Audio/Visual requirements. What is needed and who will supply it?

- Photographer/Video. Who will hire the person? Will press be admitted to take photographs?

- Room setup, explanation of diagrams, head tables and other requirements such as committee tables at the entrance, tables for gifts or display decorations and prizes.

- Flags and banners. Who will supply and hang them?

- Programs, printed material. When is the printer's deadline, who will proof read the menu, who will handle delivery and distribution? Who will pay for printing? Is there a house policy regarding advertising in journals?

- Sales tax. Is the event tax exempt? Is the certificate on file?

- Are service charges and extra charges properly explained?

- Seating list. If the seating is formal who will supply the seating list? Are place cards needed? Who will supply the master seating lists and where and when will they be available?

- Master of ceremonies/announcer. Are speeches expected, and what is the length of the speeches? Is a TelePrompTer needed, will the speaker rehearse?

- Security. Will the guest of honor or other attendees require extra security? Are the city police or Secret Service involved?

- Mechanical requirements. Are the services of spotlight operators, electricians, carpenters, upholsterers needed? Who will give lighting instructions to the electricians? Are there special stage lighting instructions?

- Telephone and computer hook up. How many telephone lines are required? How to charge for calls?

- Permits. Are special permits needed to comply with local laws? Is special insurance needed for displays?

- Arrival. Any special arrival instructions, what entrance should be used? Are extra doormen needed to control traffic?

- Parking. Are parking charges paid by the host? How many cars are expected?

Medieval Dinner

Dried Fruits and Nuts
Parsley Bread, Popover
Oreoles
(Elder Blossom Funnel Cakes)
****

Sorrelye
(Sorrel Soup with Figs and Dates)
White Port Wine

****

Porpoise Pudding
(Oat stuffed Pike)
Ale

****

Farsed Goose
Rapes, Flore Frittours, Joutes
(Stuffed Goose with Lentil Cakes, fried
Squash Blossoms and Beets)
Casks of Red Burgundy

****

Sallat
Abbay de Cîteau
Dried Fruit Salad with Cabbage and St. John's Bread

****

Desserts
Marchepane Pye, Bolas, Faun Tempere
(Marzipan Pie, Wild Plum and stuffed Pear, Gilli-Flower Pudding)
Pitchers of Mead

Fun dinner. The diners were asked to come in costume, a herald announced each guest and each course. The soup was served in hollowed out bread loaves. The roast goose was paraded around the room on a stretcher and ceremoniously split with a sword.

Costs and Credit

In most cases, the *Banquet Sales Associate* will ask the client about general budget expectations, but the *Banquet Sales Associate* should avoid talking about specific costs until the format of the party is established. Most guests have a general idea about the price structure in the establishment; price is something that should be discussed after the client is convinced that only your establishment can make the affair successful and memorable, and after the *Banquet Sales Associate* has shown genuine interest in the event.

Occasionally, a client will volunteer a price quote from a competing establishment. Such a quote might not be comparable. A banquet bill consists of many charges. What is included and what is not? Lowering the price to beat the competition is not a good policy. If the price is lowered, the customer might feel that the original price was too high. On the other hand, it is painful to lose business because of a small price difference. If a concession must be made to get the business it is best to make it in kind, such as offering a glass of sherry before the party or upgrading the menu slightly. Experiences with pricing are a good discussion topic for banquet sales meetings.

Credit Policies

After the price is agreed upon, the terms of the banquet contract are discussed. Credit policies vary, but they should be spelled out clearly to every *Banquet Sales Associate* who should follow them exactly. As a matter of policy, all inquiries are referred to the credit department for comments. If the credit of any client is questionable, no space should be confirmed until the credit is approved.

In terms of credit, there are basically four groups of clients.

- Commercial customers with established credit. These customers are on direct billing, and are billed after the party. The credit department should be notified every time the client re-books to make sure the account is up to date. Normally, no deposit is required. In large corporations it might be necessary to get a purchase order number because not all divisions use the same entertainment budget. Even when a large corporation has established credit some divisions might not have credit. It is important to inquire who will be responsible for all charges and who is authorized to approve the bill.

- Commercial customers with no established credit. As soon as the space is reserved, the client is sent a credit application. If the credit department approves the credit, the customer is put on direct billing, but a deposit is usually required.

- Customers with good credit rating, but no established credit. Many customers have a good credit rating, but are not frequent clients qualifying for direct billing. In such a situation, a deposit of at least 10% of the estimated bill should be required when the space is confirmed, and the rest of the charges due in installments, paid in full prior to the party.

- Customers with no credit rating. At least 15% of estimated charges should be payable when the space is confirmed; the rest in installments, to be paid in full prior to the party.

As a general rule, most parties should be paid in advance. In particular social parties, fundraisers, political functions, and parties given by foreign groups should be completely paid before the function takes place. Naturally, there are exceptions to the rule, and each case has to be evaluated separately. A wedding booked by a prominent businessman with an excellent credit rating might not be a bad credit risk. As general policy, however, money up front should be required.

Banquet Staff Meetings

It takes a team to run successful banquets and good communications are important. All members of the team should always be aware of how things are going. In large banquet operations, it is important to have formal banquet meetings once a week attended by the *Banquet Sales Associates*, the *Director of Service*, the *Executive Chef* or *Banquet Chef* and the *Head Houseman*. In smaller operations, the banquet meeting can be a friendly get together over a cup of coffee to evaluate past functions and to discuss problems.

Note:
At Conference Centers and Convention Hotels the meeting is usually conducted by the Conference Center Office Manager.

Effective format for banquet staff meetings:

- Attendance at weekly meetings are mandatory; appointments to be scheduled around the meetings.

- Meetings must start on time and should not last longer than 45 minutes.

- All *Banquet Sales Associates* must attend.

- Minutes should be taken and sent to all persons who attended before the next meeting.

- The minutes of the previous meeting should be read and any action taken should be noted. Suggestions should be either followed up or denied. It is discouraging when employees make suggestions but they are ignored.

- The *Executive Chef* should attend at least every other week.

- Other department heads should be invited occasionally such as Purchasing, Housekeeping, Laundry, Security, and Engineering.

- The *General Manager* or *Resident Manager* are automatically invited. They should get copies of the minutes.

- At least one person from the *Sales Department* should always attend.

- The *Director of Catering* should open the meetings by discussing the financial results of the previous week compared to forecast.

- Review of banquet profit and loss reports.

- Weekly review of upcoming business made by each *Banquet Sales Associate.*

- Review sales goals for each *Banquet Sales Associate.*

- Lost business reports.

- Evaluation and comments about food and service.

- Review of high cost food items.

- Comments about office procedures, distribution of menus.

- Problems concerning guarantees.

- Report about repairs and condition of banquet spaces.

- Engineering charges and comments.

- Condition and availability of equipment, shortages of china, linen, flatware.

- Update on banquet marketing plan.

- Acknowledgement of complimentary comments and letters.

- Response to letters of complaint.

A meeting should not be a gripe session. If a subject comes up which is not of mutual interest, it should be discussed with the individuals but not at the meeting.

Summary

This chapter discusses the importance of setting sales goals and developing a realistic marketing plan. There are various components in the plan, including identification of needs, potential sources of business, scrutiny of space utilization, evaluation of the competition, and the assessment of own operation.

Preparing the forecast is an important responsibility of the *Director of Sales*.

When the marketing plan is in place, it becomes an action plan for increasing business. The performance of the *Banquet Sales Associates* is monitored against revenue forecast. Various sales tools are necessary for the salespeople to sell successfully, such as knowledge about their own operation, knowledge about the strength and weaknesses of the competition and genuine interest in the needs and expectations of the guests.

The credit policies common in the hospitality industry are discussed. There are techniques for handling inquiries, for soliciting business and for maintaining the banquet files. Banquet staff meetings are important for communication, and there is a proven format for success.

Discussion questions

- What is the meaning of the term banquet room utilization?

- List the three methods of calculating banquet room occupancy and use.

- What is a marketing plan and how is one developed?

- What is a forecast or plan?

- What information is used to make a revenue forecast?

- How are financial goals developed?

- How are financial goals monitored?

- List potential sources of business.

- Is evaluation of your own operation useful in selling? Should the competition be evaluated?

- How is the average check calculated?

- List various types of banquet setups and list useful technical information about banquet space.

- Describe how inquiries are handled.

- List some methods of soliciting business.

- What information is contained in the banquet files?

- Discuss why image is important, and how it is best expressed.

- Give examples of useful information the sales person should gather.

- List the format of effective banquet staff meetings, and list some appropriate discussion topics.

Chapter Four
MANAGING PROFITABILITY

MODERN ELEGANT DINNER MENU

Consommé of Carolina Quails
Nest of Poached Quail Egg
Sesame Twists

****

Lobster and Maryland Crab Meat with Pernod
Polenta Rounds
Suggested wines:
White Burgundy or other Chardonnay

****

Calvados Sorbet

****

Roast Veal Tenderloin and Foie Gras Wellington
Sauce Perigourdine
Bouquetiere of Baby Vegetables
Suggested wines:
Bordeaux or Merlot

****

Salad of Assorted Greenhouse Lettuces
Blue Cheese Pithivier
Pepper Orange Vinaigrette

****

Chocolate Cream and Pear Napoleon
Seasonal Berries
Rum Custard Sauce
Suggested wines:
Champagne or Port

****

Demi Tasse
Mignardises
Cordials, Cognac or Vintage Tequila

Chapter Four
Managing Profitability

Objectives

- To understand the value of space.

- To learn how to manage space.

- To learn about the banquet contract.

- To understand the concept of loss management.

- To learn about the banquet diagram.

- To learn about guarantee policies.

- To understand the importance of precise communications.

- To understand the importance of timing.

- To understand how to control operational losses.

- To understand how to control other losses.

- To learn how to manage time.

Introduction

Years ago, volume was the only yardstick by which the performance of *Banquet Sales Associates* was judged. Profit making was left to the people operating the facility. Hoteliers used to say, "*Volume buries a multitude of sins*". This is no longer true. Today the *profitability* of the business booked, rather than sheer volume, is the major concern, and all business booked must be scrutinized by this standard. Unprofitable and marginally profitable business must be identified in time to correct the situation. It can be better to conduct a small volume of profitable business than a large volume of marginal business. However, customers do not feel comfortable when they come to a facility and find numerous banquet rooms empty.

Profitability is achieved by charging the right price for the services provided, and by controlling costs. The *Director of Catering* is the person responsible for the profitability of the department. This individual has to keep track of costs and how they are allocated.

This chapter stresses profitability because only a profitable business can stay in business. Yet a certain amount of generosity and hospitality is expected. Although some large hotel companies now prefer the use of the term *customer* instead of *guest,* the public still expects to feel wanted and treated like guests. The cost percentages and charges detailed in this chapter are based primarily on customary data from large New York City hotels. They may vary considerably in other parts of the country.

Maximizing Revenue

Because the banquet business is so diversified, ranging from large hotels to independent banquet facilities, to off-premise catered events, expected financial results vary. The following cost percentages should therefore be considered only as guidelines to maximize revenues, not absolute goals.

- The cost of food should be between 20% and 25% of food sales. This percentage will vary according to the mix of business. Certain types of parties, such as receptions and breakfasts have a lower food cost than full meals. In restaurants with small banquet facilities a higher food cost is acceptable because the expense of maintaining large spaces is not applicable.

- The cost of beverages depends on the type of liquor served and the mix between wine and liquor sales. Hard liquor bar sales should have a cost between 15% to 18% of sales. Wine cost should range from 25% to 35%.

- Labor cost varies widely. Direct service labor costs should not exceed 10%. All other labor costs, such as food receiving, preparation, cleaning should be 10% to 15% of total sales.

Controlling Space, the Basic Tool of Profitability

Maximizing the use of space is basic to profitability. Only one group can occupy any given space at any one time. It is essential that a space is not sold twice, or business refused because someone thought the space was already booked. At the same time empty space is lost money that can never be recuperated

Banquet space used to be controlled by a large book called the function book or diary. This book was custom printed in larger operations, and consisted of a double page for every day of the year. The book was located in its own office and a clerk controlled every entry. Function books were available for both the current year and the next year in order to reserve space in advance. In small operations with only one or two rooms to sell, the function book was a stock restaurant reservation book.

The function book has been replaced by catering software programs listing all available rooms, their capacity for diverse uses, and the day, date and time frame when the room can be sold. Every *Banquet Sales Associate* can access this information immediately when an inquiry is received. The programs show who blocked the space and whether it was booked tentatively or confirmed. Other spaces that can be sold, such as restaurant space, pool space, and even lobby space can be added. Proper programming is obviously needed.

Hotel companies and conference centers use fully integrated programs that also handle sleeping room bookings, convention space reservation and all accounting functions.

Freestanding catering software programs provide much more than space availability. First the computer will assign a banquet file number to each party and this unique number identifies the event from then on.

Some programs handle the complete booking process and provide menu choices, calculate the food and beverage costs and generate the *Banquet Event Order* (BEO). The name BEO is very appropriate because all arrangements and promises made to the customers become work orders for the executing departments. Most programs also manage food inventories, print food and beverage requisitions, calculate recipes, and provide a profit and loss statement (P&L) for each banquet. All software requires tedious programming and allows no deviations of any sort. When using these programs the booking of banquets is completely mechanized and little experience is required of the *Banquet Sales Associate*.

However the catering business is a people business. Customers like to be advised, have customized parties, have special demands and requests only experienced *Banquet Sales Associates* can handle. To achieve guest satisfaction and maximize profitability, human involvement is essential.

The Hotel *Sales Department* sells the total hotel facility, primarily sleeping rooms and banquet or meeting space. The *Catering Department* is usually responsible for selling food functions. There could be a conflict of interest and rivalry between the departments; the *Sales Department* may block space for relatively low-revenue meetings needed in connection with sleeping room sales, and the *Catering Department* may wish to use the space for high-revenue food functions. The overall profitability of the business is more important than departmental rivalries, and in most hotels the sleeping room business is more profitable, even when meeting space is used for low food revenue events, than any food function.

Managing the Space

When an inquiry for a function is received, the first step is to find out what space is available on the date requested. The most suitable space should be selected and blocked. Occasionally the customer knows the hotel and will ask for a specific ballroom, although the expected number of guests may be less than the room could accommodate. If no suitable space is available on the date requested, other dates or alternate spaces could be suggested. Space management can become very difficult. In some cases the speaker or guest of honor is available only on a specific date and therefore the date of the event cannot be changed.

Champagne Supper Dance

RECEPTION

Buffets offering seasonal Bounty and exciting Delicacies

CHARCUTERIE TABLE
Galantines, pâtés, mousses and terrines

SMOKEHOUSE TABLE
Regional hams, sausages and fowls

WHOLE BAKED FISH TABLE
Carefully basted sturgeon portioned at the table

GAME TABLE
Winter game prepared different ways

PASTA TABLE
Oriental pasta prepared before your eyes

Choice of Champagnes served all night:

Ayala Brut   Bollinger Special Cuvée
Laurent Perrier Ultra Brut   Mumm Cordon Rouge Brut
Perrier Jouët Grand Brut
Piper Heidsieck Cuvée des Amabassadors Brut
Taittinger Brut La Française

MENU
Velouté of Almonds and Fennel
Hot Cranberry Bread
****

Crisp Duckling Breast
Green Peppercorn Sauce
Glazed Chestnuts and Tiny Onions
Seedless Grapes
Turnips Anna
****

FOR DESSERT
Return to the Garden Foyer for a Splendid Dessert Display
Moët & Chandon White Star

Future:
Customers will be able to access the hotel computer and find out space availability.

Once space is confirmed it cannot be changed without the consent of the party unless the attendance no longer meets the space requirements. It can require delicate negotiations and occasionally concessions to move a party to a different room. Often a certain size room with specific mechanical requirements is needed and much imagination is necessary to convince the client that the alternate space is still suitable, or even better. The key words are: *Do not lose a party!*

Functions have been held successfully in spaces normally not classified as banquet space such as lobbies, lofts, gardens, skating rinks, kitchens and the like as long as the space is safe, legal, and delivers basic creature comforts.

There are three types of entries: prospective, tentative, and confirmed.

• *Prospective entries* are inquiries. The entry is made in the computer as an inquiry by the person making the entry and a date set when the space must be released.

• *Tentative entries* are functions for which a contract and a request for a deposit have been sent out, but not yet received.

• *Confirmed entries* are functions for which the signed contract has been returned and the deposit check has cleared.

To prevent double booking, the space must be managed with great care. Most electronic function book programs require a password to gain access to information and to change entries.

Managing space properly is crucial to profitability. Every inquiry must be carefully assessed, and the best space selected for the occasion. This is difficult, yet it is crucial to optimal utilization. Clients often over estimate expected attendance, and consequently a larger space than is actually needed is selected and blocked. On the other hand, parties can grow beyond expectation.

In large banquet operations, management specifies the minimum number of guests that should be booked into each banquet room. These numbers are guidelines and are designed to maximize space utilization and customer comfort. A small group in a cavernous ballroom can feel very uncomfortable. If more suitable space cannot be found the hotel should make every effort to make the room feel more intimate, providing screens, folding walls, and planters. There should be no charge for these extras.

The suggested minimum amount of business for each room can vary according to the season and/or the meal period and can be tied to required minimum revenue. This will encourage the *Banquet Sales Associates* to sell higher priced menus during high season.

The utilization of space must be reviewed constantly, and entries that are prospective or not confirmed and have been pending for a long time should be removed if the client cannot be reached. Because this cannot be done arbitrarily, both the *Director of Catering* and the *Director of Sales* should evaluate the bookings at scheduled meetings. The status of every account should be reviewed regularly, and space unused or no longer needed should be released as soon as possible. Clients often ask convention planners to block more space than they will actually need, in order to be sure space is available for the planned programs. It takes a good relationship with the client to get the unnecessary space released as soon as possible.

Rental Charges

The operator is entitled to rental charges to recuperate the investment in space, maintenance costs, cleaning costs, and utility costs. Space is not free, and should not be given away freely. There is often demand for free space from regular customers, civic groups, and charitable organizations. With this in mind, every house should set rental policies. These policies are guidelines and should be flexible, for when and whom to charge is a tricky question. Giving free space is a tactic often used as a reason to create good will or lure groups into the facility who might patronize the bars and restaurants after the meeting. However, when groups are accustomed to getting free space many may take it a step further, eventually asking for additional favors.

The rental charge policy in many hotels allows a certain amount of free meeting space with a certain number of room nights. Rental is not normally charged for food functions. Rental is charged for meeting space not connected with room sales, for reception space (unless the food and beverage revenue is high), and for any other use of space.

There are labor costs connected with rental income. Furniture setup and removal, cleaning, and often supervision are required. In most hotels rental income goes directly to the bottom line, and the *Food and Beverage Department* is expected to absorb the labor cost and related expenses.

Pricing

Pricing policy should be dictated by the law of supply and demand and should be flexible. Maximum occupancy of space with profitable business should be the goal, so it is only common sense that a function room should produce higher revenue during the busy season than during the slow season. The same thinking is used in the *Rooms Department*, in slow seasons rates go down, during high season rates go up.

Note:
Few customers pay rack rate for sleeping rooms because many have special packages. In addition room clerks have considerable freedom to reduce rates late in the evening if many rooms remain unsold. It is justifiable to have flexible room prices for banquet guests.

Profit and loss statements should be generated for every party. The cost of food, beverages, and labor can be calculated rather easily; calculating the value of space is more difficult. Each space has basic operating expenses every time it is used, such as utility costs, basic staffing, cleaning, and other easily traceable costs. In addition, each space has associated costs regardless of whether the room is used or not. These are the costs of basic acquisition, taxes, and maintenance. To calculate a base cost for each banquet room is just about impossible because the expenses of operating banquet spaces are integrated with other operating expenses. Normally the basic operating costs charged to each party are rather arbitrarily set.

During slow times the expenses charged against a specific party should not be more than during the busy time. The basic staffing cost and the prorated room cost should be used as guidelines when making a profit and loss calculation for a specific party although a party booked during the off season might have a higher labor cost than in high season. Hotels use the slow seasons to give vacations to employees and often are not staffed to handle an occasional large party. Extra labor must then be hired to handle the business. It is a difficult decision whether to book a party with marginal profitability or to leave the space empty.

Most clients are fully aware of seasons and expect to pay less, or get some other concessions when business is slow. Clients might even threaten to take the business to a competitor. The *Banquet Sales Associates* have to negotiate very carefully to get the best price without losing the sale.

Menus

Many hotels and conference centers have two distinct markets to satisfy, the convention market called commercial business, and the local market described as social business. Business connected with booking sleeping rooms often requires that menus with firm prices are submitted to the organizers many months in advance. In the trade, these are called *Canned Menus.* The menus are usually printed on attractive stock, sometimes with pictures because they have to sell food service. They are sent to clients months in advance, change little from year to year and therefore they cannot reflect the seasons. Even local specialties are seldom emphasized, because these menus have to satisfy a wide range of clients.

Typically, *Canned Menus* offer a number of packages for each meal period such as breakfast, coffee breaks, snack breaks, luncheons, receptions, and dinners. See **Appendix A** for *Canned Menus.* The package also includes beverages. Sometimes these menus offer choices, which gives the client the opportunity to create customized menus. When clients themselves create menus a number of aesthetic problems and logistical challenges could result. Frequently clients make menu choices according to their personal tastes, which may not reflect the tastes of the group attending the function. The guests could be unhappy with the food not knowing that the hotel did not choose the menu. Menus created by clients can also result in logistical challenges in large banquet houses, because the staff would have to deal with many different choices on busy days. Some hotels do not give the client the option of choosing soups, vegetables, or starch accompaniments; they leave these choices up to the chef.

In many cases, prices are not printed directly on the menus. Instead, the menus are price coded, and a price sheet accompanies the menu package. The price sheets could vary according to season. *Canned Menus* are necessary in convention hotels, and most food functions are booked using *Canned Menus*. These menus are by necessity rather bland because they have to satisfy the average taste regardless of season and size of group.

Operations without sleeping rooms, such as restaurants, clubs, and off-premise catering businesses also submit menus for functions scheduled many months or years ahead. These menus can be more customized if the client is known. Off-premise caterers will always inspect the premises before menus are suggested. When possible prices are quoted close to the event, costs are known.

Creating menus gives the *Banquet Sales Associate* an opportunity to be creative, to make the menu fit the occasion and to maximize the price. Good *Banquet Sales Associates* should always try to make the party special, to suggest interesting food and make the occasion as customized and memorable as possible. Most custom menus are not created entirely from scratch; they are assembled from a list of components, such as particular dishes and garnishes that have proved successful in the past.

Many *Banquet Sales Associates* are very good at selling and customer relations but often lack the experience to evaluate all ramifications a customized menu can create. Pressure from clients and hesitance to refuse the customer can develop into disasters. There is not an *Executive Chef* or *Banquet Service Director* without horrifying tales. Here are some of the common problems:

- Seasonal availability is often not considered. Many parties are booked months in advance, and the person creating the menu may not be aware of which food is in season when the party takes place. The items sold are then either frozen, prohibitively expensive because they are out of season, or of poor quality.

- Group size. Certain menu items work well for smaller groups, but can be disastrous for large groups. Good communication with the chef is necessary to avoid unpleasant situations. Wrong menu choices can also affect the quality of service.

- Equipment availability. There is a limit to the amount and type of equipment available, even in the best-equipped operations. However, the lack of specific equipment should never deter the *Banquet Sales Associate* from making a sale because most items can be rented. Specific items cannot be promised to different clients at the same time.

- Equipment capacity. *Banquet Sales Associates* may not be aware that each piece of kitchen equipment has a given capacity, which can only be exceeded by abusing it or cooking ahead of time. As an example, in an oven two Rib Roasts or 40 portions can be cooked in 3 hours. The same oven yields 32 portions Roast Sirloin every hour. The same oven yields only 16 serving Duckling in 1¾ hours.

- Food that requires specific dishes or containers not available.

- Timing issues such as dishes that take too long to eat. This could interfere with the schedule for speeches and the rest of the program.

- Food not suitable for banquet service because they are too cumbersome to eat, such as bony meat and fish.

- Dishes not suitable for the group for ethnic or religious reasons.

These problems occur frequently when *Banquet Sales Associates* change jobs and bring menus from their previous place of employment. As much as fresh ideas are always welcome dishes that can easily be prepared in one place might create big problems somewhere else.

Chapter 6, Choosing the Right Menu describes how to create menus.

The Banquet Contract

When the arrangements are final, a contract is sent to the client to be signed and returned. Contracts vary, but they should contain all arrangements discussed and agreed upon, all firm and estimated charges, credit and down payment information, information about taxes and gratuities, information about gratuity distribution, and information about the limit of liability of the caterer. Banquet contracts can be produced on printed forms, or they can be generated on the word processor. Ideally, the program in the word processor is set up in such way that the banquet contract and the *BEO* can be generated without much additional typing. Most information contained in the banquet contract is also part of the *BEO*.

The Diagram

After the contract is signed and the financial aspects of the event settled, about one week prior to the function the client is given a diagram. The diagram is a floor plan of the space that will be used for the party, and shows, in scale, the number and configuration of all tables, platforms, and head tables, along with the tentative number of seats. The client is asked to review the diagram and make any changes. The signed diagram must be returned no later than 48 hours prior to the party. The number of seats indicated on the diagram, and signed for by the client will become less 3%, the guarantee for which the client will be charged, regardless of how many people attend the function. When the seating is formal the diagram will be used by the host to generate the seating.

Note:
When the events are small and fairly simple, such as meetings, no diagrams are sent, although the room arrangements must be clearly specified on the *Banquet Event Order (BEO)*.

For large receptions, diagrams should be sent out to show the room arrangements, including the location of exhibit tables, platforms, lecterns etc.

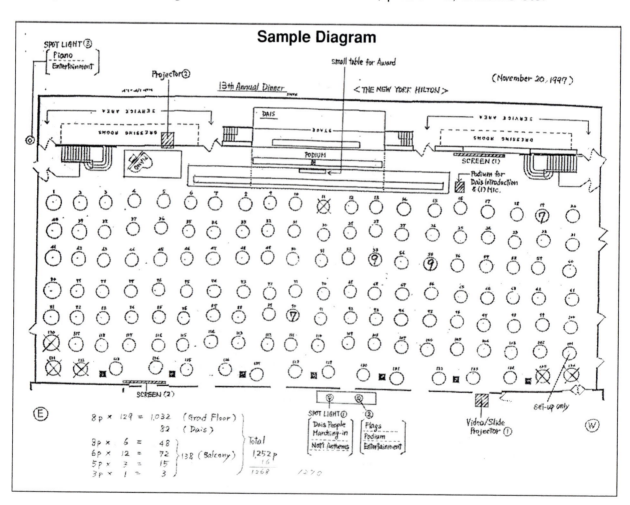

Sample Diagram

Computer software can generate floor plans but their size is based on the paper size which the installed printer can handle and how big they can be enlarged. Computer generated diagrams are usually too small to be practical.

Diagrams in large hotels are still made in the office of the *Director of Service*. The configuration of banquet rooms, especially in older hotels can be complicated. Diagrams are often in ¼" scale and templates are used to indicate the furniture. The diagram will become the basic information sheet for the *Servers'* payroll as discussed later.

New:
Special software is capable of providing floor plans showing all architectural features such as windows, doors, pillars, and adjacent spaces in scale. They require lengthy and expensive programming. These programs are helpful when booking the party to show the clients the possible space configuration.

Guarantee Policy

Catering establishments have the right to know, as precisely as possible, how many guests will attend a function. For this reason, the party giver is asked to supply a guarantee figure 48 hours before the function takes place. The number indicated on the diagram is referred to as the setup number, and the guarantee is automatically 3% less. The guarantee policy must be clearly stated on the banquet contract, and should also be explained verbally in order to avoid disputes when the bill is presented.

Guarantee policies vary. Some operators allow guarantee figures to be lowered within 24 hours of the time the function is scheduled. Other operators hold to the 48 hour rule; others have no policy at all.

Note:
Off-premise caterers often have a guarantee policy of 6 days because they have to commit their equipment needs to the rental company.

A firm guarantee policy is important. The caterer should not be asked to gamble on attendance. Some operators are reluctant to charge the full guarantee when fewer people show up. This is not fair because the food was purchased, prepared and the staff hired. The guarantee should be considered as a lease; the rent is due regardless of how many people use the facility. It is the privilege of the *Catering Director* to make concessions on an individual basis when absolutely necessary.

Guarantee increases are always welcome and should be accepted up to the last minute because they generate additional revenue. It should be pointed out, however, that large increases at the last moment are difficult to handle. Service and food quality could suffer, and the caterer may get a bad reputation because the attending guests do not know that the guarantee was significantly increased at the last moment. To maintain the reputation of the establishment, and to bring in as much revenue as possible, sales personnel should always strive to get realistic guarantee figures from clients.

When very large parties are booked the *Banquet Sales Associate* might agree to set up a number of additional tables. These tables will be staffed, and the chef will be advised, but the client will be charged only for the service labor when these tables are not used. The chef is expected to have additional food on hand, but has no guarantee that it will be used. When a guarantee is increased during the party, it must be done in writing to avoid possible disputes when the bill is presented. For this purpose, the *Charge Captain* has a special form called *Extra Charge Form*, which must be initialled by the host.

In the case of receptions and meetings, it is difficult to count the attending guests. Here it is better to charge a rental fee for the use of the room, and sell the food and beverages by unit rather than per person. Good examples are hors d'oeuvres and breakfast pastries sold by trays, coffee by the gallon, and soft drinks as consumed.

At meetings without food service the number of guests attending does not matter except that if more people attend, more seats have to be provided. If the contract with the client is a flat rental fee, the seats should be provided free of charge up to the legal occupancy limit. Usually the client wants to control attendance and requests a committee table as a checkpoint. The client normally supplies the staff. The committee table usually requires a telephone.

Portion Control

In large operations, control must be exercised over the portions taken to the banquet rooms. The chef is required to prepare the number of portions indicated on the setup, with perhaps a few additional portions in case there is spillage or the party increases at the last moment. As so often happens, *Servers* take more portions than they actually need. During pick up, in the excitement of service, some *Servers* intentionally take a few extra orders so they will not be short when they get to their station. Other *Servers* take more portions in order to help colleagues. Some *Servers* take more because they plan to eat them later. Whatever the reason, the kitchen is short, tempers flare, and in some cases the guests have to wait because more food was taken than was ordered.

It is the responsibility of the *Charge Captain* to make sure that no more portions are taken than needed. The general routine is to have the *Charge Captain* stationed in the kitchen when the food is picked up, and to control the number of portions by using the diagram which indicates the number of seats at each table. Another method is to issue meal order slips to each *Server* before the food is picked up. The *Servers* hand the tickets to a kitchen staff person, often the *Banquet Chef* who would call out the number needed. The number of portions used should be compared with the guaranteed number after the party, and differences investigated.

Extras Charges

Additional charges can become a bargaining issue during the banquet booking process. It is customary to provide a bridal suite, but housing family members at a reduced rate can become a sticky issue during high occupancy periods. At large dinners, changing rooms for committee members are necessary and it must be specified when these rooms will be vacated and put back into inventory. It is easy to give away the house.

Typical extra charges are:

- Extra napkins.

- Special china (gold service).

- Special silver.

- Special flatware.

- Special candles.

- Menu printing.

- Extra storage requirements.

- Washroom attendants.

- Coat room charges.

- Security charges.

- Cashier charges for cash bar.

- Parking.

It is important to keep track of all unexpected charges incurred during the course of the event. Occasionally additional liquor is sent to friends by the host, or other requests are made. The *Charge Captain* or *Director of Service* in charge of the party should have a pad of additional charge forms with them at all times and get every request signed by the host. This way, disputes are avoided when the final bill is presented.

Controlling Costs

There are so many costs connected with doing business that large corporations have created *Loss Management Departments* to control costs and prevent losses. Smaller operations cannot afford a whole department, but they are faced with the same task.

Hacienda Fiesta Typica
Bacalaitos
(Cod fish fritters)

Tostones rellenos de salmorejo du jueyes o pollo
(Fried plantain with land crab or chicken filling)

Rellenitos de yuca
(Stuffed cassava fritters)

Lechon asado
(Spit roasted suckling pig)

Morcillos butifarras longanizas
(Three typical sausages)

Guineos yautica ñame
con aceite de oliva y ajilimojili
(Boiled green bananas, taro and other root vegetables)
served with olive oil and Puerto Rican seasoning
Arroz con tocino
(Rice seasoned with fatback)

Habichuelas blancas
(Stewed white beans)

Gandules con bollitos de platano
(Pigeon peas with plantain dumplings)

Pavochon
(Spit roasted turkey)

Cabrito estufado
(Roasted kid)

Ensalada de aguacate, berros Y papaya
(Avocado, watercress and papaya salad)

Ensalada de chayote
(Mirliton salad)

Pastas de frutas surtidas con quesos de pais
(Assorted fruit tarts with local cheeses)

Cafe de Puerto Rico, ron perfumados dulces
(Coffee and assorted rum scented petits fours)

Losses can be classified as:

- *Operational Losses.*
- *Direct Losses.*
- *Potential Losses.*

Operational Losses

Operational losses are unavoidable, but can be controlled by vigilant management. Example of losses are:

- China and glassware breakage. It can be considerable and must be controlled. The controls involve employee training and providing proper equipment. Most breakage occurs during bussing and breakdown. Kitchen planners often underestimate the space needed to accommodate the deluge of dishes arriving in the dish room simultaneously, especially when a number of parties are taking place at the same time. Space restrictions may prevent the installation of sufficient soiled dish tables. Some detergent companies have trained employees to evaluate the operation and suggest solutions.

- Flatware loss has two causes, carelessness at the dish table when employees scrap flatware into the garbage cans, and pilferage by employees and guests.

- Linen loss and abuse is caused by employee carelessness, especially by kitchen employees when they use napkins and tablecloths as cleaning rags. Waste also occurs when linen is poorly maintained, because *Servers* cannot use linen with holes and stains. If this linen is not separated at once it will be automatically washed again and recycled. Quality and proper washing procedures are also important issues.

- Food over-production is caused by lack of precise information about attendance, and poor kitchen management such as lack of scales and measuring devices, poor portion control, and inadequate instructions from the *Banquet Chef* specifying quantities. Without direction, cooks frequently produce extra food, partly because they have time, and because they do not want the food to run out.

- Beverage over-pouring can be a problem when packaged parties are sold that include unlimited beverage service. Some bartenders and *Servers* are careless and pour more than customers really want. Another *Server* habit, expensive to the house, is removing partly filled glasses too fast, so that when guests come back to the tables the drinks are gone before consumed. There is a fine line between giving too much service and not being attentive.

- Poor food purchasing is a common problem in small operations when food is purchased without clearly established specifications. Some operators believe that the least expensive is best, or that by paying the highest price then quality is assured. Food purchasing is an exact science and should not be left to an untrained employee. Besides getting the quality for the price, getting the right quantity and yield is of equal importance. Poorly written *BEOs* lacking precise time and attendance information can also lead to over buying.

- Poor receiving practices are common. Although most food is packaged with precise weights at least the packages should be counted and checked against the invoice. Receiving is often delegated to anyone who happens to be around and is willing to sign an invoice. In some cases purveyors are asked to leave food at the door or inside the kitchen, where it remains unattended until it is stored. Food losses do happen and are often not discovered until a cook starts looking for it. The responsibility for receiving and storing food rests with the *Executive Chef* or *Steward*.

- Lack of inventory rotation is mostly caused by inadequate storage space. It is difficult to rotate stock when the coolers are packed to the rafters with food and employees are in a hurry. This in turn makes it very difficult to control inventory and buy only what is needed to take care of the immediate business. Caterers are occasionally prompted to buy ahead to ward off announced price increases. As a rule there should not be more merchandise in the house than is used in one month. The best operation is a lean operation.

- Waste of auxiliary items is often overlooked, because operators concentrate on controlling the losses of the "*big four*": china; silver; glassware; and linen. Auxiliary items are paper goods such as cocktail napkins, matches, stirrers, doilies, towels, and kitchen paper items. Control should be exercised over the use of candles and canned fuel. Cleaning supplies are often wasted. Everything costs money, even a paper doily wasted because it was not properly separated.

- Utility waste can be caused in the front of the house as well as in the back. One common practice of banquet sales and service personnel is to leave the lights on when showing a banquet room or after setting it up. In all fairness older hotels have electrical circuits which are cumbersome to operate and require an electrician to turn lights on and off. Cooling or heating units are often left on when the space is not in use; in large old hotels they are part of the central system and cannot be individually controlled. Utility waste in the back of the house can consist of hot water and steam waste when dishes from small parties are washed right away rather than storing them until a large amount is washed at once. It can save on labor and utilities.

- In operations with wild fluctuations in business, some heating and refrigeration units can be turned off when not in use. Many cooks are in the habit of turning on all stoves and ovens when they come in to work, regardless of whether or not they are needed. This practice not only makes the kitchen needlessly hot, but wastes a lot of energy.

- Both employees and guests cause pilferage. Some guests will steal flatware, ashtrays, and other small items as souvenirs. Occasionally rogue employees steal flatware, beverages, and food. In many operations, the function rooms are not locked and are easily accessible to everyone. This practice presents an opportunity for theft and also for vandalism. Hotels are like sieves and in many properties people can wander around without being challenged. The best solution is to keep all equipment under lock and key when not in use.

- Lack of preventive maintenance can result in major losses. (This subject is also discussed more extensively under accident prevention). Poor maintenance is often encountered in banquet kitchens. Since the equipment is used intermittently, maintenance and replacement are often deferred with the result that in some kitchens none of the equipment works properly. The kitchen is the production plant of the operation, and if it is not kept in good repair, the results could be disastrous. Roasts may be overcooked, food not served at the right temperature, and even large amounts of food lost on account of equipment failure. There are chefs with foolish pride who think that they can work with dilapidated equipment. This gives management no incentive to make replacements or repairs.

- Improper scheduling of employees is a major operational loss factor. Payroll costs and related benefits are the highest single cost in most operations. Many scheduling mistakes are the result of sloppy planning by the *Banquet Sales Associates*. The *Server's* payroll is based on the number of guaranteed guests expected to attend. If this guaranteed number is not transmitted to the *Director of Service*, and the final number is smaller than that originally transmitted, it is possible that too many *Servers* will be scheduled. The same is true for the kitchen staff, although small variations in attendance do not directly affect kitchen staffing, but payroll expense can be wasted here too if the function schedule is not clearly specified. Almost every function has a number of time segments, such as when the party starts, when service is expected to begin, when service is expected to end, and when the party is over. In the catering field kitchen time can easily be spent waiting around. If the *BEO* is explicit, the kitchen and *Steward* staff can be scheduled much more efficiently.

- Waste of office supplies is common, although it does not involve large amounts of money. The use of stationery, order blanks, stamps, and the copy machine should be controlled.

- Lack of telephone controls can be costly. Telephones accessible to guests, such as those placed in function rooms, must be restricted by having to dial the operator to get an outside or long distance line. These phone lines may be used to hook up to other computers or the Internet and long distance charges can appear unexpectedly. Portable telephones have, however, largely eliminated the problem of guests using the hotel telephones. Controlling and restricting the telephone extensions in the back of the house are a major operational issue. Employees could easily get telephones, plug them into jacks in function rooms, and make unrestricted calls.

Dinner Menu Prepared by Culinary Apprentices

RECEPTION

Home Cured Smoked Salmon   Oysters on Half Shell
Raclette
Maine Shrimp Tempura
Assorted Canapés passed Butler Style

DINNER

Smoked Maple Leaf Duck
Peppered Watercress and Apple Salad
Papaya Pineapple Chutney

****

Pan steamed Maine Lobster
Served in its Saffron Broth
Green Asparagus Tips

****

Champagne Sorbet

****

Veal Loin Medallions
and Chicken Mousse
Stewed dried Apricots and Orange Zest
Natural Juice with a Scent of Apricot Brandy

****

Seasonal and imported Greens
Raspberry Vinaigrette

****

Hazelnut and White Chocolate Pudding
Custard Sauce with Jamaican Rum

****

Home Made tiny Cookies

****

Coffee

Direct Losses

Direct losses are revenue losses, and can come from a number of sources.

- Uncollectable bills are direct revenue losses and happen in all operations, even when credits are carefully checked, and a comprehensive credit policy is established. It is the nature of any business to take risks, and it is the aim of management to reduce these risks. The *Banquet Sales Associates* are responsible for following policies and contacting the client when charges are outstanding. Larger organizations have credit meetings during which all outstanding accounts are discussed and the reasons why some accounts cannot be collected are reviewed.

- Careless booking which results in disputed charges. The disputed charges could be the final guarantee, additional charges that were requested but assumed to be free, or items ordered additionally during the service but not documented. Careful selling and good documentation is the best defence.

- Complaints. Revenue loss caused by complaints should not happen but does occasionally. Some clients demand a discount for trumped up incidents. Complaints should be taken seriously and followed up by the *Banquet Sales Associate* with a telephone call, or if necessary with a personal visit. A bland letter of apology will not do. First, any complaint should be reviewed with all parties involved, and the facts documented if possible. Rebates because of complaints should seldom be extended. If word gets out that a refund will placate a complaint, the operation could receive many trumped-up complaints. If the complaint is valid, a small rebate can be negotiated. Most parties are prepaid, and the amount of the refund is normally small.

Potential Losses

Potential losses are losses which do not directly stem from the operation but are caused by poor management, lack of insurance, and lack of accident prevention. These losses could be larger than any one of the losses described above. Insurance is available against most potential losses. Premiums are calculated on many factors, among them frequency of occurrence and amount of settlement. In all instances it is important to make out a detailed accident report as soon as possible. The report should include witnesses if any, photographs of the scene, measures taken, and statements made.

Guest accidents can be caused by poor maintenance such as falls caused by wet floors, slippery dance floors, open carpet seams, poorly lit staircases, poorly lit and maintained parking lots, and icy sidewalks. Guest accidents caused by employees are usually burns and food spills.

Food poisoning is very serious, not only because of the suffering and the grave health hazards, but it can also damage the reputation of the catering operation and can be used as a reason for canceling tentative parties. Every precaution must be taken to avoid food contamination. In the catering business, with large swings in business volume, refrigerated storage facilities are often overtaxed. In some instances, food is prepared too far ahead of time and not properly stored. This is especially true in off-premise situations, where facilities can be primitive and makeshift. It is imperative that the operator insists on the most stringent sanitary practices. Feeding large numbers of people is a great responsibility, and must be taken very seriously. The old kitchen rule should be followed: *"when in doubt, throw it out".*

It is important to recognize that it takes 24 hours before food poisoning symptoms appear. If a guest complains shortly after the party took place and no other guests complain, then the caterer did not cause the incident.

Allergies are fearful phenomena for the sufferer and for the food service provider. It is just about impossible to list all ingredients going into banquet food. The *Banquet Sales Associates* should inquire when booking the party whether any guests have known allergies. If they do, it should be clearly marked on all BEOs. The *Banquet Service Director* should identify the person and discreetly serve a special meal.

Foreign objects can be found in food even in the best run operation. The foreign objects most frequently found are shreds of glass. This happens when dishes are stacked carelessly, especially when ice cream dishes are stacked in freezers. Glass is also found in ice and gets into the bin when employees use glasses to scoop out ice instead of the ice scoop which seems to have a habit of disappearing. Occasionally steel wool shreds, outlawed for pot washing in many states, are found in food. Sometimes objects such as wire clips, wood splinters, and worms are found in poorly washed produce.

When a foreign object is found, the person in charge should personally handle the situation. The guest should be made as comfortable as possible. In case of injury, an ambulance should be called and an accident report made out. The cause of the incident should be carefully investigated. As a basic rule when glass breaks in the kitchen, throw out all food that could possibly have been affected. It is important to find the object. It will help the operator to identify where it came from and eliminate a reoccurrence. It will also protect the operator in case of a lawsuit.

Employee accidents can have many causes. Falls on wet floors or on worn stairs, back problems caused by improper heavy lifting, and cuts and burns are the most frequent accidents. Accidents also occur because of improper handling of cleaning chemicals, and federal law stipulates that the composition of all chemicals and the remedies in case of accident be clearly posted. It is the responsibility of the operator to provide a safe working environment, and to educate employees in accident prevention.

Discrimination allegations are a serious matter. There are two types of discrimination of concern to the catering operator: guest discrimination and employee discrimination. Guest discrimination is a lesser problem because the operator has no control over the guests being invited to a private party. It can become an issue if a guest claims to have received bad service. Handicap discrimination suits are possible based on lack of access. The American Disability Act is now a number of years old and all new construction and building renovations must conform.

More frequent are employee discrimination claims. The most common of these are age discrimination, followed by sex and race discrimination. It is necessary to keep all employment records up to date and conduct training classes for all supervisory personnel.

Fire losses can be caused by poor maintenance of kitchen equipment, especially filters and ducts. Most fires in food operations start in the kitchen. Building codes in most communities specify the use of flameproof materials in public spaces. Many communities also require sprinklers in all banquet rooms. Bad housekeeping often causes fires in function rooms. Debris may be allowed to accumulate in storage closets, or may not be cleared away promptly after a meeting or trade show. Smoking by employees is often the cause of fires in these areas. It is the responsibility of the *Director of Catering*, and the *Director of Security* to make sure that emergency exits are never blocked, that all signs are lit, and that the function rooms are not filled beyond the legal capacity.

Some hosts, especially sponsors of dances with ticket sales will be concerned about gatecrashers, and want to block entrances. This should not be allowed under any circumstance. If necessary, the party giver should hire guards to secure the doors.

Accidents can be caused by contractors. Depending on the size of the project, contractors should not be allowed to make repairs without the supervision of the engineering staff or an architect. All contractors, regardless of the size of the job, must provide a hold harmless form and submit proof of insurance coverage. Decorators must certify that all materials used are flame proof. Fresh Christmas trees and wreaths are not permitted in any public building in New York City.

Liquor consumption lawsuits are often filed when consumption of alcoholic beverages leads to an accident, or when infringements of the liquor laws are observed and reported. In order to avoid problems, all staff must be instructed that no alcoholic beverages can be served to minors, those under the age of 21, or to those already visibly intoxicated. This is sometimes very difficult to enforce at private parties when liquor is free. Catering operators should not sell whole bottles of liquor placed on tables because it invites abuse and removes control. Drinking of alcoholic beverages by employees should be prohibited and made part of the house rules.

Liquor consumption lawsuits can even affect company receptions taking place in hospitality suites. There have been cases when the host company was successfully sued when a serious accident was caused by a guest or employee attending the event. The employee was considered working while at the party.

Bad publicity is a potential loss and should be avoided. As a house rule, no employee should be allowed to give an interview or make statements on or off the premises about the operation, or about guests attending a party. Journalists and photographers need the permission of management to be present on the premises in an official capacity. The host of a party can request that no press be allowed to enter the function room where the party is held. A designated management employee should handle all press contacts.

Certain parties, such as rock concerts, carry the risk of bad publicity, besides the potential risk of damage to the facility. Before these parties are booked, management should be consulted. Booking opposing political or different ethnic groups at the same time can also result in bad press and major problems. It is difficult to choose between questionable business and an empty ballroom.

Giveaways

The hotel and catering industry is in the hospitality business and generosity is expected and appreciated, yet expenses can easily get out of hand. In any business, incentives and considerations are given to close a sale. Some are already mentioned in *Extra Charges*, but they are listed here in more detail because it is easy to give away something from another department. Everything has a cost attached, and many sales people do not understand the value of a giveaway. They would be shocked if they were to find out the true costs of something given away casually. Most giveaways have two costs, the direct cost to the operator, and the potential loss of revenue. A suite given away during a sell-out period, or a banquet room given without rental charges can represent a large dollar amount.

The *General Manager,* the *Director of Catering* or *Director of Sales* should always approve giveaways. The problem with giveaways is that it is difficult to take them away when the client has been given them once and books again. However, conditions change, and something that had inconsequential costs attached can become expensive. The reason for giving them has to be evaluated carefully each time.

Good examples for casually given perks:

- Free banquet space. It is difficult to charge for space when it is empty, but there are setup, cleaning, and utility costs.

- Free welcome reception for a group can create goodwill, but an internal charge should be made to give the *Food and Beverage Department* the proper credit for material and labor.

- Free use of the sports facilities cost little beside laundry charges.

- Complimentary wine with the meal is a double-edged sword because it deprives the house of revenues and has a cost attached. In hotels with a collective bargaining agreement there is usually a labor charge for pouring wine, even when it is complimentary.

- Free sleeping rooms in connection with social dinners, such as a bridal suite or rooms for parents. Sleeping rooms, even when the occupancy is low carry a laundry cost, an amenity cost, and the cost for making up the room.

- Free changing rooms also carry costs.

- Free use of a reception room for a press conference. In just about all cases it is good business and publicity productive but it should not be an automatic giveaway.

- Free hors d'oeuvres are so easy to give away and many *Catering Directors* consider them a nice gesture. The labor and food costs can be considerable and proper credit should be given to the *Food and Beverage Department*.

- Complimentary flowers. Hotel florists are usually concessionaires and rather expensive. It is so tempting to pick up the telephone and send somebody a nice flower arrangement without considering the cost.

- Free limousine service. Casual pickup at airports or using the limousine to run errands can be costly.

- Fruit and cheese baskets sent to rooms. Besides the basic material cost are a delivery labor charge, pick up expenses, and the potential flatware loss.

- Champagne sent to guest rooms is an elegant way of welcoming important customers but there are costs attached which go beyond the basic material cost.

Time Management

The Internet offers a number of web sites dealing with the catering industry. They can help to manage time more efficiently if used judicially. Surfing the Internet can also be incredibly time consuming. *Banquet Sales Associates* should not be glued to the computer. Banquet business is a people business and personal service and attention is crucial.

Web sites for the catering industry can be classified broadly into the following groups:

- Web sites providing links to suppliers. If special props or equipment are needed, the web can be a great time saver.

- Web sites providing theme ideas and specific issues, such as etiquette or help in party planning.

- Discussion groups, exchange of ideas and networking. The catering business is intensely competitive and time consuming. Most catering sales personnel cannot spend much time on the computer chatting away. There are also privacy issues to consider, and the possibility of divulging trade secrets or leads.

- Web sites designed for clients dealing with organizing, planning, and execution of events. The menus are interactive and huge, and offer a smorgasbord of services and event promotions. Related sites help meeting planners to find worldwide facilities. Some sites specialize in specific theme events such as golf outings, trade shows, or picnic sites.

- Web sites linking clients directly with participating hotels and providing reports, room diagrams, supplementary vendors' information, and other material.

The Internet industry is young and technically amazing, yet not foolproof. Accessing information can be confusing and requires learning. Few event planners will completely entrust the planning of an event to computer generated software. Social business, especially weddings, will always br booked by personal contact. One major advantage is that the experienced *Catering Manager* understands the needs of the client and will custom tailor the event accordingly.

Summary

The profitability of any business depends on the ability to generate the revenues needed to pay for expenses, amortize the investment, and render a fair profit. In house catering is a space intensive business, and the optimal utilization of the banquet space is crucial. Space is controlled through the computerized space management programs, and policies aimed at maximizing space must be well defined. An important aspect of profitability is the ability of selling the most suitable menu and charging the right price, although many operations deal strictly with printed menus and discourage changes. The banquet contract must explain the guarantee policies and the charges for extra items. Controlling attendance through the diagram, and enforcing guarantee policies are important to profitability.

Being able to control losses is important to achieve profitability. Losses can be categorized into operational losses and potential losses. Operational losses include breakage, theft, faulty purchasing and storing practices, food over-production, lack of portion control, and general waste. Operational losses can also result from improper scheduling of employees. Potential losses could be accidents, food poisoning, foreign objects found in food, lawsuits, fires, and bad publicity. Large companies may employ a loss prevention manager, or a profit enhancement department to prevent potential losses.

A Robert Burns Supper

RECEPTION

Smoked Moray Firth Salmon
Finnan Haddie Mousse
Potted Shrimp
Pickled Leeks
Scotch Quail Eggs
Alloway Game Pie
Glenmorangie Scotch
Rüdesheimer Bishofsberg Riesling Spätlese

DINNER

Cock a Leekie Soup

****

Cod Fillet rolled in Oats
Served with Pease Pudding
Graves: Château de Bellefont 1996

****

Kirkcudbright Haggis
Served with Bashed Neeps
Presented by Dancers and Pipers
Glenlivet Scotch

Epigram of Lamb
Served with Rumbledethumps
And Smothered Kail
Claret: Les Forts de Latour 1994

****

Stilton Cheese with Ruby Port

****

Lemon Curd and Walker's Shortbread
Hock: Niersteiner Orbel Auslese 1986

Discussion questions

- List three methods for maximizing revenue.

- Explain space control, its importance for profitability, and list three types of entries.

- Explain potential areas of conflict between the *Sales Department* and the *Catering Department*. How are such conflicts usually resolved, and why?

- Why are rental charges flexible?

- Explain pricing philosophy.

- Explain the term *Canned Menus*.

- What is the diagram and what is its function?

- Explain the purpose of a guarantee policy.

- List some typical extra charges.

- What are the big four?

- List causes of revenue loss?

- Explain the term potential losses. How do they compare to operational losses?

- What is the purpose of giveaways?

Chapter Five
LOGISTICS

Dinner to Compliment Wines

Veal Pot au feu in Aspic with Vegetables

****

Duck Consommé with smoked Duck Dumplings

****

Sautéed Red Snapper Fillet
Fresh Thyme and Noilly Prat Butter

****

Wild Strawberries Melba

****

Coffee, Tea

Wines:

Shafer Chardonnay Napa Valley 1980
Shafer Chardonnay Napa Valley 1982
Shafer Chardonnay Napa Valley 1984
Sonoma Cutrer Chardonnay Les Pierres 1985
Chateau Souverain Chardonnay Reserve 1986

****

Château Rauzan-Gassies, Margaux 1975
Château Croizet -Bages, Pauillac 1975

****

Johannisberger Klaus Riesling Auslese
Schloss Schönborn 1971

Chapter Five
LOGISTICS

Objectives

- To understand the customer's expectations.

- To learn about the importance of correct communication.

- To understand the purpose of the Banquet Event Orders (*BEOs*)

- To learn about the guarantees and the daily sheet.

- To understand operational logistics.

Introduction

Booking banquets requires the ability to understand the customer's needs and wishes, and to communicate these requirements to the employees who will carry them out. This is not easy, and this chapter explains the importance and techniques of internal communication. In larger banquet houses, where numerous parties take place at the same time, precise and timely communication is crucial to the success of the department. Good communications are also an important aspect of profitability; not charging for the exact number of guests because a change in guarantees was not communicated in time is a good example. Operating a party involves many logistical challenges, from staffing and timing, to the availability of equipment and the ability to turn space.

Communications

Client communications

Every function is important, and some functions are very detailed and quite complex. It is imperative that all instructions, changes, and additions be confirmed in writing and sent to the client as soon as practical. In some cases, the most efficient way of sending this information is by fax or e-mail. Menu requests and proposals should be sent by messenger or by overnight mail. The catering operator should do everything possible to respond to requests in a speedy, efficient, and precise manner.

Communication between departments.

Communicating effectively within the operation can be challenging. Menu and attendance changes should never be made verbally unless they require immediate attention.

Banquet Sales Associates should respect the chain of command and never ever give any instructions directly to rank and file employees!

Even when changes were made orally they should be followed up with writted confirmation. E-mail makes it easy to confirm what has been said over the telephone. The phrase "they said" is common when information is passed on. Often the information is false, or only half true. In addition, language barriers hinder communication even more in many operations. The telephone should not be used to give instructions to executing departments, such as the *Kitchen Department*, the *Steward's Department* and *Service Department*, unless the absence of time dictates. Telephone calls interrupt the work of the person receiving the call, and at the same time obligate that person to interpret the information and write it down so it will not be forgotten and passed on to co-workers. It is easy for a *Banquet Sales Associate* to pick up the telephone, issue instructions, and place the burden on the executing staff saying "*I told them in the kitchen that we will need extra fish*". This is not a professional or reliable method of communication.

New:
Computers have made internal communication efficient and instantaneous. Departments can be notified by e-mail about any changes, additions and other information.

The basic information tools are the *BEOs*. They are *work orders* and what is not written down will not happen! *Banquet Sales Associates* should never assume that somewhere and somehow all will work out. All of the arrangements made with the client must be written down in great detail so all personnel involved are informed.

In large hotels, the *BEOs* are distributed to many departments, and sometimes up to 50 copies are made. Even in smaller operations, at least 5 or 6 copies are needed. It is cheaper to make extra copies than to have employees running around borrowing the *BEOs* to get the information they require. To make sure that no department is forgotten, a distribution code should be printed at the end of the document.

New:
Some companies no longer distribute *BEOs*. The major back of the house offices such as Chef's, Steward's and Service offices are connected to the Banquet Sales office and are equipped with printers. The department heads are responsible for printing out the *BEOs*. It is not much of a labor saving and merely shifts the work from the Banquet office to the Executing Departments.

Instructions from the banquet office should be clear, precise, and to the point. The *Executing Departments* should not have to guess; they should be instructed precisely. A memo stating: "Have some fish available as substitute meals" is useless to the chef. It places the burden of estimating the proper amount on a person who has no direct guest contact. The *Banquet Sales Associate* should estimate the requirements, and pass this information on. The word "some" should not exist in banquet operations. Phrases such as "give me some sauce" or "I need some canapés for the head table" are used everywhere. It is difficult to break the habits among rank and file employees, but department heads at least should think about communicating more precisely and effectively.

Banquet Event Orders

When a function is booked and confirmed, a *BEO* is sent to all pertinent departments. The *BEO* should be sent out whether or not a function needs food service. When there is no food service it should be stamped prominently "No Food and Beverage Service Required". Functions without food service might impact restaurant and bar business or cause nagging concerns that maybe somebody forgot to send out menus.

BEOs are the most important communications sent by the banquet office to other departments. They should be treated with the greatest care by all receiving departments. It is not acceptable that a function is forgotten because a *BEO* was lost. It is imperative that the same format always be used, regardless of the size of the party. The information should be in the same place all the time, so that employees get used to looking for it. There should be no excuse for not seeing information because it was placed in a different spot, or in a different sequence than normal.

BEOs must list the day and date of the event, not just the date. It would be catastrophic if a bridal party arrived and the date on the *BEO* was wrong. Employees look less for the date but rather for the day of the week when they can be off, or working. Computer programs have fairly eliminated this problem.

The format of the *BEO* is different in various operations and also between different catering programs. Some catering houses use preprinted forms, but since the information can vary greatly from party to party, printed forms are often too small.

Most catering software programs generate the *BEOs* automatically as soon the party is booked and all details are confirmed. Often these *BEOs* do not provide sufficient detail, or even space for details. They are cookie cutter approaches and work for operations with limited menus and few extra arrangements.

As a rule, *BEOs* should be available to the respective departments at least two weeks prior to the function date. Of course that is not possible in all cases, since the information is not yet available. Sometimes clients cannot decide about some details, or the credit check or the payment is late, or the function is a last minute booking. When this is the case the department heads should be alerted by e-mail. It is better to call the chef and tell him/her that tomorrow a luncheon requiring 100 chicken breasts will be needed than to wait until late afternoon when the *BEO* is ready.

The same is true for other departments affected by a late pickup, which have to schedule employees. The department heads in the kitchen, the service office and the *Steward's* area do not spend much time on the computer because they are physically supervising employees. It cannot be assumed that once a party is booked and in the computer that the information will be immediately noticed.

Banquet Sales Associates are by temperament, necessity and training imaginative, flexible, customer oriented and always ready to say yes. The result of their work is on paper.

Chefs, Stewards and *Service Supervisors* are realists; they have no time for wishful thinking. Chicken will not turn into fish, 600 dinner plates set out for a party will not turn magically into a different pattern, 1000 blue napkins requisitioned from the laundry will not turn red. Food must be ordered in advance. Food needed for lunch functions scheduled on Monday must be ordered on Thursday and delivered on Friday or very early Monday morning. When there is a holiday weekend, the food for a Tuesday luncheon should be in the house on Friday to make sure that it is ready on time. In some parts of the country, delivery schedules are even longer. In many locations, beverage distributors deliver only on certain days. Sometimes, wine must be ordered weeks in advance to get the right vintage and in the quantity needed.

Advice to *Banquet Sales Associates*: Never leave anything to chance!

Most catering operations employ extra staff on call, especially in the service departments. These employees must be notified when they will be needed, and their availability confirmed. Other supplies, such as linen, uniforms, and other equipment must be ordered. Off-premise caterers, who rent much of their equipment, have to give advance notice to the rental company to get the right equipment delivered on time.

Typical BEO Distribution

Regardless of how the *BEOs* are distributed many departments should get copies to make sure the event will materialize as planned. In large hotels the *BEOs* are distributed to:

- The banquet file.

- *Credit Office/Accounting Office.*

- *Chef's Office.* In large operations, up to 10 copies are needed, in smaller houses, one copy each is needed for the chef, the cold kitchen, the hot kitchen, and the pastry department.

- *Purchasing.* Copies for the person who does the purchasing, receiving, storing, and issuing.

- *Service Department.* Copies for the *Director of Service*, for the *Captains,* for the person making the payroll, and for posting on the bulletin board.

- *Convention Service Department* if not combined with the *Catering Office.*

- *Banquet Housemen.* Sometimes *Housemen* report to the *Director of Service* and get their copies from the service office.

- *Beverage Service.* Copies for the person purchasing, storing, and issuing the beverages. Copies for the bartenders.

- *The Steward's Office,* a number of copies are needed.

- *Food Control Office.*

- *Housekeeping.* Housekeeping is usually in charge of linens and uniforms.

- *Engineering.* The *Engineering Department* should get a copy, even if the function does not need their services. If a number of different services are needed, for instance carpenter and electrician work, one copy for each department is needed.

Price Information

In some operations it is policy not to put the menu price and all other charges on the *BEOs,* and occasionally charges are put in code. The reason for this is so that employees do not know how much the client is charged, and how much revenue the operation is generating. This rationale is counter-productive. Employees will figure out the code very quickly. When there is no code, they spend time guessing how much the client pays. *Servers* who get paid a gratuity share have a right to know how much the guest is charged, so they can check the accuracy of their pay. The chef should know the menu price in order to calculate the food cost. The *Director of Service* is responsible for making the final banquet bill, and must know all charges.

Prices are not confidential. Every item on the *BEO* for which there is normally a charge should show the charge, and when there is no charge it should also be indicated, to eliminate guesswork.

Summer Brunch

New York State Mimosa passed

CONTINENTAL BREAKFAST STATION

Orange and Grapefruit Juices
Miniature Croissants, Danish Pastries and Muffins
Imported and Local Preserves

THE BISTRO TABLE

Assorted Fruits   New York State Cheeses   Goose Liver Mousse
Saucisson in Flaky Pastry, Dijon Mustard
Baskets of Breads and Biscuits

NORTH COUNTRY FARM STATION

Honey Smoked Turkey Breast
Maple Sugar Glazed Ham
Cranberry Relish, Apple Rhubarb Chutney, Whole Grain Mustard
Cabbage Slaw with California Grapes
Buttermilk and Baking Soda Biscuits

NEW YORK STATE STATION

Free Range Chicken, Smoked Pheasant and Duck Confit
Served on Roasted Potatoes and Tomatoes with Rosemary
Organically Grown Field Greens
Sprinkled with Dried Cranberries, Walnuts and Coach Farm Goat Cheese

HUDSON VALLEY SWEETS

Warm Sour Cherry Cobbler
Five Cent Pretzel Rods dipped in Bittersweet Chocolate
Assorted Ice Creams with Sprinkles, Jelly Beans, Reese's Pieces
Bowls of Strawberries, Raspberries and Blueberries
Heaps of Whipped Cream

COFFEE STATION

Extra Strong Coffee, Regular Coffee, Decaffeinated Coffee

Cancellations and attendance changes should be transmitted as soon as possible to the most important departments involved, normally purchasing, kitchen, steward, and service. These changes are always tentative and can go up or down. It is not unusual for receive many changes in expected attendance before the event actually takes place.

The final guaranteed number is very important and must be treated with great care. Purchasing and staffing decisions are based on the final guarantee. Since every cover is important, there should be no ambiguity or guesswork concerning guarantees. Guarantees should always be given for the specific room and function, not under the name of the group. One group of guests can only occupy one space at any given time. A large group, especially a convention or a company, could occupy many rooms for meetings and other functions. If the guarantee is given under the group name, it is not clear what part of the group is meant. Giving the guarantee for a room and function is much clearer. Since speed is critical, guarantees are often transmitted to the most important operating departments over the telephone and by e-mail. If possible, a record of the guarantee changes should be kept.

New:
In most computerized systems guarantee changes are no longer identified by room and group but only by the *BEO number*. Department heads must access the information in the computer to find out that a party increased or decreased.

Guarantee Sheets

Catering facilities with more than one banquet room generate a final guarantee sheet 24 hours before every date. This sheet serves two functions. It is a final written record of all parties taking place on the specific day, and it officially lists all guarantees that might have been transmitted previously. The guarantee sheet lists the name of each group, the room they occupy, the time frame and type of function, the final guaranteed number, and sometimes the linen color to alert the laundry or the *Housekeeping Department*. To emphasize the importance of the guarantee sheet, it should be sent out on a different color paper to that used for the *BEOs*.

The guarantee sheet ties all the *BEOs* together. It is a final check that all departments have the proper *BEOs* and that no party is forgotten and no space is double booked. If a department discovers a function on the guarantee sheet without having the *BEO*, which can happen in large operations with many last minute bookings, it is not too late to make the necessary arrangements. The guarantee sheet should be issued every day, even when no functions are booked on that day. It would say: No functions booked today. This practice gives continuity to the system and allows the security department to lock all banquet rooms. The guarantee sheet is an important check for the accounting department when the bill is sent. If the bill submitted by the *Director of Service* is for a lower number of guests than indicated on the guarantee sheet, the bill can be questioned.

The distribution of the guarantee sheets varies. In addition to the departments on the *BEO* distribution list, the following departments should receive the guarantee sheet:

- The managers office. Copies for the *General Manager* and for the MOD (Manager on Duty).

- The food and beverage office.

- Front service is responsible for posting and listing the parties on the reader boards and for printing the *Daily BEO* for posting in elevators and other suitable locations. Obviously the sheets should be attractively printed and placed in frames, never ever posted with tape on doors or walls. Front service is also responsible for scheduling additional doormen and parking lot attendants. All bell persons should have copies in order to direct guests. Large functions and events attended by dignitaries can pose challenging traffic problems, which must be solved without undue inconvenience to the guests staying in the hotel.

- Security managers must know which function rooms are occupied. All officers should have copies to be able to answer questions about functions. Occasionally security guards and the involvement of the local police department or Secret Service is required.

- Telephone department. Guests may call for information.

- Room Service. Guests may call for information.

- Restaurant managers. Guests may ask for direction to function rooms.

Weekly Banquet Resumés (see sample on next page)

The Catering Manager or Convention Service Manager is responsible for sending out the *Banquet Resumé* in the middle of the week.

The weekly *Banquet Resumés* have the same distribution as the *Guarantee Sheets*.

THE TALL TIMBER IN HOUSE EVENTS
THURSDAY JANUARY 29, 1998 THROUGH WEDNESDAY, FEBRUARY 11, 1998

Name	Time	Function Room	Attendance
Thursday, January 29, 1998			
Circus, Elephant Division			
Meeting	7:00 AM - 3:00 PM	Stable Room	25
Breakfast	7:00 AM - 8:15 AM	Foyer	50
Meeting	8:15 AM - 3:00 PM	Tent Room	50
Lunch	12:00 PM - 1:00 PM	Bamboo Room	50
On Time Airlines			
Breakfast	6:00 AM - 7:30 AM	Sky Lounge	120
Meeting	8:00 AM - 12:00 NOON	SkyLounge	120
Friday, January 30, 1998			
Tall Timber Sales			
Meeting	9:00 - 11:30 AM	Red Room	25
Organic, Inc.			
Breakfast	7:00 AM - 9:00 AM	Chef's Office	15
Meeting	9:00 AM - 1:00 PM	Garden Room	50
Lunch	1:30 PM - 2:30 PM	Veranda	75
Saturday, January 31, 1998			
Pickle Packers			
Dinner Dance	8:00 PM - 11:45 PM	Green Room	350
Sunday, February 1, 1998			
Pickle Packers			
Breakfast	9:00 AM - 11:00AM	Veranda	350
Monday, February 2, 1998			
No functions scheduled			
Tuesday, February 3, 1998			
Balloon Galore			
Picnic Lunch 12:00 noon		Take out	560

Timing

There are several aspects of timing. The first concerns the smooth progress of the function. Many functions are very simple: guests arrive a certain time and leave when they are supposed to. Other parties require minute-by-minute timing. "The timetable was made for a dinner with 1800 guests, and involved a short entertainment interlude and a number of speakers." Precise timing is crucial when the event is televised.

Schedules requested by the client must be reviewed, and changed in the event they do not work. A party is a joint effort, and almost all clients will respond to reasonable objections to a suggested timetable. *Banquet Sales Associates* are more than order takers, they are the professionals, experienced in running parties, and should point out to the client when a timetable does not work. This needs a climate of trust and a good rapport between the client and the *Banquet Sales Associate*.

I remember a fund raising supper given by a socialite scheduled for 9 p.m. She insisted on doing the fund raising, with all speeches and awards ceremonies, before anything was served to her guests. The *Banquet Sales Associate* went along with her schedule. By 10.30 p.m. her guests were so hungry and unruly that some bribed the *Servers* to bring them rolls to eat, and others sent their chauffeurs to the local deli for sandwiches. When the supper was finally served at 11 p.m. there were 800 very unhappy guests.

During dinner dances, the responsibility of coordinating the music with the kitchen and service requirements rests with the *Charge Captain*, who advises the bandleader when to stop the music so the food can be served. Any conductor who does not co-operate with the *Charge Captain* should not be encouraged to come back. Timing is also crucial for luncheons, because most people have appointments in the afternoon. They come to hear the speaker or to attend the presentation. The caterer must make a real effort to stick to the established schedule.

Timing Functions to Maximize Banquet Space

The other aspect of timing is the multiple use of function space. Since space has value, it should be used to maximum capacity. All parties booked should have an estimated closing time, so the room can be made available for other functions. In some wedding facilities, weddings are timed so that parties use reception and banquet rooms in rotation. When weddings take place in hotels, two banquet rooms are normally reserved. The wedding ceremony takes place in one room, while in an other room the reception buffet is set up. While the guests are enjoying the reception, the first room is set up for dinner and dancing. During the dinner, the reception room is set for the dessert buffet. All this is possible with good timing.

Timing To Coordinate the Back Of The House

Another aspect of timing has to do with food quality and logistics in the back of the house. All parties have a starting time, but this time is never the serving time. The *Banquet Sales Associate* should give as precise an estimate as possible when food service starts. If there is dancing between courses, or speeches during dinner, this information should be marked on the *BEOs*.

In order to time food service properly, the *Banquet Chef* has to know the serving time as close as possible. The *Charge Captain* should always confer with the chef about timing, and work closely with the kitchen. Nobody likes surprises, so the more communication between service and kitchen, the better. *Servers* should not march into a kitchen and cry "pick up" without the chef having been notified. *Servers* should not tell any cook to start slicing the meat or dishing out the vegetables. The communication is between the *Charge Captain* and the *Banquet Chef* in charge. All orders concerning service should come only from the *Charge Captain*. All employees should be aware that orders come only from the *Charge Captain* and the *Banquet Chef.*

Some large banquet houses have discreet signal lights over the service doors to alert the *Servers* when to start serving and when to start clearing off. Bussing dirty dishes is always connected with unavoidable clatter, and the *Charge Captain* must time things so that this clatter does not interfere with the program. It is possible that a party is running late, and some *Servers* might not manage to clear their tables in time. If this is the case, then the *Charge Captain* should instruct the *Servers* to be as quiet and as unobtrusive as possible, and not to block the guest's view.

New:
Many large hotels provide *Banquet Captains, Banquet Chefs,* and *Head Banquet Housemen* with walkie-talkies. It is certainly an efficient method to communicate, but not very elegant when employees in tuxedos have bulky antennas sticking out of their back pockets.

Large hotels have a number of service kitchens on different floors. Teams of cooks are assigned to specific kitchens to serve a party. If the serving time is not indicated on the *BEOs* then these employees are sent too soon to the service kitchens, while they could do some work somewhere else.

Staffing

The plague of the restaurant business is absenteeism. The catering industry is dependent on extra or casual employees. These employees have in most cases other career goals or interests. Their first choice of employment, or school, takes precedence over working for a caterer. Little can be done about this situation except slowly weeding out late or no-show employees, and replacing them with dependable ones. Good pay, good working conditions and strong discipline help. Better employees like to work in an environment with set rules, established procedures, and clear lines of command and communications. Morale suffers when lazy employees are not reprimanded, and good employees are continuously asked to pick up the slack. There is more said about this in **Chapter 8, Service.**

Equipment

Equipment is anything that is not edible. Equipment represents an investment and it should be maintained. Even the best equipped operation runs out of equipment occasionally. If all parties on a given day order buffets, it stands to reason that buffet equipment will be in short supply, and some pieces will have to be improvised, rented, or substituted.

Every *Banquet Sales Associate* should be familiar with the size and shape of all equipment, its condition, and the number of pieces available. Equipment needs should be co-ordinated, so that one *Banquet Sales Associate* does not promise something already committed to somebody else. Equipment can be shared between parties, if the timing is co-ordinated. Often, a slight adjustment in timing allows for multiple use of specific pieces when necessary. However, the best-laid plans do not always work out, and depending too much on perfect scheduling can lead to equipment shortages.

Dinner Menu Given in California

FIRST COURSE
Seared Ahi Tuna
with grilled Endive
(Chappellet Signature Chardonnay 1998)

SECOND COURSE
Ravioli filled with Mascarpone Cheese and Porcini
Garden Peas Braised with shredded Lettuce and Pancetta
(Grgich Hills Napa Valley Chardonnay 1997)

MAIN COURSE
Roast Loin of Veal
Natural Juice with the Scent of Sage
Fava Beans, Fiddlehead Greens and Ramps
(Heitz Bella Oaks Cabernet Sauvignon, Magnums 1995)

DESSERT
Lemon Crème Brulée
Blackberry Coulis
(Far Niente Semillon/Sauvignon blanc 1991)

Almond Cookies
Coffee
California Brandy

Tables

Banquet tables are called *lumber* in the industry because they are made of plywood or a composite material, have foldable legs and are always being taken somewhere, or stored, or being used. They take a lot of abuse and sometimes are in deplorable condition. In better banquet facilities the tables are foam padded or *Servers* use a light felt table cover under the tablecloth. The standard height of these tables is 30 inches.

Knowing the sizes and capacity of tables is especially important when booking parties that require buffets. The *Banquet Sales Associates* should know how big a buffet must be for a specific occasion, and how the tables fit into the designated space. It is helpful to talk to the *Director of Service* about specific setups. The *Director of Service* works with the equipment every day, and often can visualize the look of a setup better than the *Banquet Sales Associate*.

The size and shape of the buffet table is always indicated on the *BEOs*, and in case the table size is unusual, the buffet setup should be discussed with the chef. A poorly planned buffet table might not be able to accommodate all food displays, flowers, ice carvings and table equipment which the chef has planned.

List of Standard Banquet Folding Tables.

Table Type	Table Size	Table Cloth Size
Round Tables	2½' cocktail	54" x 54"
	3' cocktail	64" x 64"
	4½' cocktail	64" x 64"
	5', 10 people	84" x 84"
	5½', 10 people	90" x 90"
	6', 12 people	90" x 90"
Rectangular	6' x 18"	
	6' x 24"	
	6' x 30"	
	6' x 36"	
	5' x 30"	
	4' x 30"	

Table type	Table Size	Table Cloth Size
Square	30" x 30"	
Half Round	5' x 30"	
Quarter Round	30" x 30"	
Crescent	6' x 36"	

Combinations:

To make a large oval table for 16 customers combine two half rounds with four rectangular tables 6' x 30".

For hollow buffet table combine four crescent tables with sufficient number of 3' rectangular tables.

For clover leave buffet table with large center combine half round tables with rectangular and square table.

China and Glassware

Some operations have a choice of different quality china and glassware. Normally, there is an extra charge for the use of the better equipment. The *Banquet Sales Associate* should know the replacement cost of this equipment, and should discourage its use if the party is held in a location with inherent breakage problems, even if the host is willing to pay for it. In some banquet pantries, dishwashing might take place on a level many floors away and it would be foolish to jeopardize the best china and stemware. The extra charge for the equipment does not cover the replacement cost, and in some cases it cannot be replaced quickly enough.

In off-premise catering operations the equipment is normally rented. Good communication with the rental company is necessary to know what is available, and to get a commitment for the use of certain equipment before it is rented to somebody else. Speed is always important to turn over rooms; clearing dishes efficiently is considered a sign of good service. Customers do not like to sit staring at soiled plates.

Much equipment is damaged by carelessness. It is imperative that all employees treat equipment with care and respect, no matter how quickly they are moving to perform a given task. Breakage is no laughing matter. Some operations display prices for each type of china, others post the replacement costs prominently when the quarterly inventory is taken.

Linen

The linen supply is always a problem in catering houses. When there is a choice of many colors, the *Banquet Sales Associate* should know the quantities available in each color, and also who is using it on a particular day. In some houses, the daily guarantee sheet lists the linen color next to each function in order to alert the linen room, normally part of *Housekeeping* or in smaller houses part of the *Steward's Department*, about the color and quantity of linen needed. Some operations also list the linen color selected in the computer. This way, the use and availability of specific colors can be monitored.

There are a number of options available to operators concerning linen supply. Linen can be rented from commercial laundries, who normally stock a number of colors and sizes and rent linen and uniforms. The charge is by the piece delivered clean or by the number of soiled pieces picked up. In many cases quality is poor. Colored linen gets washed out and the older linen does not match the newer linen.

Some laundries offer to buy a specific quality, in certain colors and sizes for a specific operation on a contract basis. The banquet operator has no immediate linen expense, but has to sign a long-term contract, and has little leverage when the quality is poor on account of inferior washing, pressing or slow replacement. Soiled linen is not always counted when it is sent out, and seldom counted when it is delivered clean. Sometimes, the laundry sends in, and bills, for the same amount every week, regardless of actual use. In other cases, the laundry claims, often rightfully, large losses on account of abuse or low counts, and charges for these losses.

For these and other reasons, some catering houses purchase their own linen and install laundries to take care of it. The initial investment for the linen inventory, and the laundry equipment is large, especially when the operation offers a choice of colors, and quality expectations are high. All cotton linen or genuine linen requires ironing; polyester blends or synthetic fibers require little or no ironing. If all cotton or genuine linen is used, the laundry should be equipped with ironing machines. The labor cost of operating the laundry varies. In some catering operations, laundry can be done in off time, and by employees who would have little to do because there is no immediate business. Providing space and labor is available, it is economically advantageous to have a laundry.

Linen quality is a problem in many operations. Commercial laundries are highly mechanized, and often staffed with unskilled workers. Linen is seldom sorted thoroughly, and damaged or badly stained linen is washed and sent out again and charged for. If the amount of linen ordered for a specific function does not allow for a certain number of rejects, it is possible that the amount ordered will not be enough to cover the need. Rejected linen should be separated and inspected by a competent management oriented person. Rejected linen, if not fit for further use, should be taken out of circulation and not sent back to the laundry. Some employees reject any piece with the slightest defect; others use pieces with the biggest stains and holes. The quality expectations of management should be enforced by a management person, and not left up to employees.

Skirts

Tables are often skirted. The principle of skirting is to hide the table legs when the table would be visible. Tables with chairs around are not skirted, but buffet tables, head tables, the inside of U shaped conference tables, the outsides of committee tables, and the outsides of meeting tables when set up schoolroom style should be skirted. For table configurations not listed, measure the table perimeter and add six inches for the proper skirting length.

To calculate the skirting length required for round tables, use the following formula (round off to the next six inch increment):

<u>Table diameter x 3.14 divided by 12</u>

Table skirts come in many different colors and shapes. Some are pleated or ruffled; others are straight. Some skirts are designed in two parts, a lower or base part, and an overlay, which could be transparent lace, or a solid half skirt. As is the case with table linen, the *Banquet Sales Associate* should know which skirts are available, and who is using skirts of the same color on the same day. Co-ordination of the color of the tabletop with the selected skirts is also important and should be specified by the *Banquet Sales Associate*. Skirts are dry cleaned. and should be hung on special hangers when not in use. Normally, they can be used many times between cleaning.

Chafing Dishes and Hollow Ware

Chafing dishes are ornamental containers that keep food and liquids hot in front of the customers. Hollow ware are metal containers used for the service of hot beverages, but the term is also used for other metal containers, such as sugar bowls and creamers. Chafing dishes and hollow ware can be manufactured in a number of different metals, such as silver plate on copper or stainless steel bodies, copper plate, stainless steel, and other alloys. Chafing dishes consist of a frame, a water bath, and inserts. Simple chafing dishes consist of wire frames, and can even be used with disposable aluminum pans. The price varies according to the quality and sturdiness of the equipment. Silver and copper pieces require polishing, always done by hand.

The heat source for chafing dishes is in most cases canned fuel, which can be liquid or solid. The most common brand is *Sterno*, and the name has become almost a generic term. Chafing dishes can also be heated electrically. Dishes heated with canned fuel always present a fire hazard, and employees must be instructed to extinguish the flames when the equipment is no longer needed. At the same time, fuel can get burn down in the middle of service. It is important to check the fuel periodically.

Burning canned fuel gives off on unpleasant odor.

Electric chafing dishes require outlets close by. Cables can be cumbersome to work around, and can be a hazard. Electric equipment is safer than equipment heated with open flame, but it is more difficult to clean.

Chafing dishes should always be purchased with additional inserts, when possible in different sizes. This way, the food can be replenished by bringing a full pan to the table, rather than by bringing additional food in another container and then dumping it in the chafing dish. The empty container should be carefully removed, because the water in the water bath could be boiling. Chafing dish covers can cause a logistical problem. Most chafing dishes come equipped with decorative covers. They look wonderful on the frame, but they must be removed to get access to the food. Guests almost never see them, because they are removed when the guests arrive. These covers are normally large, and in most cases are stored under the buffet table. Some chafing dishes come with half covers, which can be folded back when needed. Others have self-storing covers, which fold under the chafing dish when open.

One of the most often used pieces of equipment are coffee urns. Urns are normally used in groups of three, one for regular coffee, one for decaffeinated coffee, and one for tea water. They should be clearly marked not only for the benefit of the guests, but also to avoid using coffee urns for tea water. Coffee leaves a residue that is difficult to remove, and the water will pick up the coffee flavor easily. It is best to use special urns for tea water only.

Urns come in different sizes. The *Banquet Sales Associate* should know the size of the urns, and how many are available. The sizes should be marked, because coffee is sold often by the gallon, and employees will fill up available urns without considering what the host contracted for. Coffee urns are often heated electrically, especially when used on sideboards in meeting rooms. There are exciting new coffee systems on the market, which allow coffee to be brewed directly into portable containers, often referred to as shuttles which can be placed on buffets. The product is fresher because it can be brewed in smaller quantities. Often coffee sits on buffet tables for hours in ornate urns and tastes like mud.

In many operations, some cooking is done on buffets in the dining room, such as mixing pastas with sauces, stir-frying oriental dishes, and filling crêpes. The stoves used are mostly fueled by compressed gas. Use of this equipment is regulated by local ordinances. Gas stoves are potentially very dangerous, and great care must be exercised in their use. When gas stoves are not permitted, electric hot plates can be used, but the same problems of logistics explained in connection with electric chafing dishes apply.

New:
A new device called an induction heater has come on the market. It looks

like an ordinary electric hot plate but heat is only created when a pot or pan made of a precise metal alloy is placed on top. It is perfectly safe for light cooking in a function room.

Decorations

Typical decorations are buffet centerpieces. Some are made in house from edible materials such as chocolate, bread, and salt dough. Others are fruit and vegetable displays, often not meant to be eaten, and bread displays. Ice carvings are very popular. There is usually a charge for custom ice pieces. In some large banquet operations, ice centerpieces are automatically provided for buffets free of charge. Custom ice pieces add glamor to the event. If there is nobody on staff to make them, ice pieces are available from outside contractors in most areas. These pieces are heavy; the standard block weighs 300 pounds, and the finished piece probably half of that. The buffet table must be sturdy enough to support the weight of the ice, and also of those setting up the piece, because one or two people normally have to climb onto the table to make final adjustments. Ice pieces melt at the rate of 1½ inches an hour under normal temperatures. An ice pan, equipped with a drain connected by hose to a bucket, should be used to support the ice carving. When electric lights are used, great caution is necessary. Lights should never be placed where they can get wet. Spots directed at a piece generate heat, and also could shine on guests.

Inedible decorations could be large vases, statues, risers, turntables, mirrors, and grocery store type food displays, such as jars of pasta and bowls of dry food ingredients. Display pieces should be high, so they can be seen from across the room. The trend is to put buffet food on small platters with minimal decoration so the food can be easily replenished rather than on huge platters that will stay on the buffet and look ravished in a short time.

Large shells or small boats with seafood served on shaved ice are always popular. The seafood can be easily replenished. Although we should not label cooks as "decoration" they look very decorative behind a buffet table.

Other decorative elements are candlesticks and candles. In most cases, table candles are part of the flower arrangement, and co-ordination between the florist and the house is needed to make sure there is no misunderstanding about the supply of candles and candlesticks. Many catering houses have candelabras for head tables. The *Banquet Sales Associate* should know the size and configuration of the candelabra, the quantities available, and the size and color choices of candles. There is often a charge for special candles.

The Search for Storage Space

Most operations are chronically short of storage space. The catering business is a business with greatly fluctuating demand, and equipment must be constantly moved and stored when not in use. Chairs can be neatly arranged along the walls in empty banquet rooms but tables and platforms, risers, dance floors, steps, and podiums must be stored out of sight.

The *Chef's Department* must store buffet centerpieces, dummy cakes, mirrors, and platters. The *Steward* stores table equipment when it is not in use. Storing chafing dishes is a problem in most operations. They are bulky; but some are very beautiful and expensive. They could be scratched easily, and might bend out of shape when dropped. Some operations use made to measure storage cases to protect the chafing dishes when not in use. These cases are very helpful, and do not occupy much space, because they can be stacked. Loosely stored chafing dishes occupy too much space, and could be damaged easily.

Much equipment is damaged and lost because of lack of storage space. Crowded storage spaces are a potential fire hazard, and are often used by employees for smoking or for hiding food and drink. In large operations, storage space inspections can turn up interesting finds. When service employees are hired to work two shifts a day, they need a place to rest between shifts. If management does not provide this place, they will use storage spaces to rest and to pass the time. I remember one place in which some employees had built a veritable den to hide in and to sleep in between shifts.

Finding storage space requires imagination. Sometimes it is necessary to rent off-premise storage space fpr extra equipment.

Turnaround

Tables, chairs, and other equipment are set up and removed by banquet *Housemen*. Enough labor should be scheduled to set up or break down a room as quickly as possible so it can be used again. I have seen huge ballrooms reset in 30 minutes between the time the last guests left and the next ones arrived. Tables could be ready, set with linen and china in an adjacent room, and carried in when needed. *Servers* could have all equipment for their stations inspected and ready on rolling tables, waiting in the wings like in a theater and ready to set up a room in short time. The catering business is like the theater business; the attitude must be "The show must go on".

All rooms should be cleaned and cleared as soon as the party is over. They should not be left to be cleaned until the next day, unless there is absolutely no business and nobody has made appointments to show the rooms. The banquet space should always be presentable. It should be clean, and all chairs should be lined up against the wall, unless it is set for a specific function. There should be no tables in the room if possible. If there is no storage place for tables, they should be covered with linen. Sometimes, a number of tables are set with different linen and table appointments to show prospective guests how they will look. When these appointments are scheduled ahead of time, the florist could be asked to provide a choice of centerpieces.

When showing banquet space to prospective clients, cleanliness is very important. The space is generally shown during the day or when it is fully lit. Poor maintenance, worn rugs, and plain dirt show so much more than when a room is set with furniture and the lights are dimmed. Some rooms look shabby when they are shown during the day. It is a challenge for the *Banquet Sales Associate* to convince the client that the room will look glamorous on the night of the party.

Major renovation of banquet space is a capital budget item, and is normally scheduled every seven to ten years. Scheduling routine maintenance, such as touch up of painted surfaces, and carpet and drapery cleaning, is the responsibility of the *Director of Catering*.

Other Logistical Challenges

Key Controls

Banquet rooms should be lockable. This is not always the case, but in order to reduce vandalism and theft, and when permitted by law, a program of installing locks should be instituted. It is amazing that in many hotels banquet rooms are always open, accessible to anybody able to avoid *Security* in the lobby. There have actually been cases of homeless people camping out in dark balconies of ornate ballrooms.

When possible, all banquet rooms should be keyed alike. It is very awkward for the *Banquet Sales Associate*, and for service and setup employees, to carry bundles of keys around. The banquet room keys should be on a large key ring. Normally, one ring is kept in the *Security Office*, to be signed in and out, and the other in the *Banquet Office*. Besides the keys to the banquet rooms, the rings could contain keys to auxiliary areas, such as pantries and storage rooms. Which keys to put on the banquet ring, and therefore make accessible to banquet personnel, is a decision for management. Normally kitchen keys, beverage storeroom keys, and keys to expensive equipment, including portable telephones and audio visual equipment, are not put on the banquet key ring. These keys are on different rings, and are issued when needed.

Storing of Guest Materials

It is common for guests to send printed and display material for meetings in advance of the actual meetings. The operation has an obligation to store this material and find it when needed. It is a very uncomfortable situation for both client and caterer when the client's materials cannot be located. There should be clear printed instructions on how packages should be addressed. The package room in large hotels handles many packages including suitcases and often lost and found items.

Sample of a package room information sheet given to clients.

Package Room Policies

- All packages connected with a conference or function should be addressed to the hotel in care of The Package Room and to the attention of the *Banquet Sales Associate* in charge of the party. It should state the arrival date of the group with names and dates of the conference or function and banquet rooms. The packages should be marked **INSIDE DELIVERY.**

- The hotel package room attendant or the banquet service staff will deliver the packages to the function rooms on the date indicated. Packages should not arrive more than three (3) weeks prior to the function.

- Packages will be kept up to five (5) business days after the close of the convention. The hotel is happy to return-ship packages if return labels are provided and a shipper is identified. All costs connected are borne by the client. Delicate equipment will only be shipped if packed properly by competent personnel.

- The Address of our loading dock is:

  Hotel Green Giant
  Attention: Package Room
  300 East 257 Street
  Blue Mountain, CA 09903
  (875) 993 7865

If the material is left in function rooms overnight, the *Banquet Sales Associate* should point out that it is at the client's risk. Even when the banquet rooms can be locked, the kitchen and pantry doors are often left unlocked. If the material is valuable, such as computers and other expensive equipment, the client should rent private security guards. They should not be allowed to lock themselves in the banquet room to sleep there with their equipment.

Printed guest materials should be stored for a reasonable amount of time after the party. The normal time is up to 5 business days. The client should be made aware that the caterer will not take any responsibility for the security of the material after that time, and the client should be advised to remove any valuable items as soon as the party is over.

Table favors and personal gift items, especially for weddings, should be sent directly to the *Banquet Sales Associate* or to the office of the *Director of Service*. In the case of table favors, the count should be verified in order to prevent unpleasant surprises when the party takes place.

Theft and Vandalism

Theft and vandalism are always a problem. In some cases, vandalism is just carelessness, and better supervision and education can reduce damage. In other cases, vandalism is deliberate, caused by a disgruntled employee, or by outsiders gaining access to the building or to the grounds. The best prevention is to keep the property well battened down, to provide security, and to keep everyone's eyes and ears open. Often, a cadre of loyal and devoted employees can provide information about theft and vandalism, and the operator should not hesitate to prosecute the perpetrators to the full extent of the law.

In the catering business, many extra employees are used, and their records are not always checked or checkable. It is not unusual for any warm body recommended by another employee applying for work is hired. This person could have a drug habit supported by stealing. There are a number of different kinds of thefts. One is theft from the lockers of other employees. Another is theft from guests' purses, although this is rarer because it is easier to trace. Large and small theft is possible and quite common. It ranges from the cook taking home a few steaks or some packages of coffee, the bartender or other employees taking some bottles of liquor, or some employees systematically taking china and flatware until they have a complete setting at home. It is prudent to conduct unannounced locker inspections. These inspections should always be done by at least two members of management and employee representatives.

Theft can also be theft of services. In à la carte situations, it is possible that *Servers* charge and collect from the client for beverages, but use the same check a number of times. In order to do so, they could be operating in collusion with the bartenders, or they could bring bottles purchased at the liquor store and sold at a hefty profit. Theft can also take place when the person receiving food makes a deal with the purveyors or their drivers to deliver merchandise somewhere else, but have the catering facility pay for the full amount. Short weight and direct kickbacks are also possible. Only strong management and good supervision can reduce or eliminate theft.

Summary

Because all parties have special requirements, good communications with the client is very important. Then all the information must be clearly transmitted to the employees who will carry them out. The main tool is the *BEO*, which must be very detailed and precise. The *BEO* is often updated with new and additional information, which must be effectively communicated. The final guaranteed attendant numbers are then conveyed on a guarantee sheet. Timing at functions is important, and a realistic timetable must be established to meet the goals of the host, and the requirements of the caterer. Staffing in the catering business is full of challenges, because many employees work part time work force only. The availability of equipment, their care and storage needs are of concern to all operators.

Other challenges of logistics are turning around banquet space efficiently to maximize space utilization, showing banquet rooms clean and tidy, controlling keys, preventing stealing and vandalism, and storage of guest items.

Discussion Questions

- Why are good rapport and precise communication with the host so important?

- What is a *BEO*? Which departments receive copies?

- What is a guarantee sheet? Which departments beside the Food and Beverage Department should get the guarantee sheet?

- How are guarantee changes handled?

- Elaborate on the importance of timing.

- What is consumable equipment?

- What is hollow ware?

- List some possible problems with linen.

- Explain the need for storage space.

- Explain the importance of quick turn around of banquet space.

- Elaborate on key controls.

- Discuss stealing and vandalism and how it can be prevented.

- How long should guest items be stored after a funct

Chapter Six
CHOOSING THE RIGHT MENU

Festive Viennese Christmas Dinner

**Hot and cold Hors d'Oeuvres, Appetizers and Leckerbissen
from the Realms of the Austrian Hungarian Empire**

*Moet et Chandon Magnums
Bollinger Special Cuvée
Piper Heidsieck
Schlumberger Austrian Sekt
Servus Austria White Wine*

Dinner Menu

**Warm Duckling Salad on a Bed of crisp Greens
Balsamic Vinaigrette Dressing**

1991 Riesling Federspiel, Wachau, Austria
****

Hearty Oxtail Broth

Sandeman Don Fino Sherry passed
****

**Veal Medallion
Ragout of wild Mushrooms
Hungarian Tahornya
Savoy Cabbage**

1986 Bonne Mares, Burgundy
****

**Sacher Torte, Strudel, Dobosh
and other legendary Desserts**

1976 Winkler Hasensprung Riesling Auslese

The dinner menu combines central European flavors with generally accepted elegant banquet food. The menu was designed to please a sophisticated New York audience and was not intended to be an old fashioned ethnic dinner.

Chapter Six
CHOOSING THE RIGHT MENU

Objectives

- To understand the importance of writing a menu that meets the guest expectations and maximizes the potential of the operation.

- To understand factors to consider when choosing a menu such as the location of the function room in relation to the kitchen.

- To understand pricing methods and philosophies.

- To understand the concept of unit pricing.

Introduction

This chapter deals with choosing the menu most suitable for the occasion, maximizing revenue and minimizing possible disasters. The rules for menu construction are detailed in **Chapter 10, Basic Rules of Menus Construction.**

One of the most important aspects of booking a party is writing a menu. First, the guest expectations must be evaluated. This takes patience, understanding and the willingness to keep the goal of the party in mind. Successful *Banquet Sales Associates* always think first what is important to the host. After the goal of the party has been clearly understood, and a rapport is established, the other details of the menus can be discussed. Obviously, budget is an important consideration in almost all cases, and working within a budget can be a challenge. In some cases it is advantageous to get the chef involved in the menu making process. However, the *Executive Chef* should not have to spend more time then absolutely necessary in the *Banquet Office*. He or she has many other important duties.

> **Note:**
> **Most operations discourage *Banquet Sales Associates* from creating custom menus. A choice of menus is set up in the computer, attractively printed. The customers are given the package and ask to select the menus. Changes and deviations are strongly discouraged because they would upset the system. This chapter is written for the operations who still write custom menus.**

When the budget is strained the chef can be asked to recommend in writing menu choices or the *Banquet Sales Associate* can make an appointment to see the *Executive Chef* or *Banquet Chef*. Assessing the quality expectations of both guests and management play an important role in menu making. Since the *Banquet Sales Associate* is judged by profit contribution, calculating costs is very important. When menus are created, other considerations besides costs come into play, such as staff capabilities, the seasons when the party takes place or the distance from the kitchen to the dining room. Whether to sell by the unit or by the person is also important.

Evaluating Guest Expectations

In order to sell banquets successfully, and to create the right menu for the occasion, good culinary knowledge is necessary. For this reason, many hotels make the *Sales Department* responsible only for booking the sleeping rooms and delegate arrangements for food functions to the *Catering Department*. The possible drawback is having to deal with two individuals in the hotel, one making sleeping room and standard meeting arrangements and the other making food arrangements. Despite the slight drawback this arrangement is best for the client, because most employees in *Sales Departments* are not comfortable or knowledgeable enough to handle food events.

No party is routine. Experienced *Banquet Sales Associates* must therefore have an inquiring mind and begin a process of communication with the client that will result in getting as much relevant information as possible about the planned function. The expectations of the prospective client should be assessed, and the right questions asked about the people to be invited. Honest answers must be given to questions asked by the client. The party should also be considered from the client's perspective. The *Banquet Sales Associate* sells an event, but also sells hope to the client, that the upcoming event will be unique, memorable, and successful.

The client may not be familiar with all aspects of social etiquette or the customs of the catering business. Good *Banquet Sales Associates* will counsel and, if necessary, strongly advise the client of the suitability of their proposed plan, menu or schedule. The makeup of the group is important. If the group is mixed between Jewish and gentile guests, it might be important to advise the kitchen to be prepared for requests of well done meat or for plain meals. If the group is of a particular ethnic origin, once again there may be special food preferences. The more that is known about the group, the better.

Keeping the Goal of the Party in Mind

Every party has a focus, and it should be kept in mind when making the menu. At weddings the focus is obviously the bride, the groom, and the immediate families. All efforts should be made to please them. Most weddings have dancing, so the food should be such that it can be held in the kitchen if the schedule is delayed. Food should be chosen that is easy to serve and uncomplicated to eat. When speeches are scheduled, the timing of the party is vital. Food that cannot wait, or takes too long to eat, or distracts from the purpose of the event, should not be recommended. If the event is given in someone's honor, the *Banquet Sales Associate* should try to find out the food preferences of the guest of honor. It may not be appropriate to serve to the others, but the special dish could be provided for the guest of honor.

Working within a Budget

Before prices are mentioned, the *Banquet Sales Associate* should try to sell up! The primary goals are to create a most memorable event and to maximize revenue. In many cases, however, the host has a specific budget in mind. The *Banquet Sales Associate* allocates the money in the budget to the various segments of the package to get a mix that both satisfies the client and meets the profit goals of the establishment. When there is a fixed budget, the charges payable to the establishment must be calculated first. Most operations have standard gratuities, and many areas have city and state sales taxes. If, for example, the gratuity is 19% and the sales tax is 8.25%, the budgeted sum per person must be divided by 127.25% and multiplied by 100 in order to arrive at the sum available for the party. If the checkroom is hosted, that charge must be deducted. There may be a fixed parking charge. After all additional fixed charges are deducted; the net budget figure is available.

The next step is to allocate the money between beverage and food. This decision is made with the client. If the event is a reception, the balance between amounts of food and beverage must be discussed. Are the guests expecting more beverages, or would they like more food? When it is determined how much to allocate for food and beverage, service styles and beverage brands can be discussed. If *Servers* pass the liquor, then house brands, which are less expensive than brand names, could be substituted. If the reception requires bars, the client might not wish to serve house brands, which are generally cheaper. Bartender charges are normally additional and the client can save money by passing beverages on trays.

When the reception is followed by a sit down dinner, hors d'oeuvres passed butler-style during the reception could be adequate, because they cost less than a buffet. More money could be spent on the dinner itself. On the other hand, certain types of parties are only successful when the receptions are lavish and have buffets. The food served at the dinner itself could be less important.

Should beverages be served during dinner? Would one variety of wine be sufficient, or should there be a choice of wines, or different wines served with each course? If there were no money in the budget for beverages during dinner, would the host allow à la carte beverage service? (The *Servers* would take drink orders at the table, to be paid by each individual). Would the host pay for the cashiers and bartenders needed for à la carte sales? At weddings today, it is also acceptable for the Champagne toast to be provided by the host, and for the guests to pay for their other drinks as they order them.

Could money be saved on flowers and decorations, and put into food or beverage?

It is a challenge to work within a budget and it takes serious investigation and imagination to make the best possible arrangement for both the client and the house.

Getting the Chef Involved

As a last resort the chef should be involved in the menu-making process when the budget is tight.

When the chef is helping to make the menu, the client gets the benefit of up-to-date, market oriented advice. Chefs might know seasonal price fluctuations of food better than many *Banquet Sales Associates*, and can suggest dishes that meet the budget, because the main ingredients will be cheaper by the time the party takes place. A chef might also be able to suggest dishes or cuts of meat not considered by the *Banquet Sales Associate*. These suggestions are useful, but they should be evaluated carefully by both client and *Banquet Sales Associate* in order to avoid serving experimental dishes. The advice of the chef is usually kitchen oriented, and seldom takes the overall purpose of the party into consideration. Some chefs suggest only what they like to cook and not what the customers expect.

Canned vs. Custom Menus

Canned menus are printed menus, sent to prospective clients months before the party takes place. Canned menus are carefully crafted to meet the expectations of a broad spectrum of customers and present different price ranges. The items on these menus can be taken off the shelf and require little extra time, because they fit into the existing work flow of the operation. They are routine menus to process, to prepare, and to serve.

Custom menus are, as the name indicates, made to order to fit specific occasions. They are more expensive than canned menus. Custom menus need more labor, because the food has to be specially ordered, received, and issued. Preparation is more complex and requires more supervision. Custom menus could require overtime because the preparation is complex. Serving might require more equipment, and more skilled service staff.

When the quality expectations of the management are clearly defined, the client's budget limitations can be put into better perspective. Some establishments might be just too expensive for certain clients.

The quality standards of the operation should never be lowered!

It would be wrong to lower quality levels to satisfy a specific group. The logistics of buying, for instance, a cheaper grade of meat or lesser quality vegetables to provide a cheaper meal is not practical. Quality is not confined to a single product, but is the combination of all products in use, from the brand of spices to the freshness of dairy products, and the brand of chocolate used in the bake shop. Cutting portion sizes to meet a budget is also wrong. The food cost is only a small part of the overall cost, and lowering the cost of one component of a meal makes little impact on the overall expenses of the operation.

128

Lowering quality standards is a self defeating policy. A quality level, once established, should never be compromised. The guests attending the function know about the establishment, and it is better to dazzle them than leave them disappointed. Even if the expected guests are not sophisticated in culinary arts and their expectations are low, the quality standard of the house should never be compromised.

Calculating Costs and Profit Contribution

The costs of food, beverage, and labor should be calculated for every function. If the costs cannot be established immediately, the *Banquet Sales Associate* should have the menu costed out before making a final commitment. Many catering houses provide cost sheets for the most common main courses. They can easily be updated weekly by computer. The *Banquet Sales Associate* should also be familiar with portion sizes. Beverage prices do not change frequently. A standard cost information sheet will help in calculating the beverage cost. Wine prices fluctuate according to the vintage and must be verified before a commitment is made. Some catering programs calculate profits down to the last penny which is unnecessary.

The labor cost of service is normally rather low, because *Servers* are compensated through gratuities. This cost is also quite standard, although special menus might require additional *Servers*. The *Banquet Sales Associate* should keep pricing in mind when additional bartenders and buffet *Servers* are needed, or when smaller tables than normal are requested.

Kitchen and *Steward* labor can be very much affected by menu choices. A breakfast calling for fried eggs or omelettes requires much more labor than a breakfast with scrambled eggs. Meat carved at the last moment, such as roasts, is more labor intensive than meat portioned ahead of time, such as steaks. When carvers are needed in the dining room, either at the buffet or to cut meat at the head table, this cost should be calculated. In many houses there is an extra labor charge for these services. Items plated ahead of time, especially cold plates, require less labor than food that can be plated at the last moment. Service from silver platters is much more labor efficient in the kitchen than plate service. China and glasses requiring extra handling or hand washing increase the labor cost of the *Steward's Department*. Late parties could increase the labor cost. While overtime cost for *Servers* is part of the contract and is usually passed on to the client, kitchen and *Steward* labor costs are seldom included.

Salespeople should keep in mind that a small concession or promise made to the client could have enormous effects on the labor cost. The only way to guard against this situation is by making the *Banquet Sales Associate* as cost conscious as possible. A good example of little extras would be *Dainty Bundles of Asparagus tied with Leek Strings*. That sounds wonderful but could add a considerable overtime to the kitchen payroll.

Staff Capabilities

Selling should never be handicapped because of staff shortages or other staffing problems. However, the capabilities of the staff and the resources available should be kept in mind when menus are made. Although just about every conceivable food product can be purchased, there is a limit to what can be handled in different stages of preparation, especially when the operation is working with a corporate purchasing office or with a full service provider. The *Executive Chef's* hands are tied, only items approved and readily available can usually be purchased, and special orders and buying from outside the system is discouraged.

If the operation is not equipped with a butcher shop, certain cuts of meat and fish might be hard to obtain. When there is no bakeshop, all desserts must be purchased from local bakeries. They might not be able to provide certain specialty items. If the kitchen is short on artistic talent, custom-made centerpieces should not be recommended.

If the service staff is not very experienced, it would not be wise to let them carve individual roasts for every table. If they are not proficient in silver service, don't let them serve soup from tureens. A good *Banquet Sales Associate* keeps the staff limitations in mind when making menus.

At the same time, the *Banquet Sales Associate* should keep staff strengths in mind when creating menus. The menus should be based on the strengths, rather than on the weaknesses of the staff. Honest evaluation of the staff is essential, and good communication between all personnel is necessary to assess the available talents. The staff should be challenged within reason to perform at more than the routine level. The spirit of the operation should be "We can do it". However, it would be foolish to promise the client something that cannot be achieved.

Keeping Seasons in Focus

Banquets are often booked months in advance. When making menus, the time of the year and season when the party takes place should be kept in mind. Food choices are different in parts of the country where seasons are pronounced. Heavy, substantial food is more suitable for winter meals than summer meals. Although most fruits and vegetables are available all year, some have distinct seasons. This is the time when they are best, and normally cheapest.

It is nice to take advantage of locally produced specialties. This should be carefully checked because the purchasing offices in large corporations are often reluctant, and may even be prohibited from dealing with small purveyors or unapproved products. It is a pleasant touch when the menu reflects local seasonal food. The quality is normally excellent, and the cost could be low. The season should also be reflected in other ways. It could be reflected in the menu language, in the garnishes and in the composition of the menu. A fruit appetizer or cold soup for example are more appropriate in the summer than in the winter.

The beverage choice could also reflect the seasons. A blush wine in spring and summer could be more suitable than a heavy red wine. A slush drink could be more fun than standard drinks on a summer buffet.

When making menus, holidays should also be taken into consideration. Serving rabbit stew on Easter Sunday shows insensitivity as does baked ham on a Jewish holiday. Although catering houses are normally rigidly neutral in religious matters, it would be prudent to remind the client about eating habits when a function falls on a specific holiday. The wrong menu could affect attendance and cause embarrassment to the client and the establishment.

I remember a party taking place on Good Friday, a day abstinence from meat for many Christians, with a meat dish as main course. A large number of guests requested fish substitutes, which threw the kitchen and service staff in a tailspin. The *Banquet Chef* could have planned for extra fish and cooked fewer meat portions, but the basic responsibility about advising the kitchen to have fish substitutes available should have fallen to the *Banquet Sales Associate.* Some political groups have a defined constituency. On one occasion the *Banquet Sales Associate* sold Roast Rib of Beef to a large mostly Jewish group, and all wanted outside cuts and well done meat. The kitchen became a battleground between frustrated *Servers* and equally frustrated cooks.

Taking the season into consideration is very important for off-premise caterers, since it could affect not only transportation, but also menu choices. If the meal is served out of doors in the summer, gelatin-based desserts and ice cream are difficult to serve unless adequate refrigeration is provided. Some foods, such as delicate salads and cold appetizers, are more in demand in summer than in winter, but require more refrigerated equipment to keep plates and ingredients cold. Tents that are not air-conditioned can be very hot in the summer. When serving meals under tents, menu choices as well as staff uniforms must be considered in light of the heat. Cooking and keeping food hot under makeshift conditions, frequently encountered in off-premise catering situations, is more difficult in the winter in than in the summer. It can be a challenge to serve a meal hot.

Timing

The subject of timing has been addressed in a number of places in this book. In order to stay within a prescribed time schedule established by the client, compromises of menu choice and service style may occasionally be made. When service time is short, appetizers can be preplated and set on tables before the guests arrive. At some luncheons, desserts and coffee can be placed on the table for the clients to serve themselves. Salads served with the main course are faster to serve than salads served as a separate course. Wine service takes a few precious minutes. If time is very short, the open bottles can be placed on the table.

The time required to dish out food should also be taken into consideration when time is short. When food is dished out, whether in the kitchen or in the dining room, the shape of the food can make a big difference. Whole stalks of asparagus and whole stems of broccoli are harder to dish out than walnut-shaped pieces of vegetables, such as zucchini chunks (not slices) and whole tiny carrots, mushroom buttons, and other vegetables that can be scooped up quickly. Long pasta takes more time to plate and eat than short pasta, such as tortellini, shells, and spaetzle.

Service from silver platters, commonly called French service, is much faster than plate service. Each *Server* gets a platter of food for each table. This service is especially fast when serving soups, but it requires a large investment in utensils and a trained staff. Portion size has little impact on how long it takes to eat a meal. However, the type of food served has a clear impact. Boneless meat and fish pieces are fastest to eat. It takes much longer to eat pieces with bones attached. Fruit cut up in the kitchen can be eaten faster than half melons or fruit baskets. Baked potatoes take a long time to eat.

Offering a choice of more than three vegetables at large banquets slows up service. Cheese trays or plates with more than three choices also slow service tremendously. When fruit is served with cheese, it should be pre-cut in manageable chunks. The best fruits are grape clusters, which can be purchased ready portioned. Other elegant and easy to handle fruits are fresh figs, cut in half, or peeled pear wedges, cut ahead of time, and kept in lemon water to prevent oxidation.

Distance from the Kitchen to the Dining Room

Large operations have function rooms on different floors, some of them far away from kitchens and pantries. Off-premise caterers often have to put their temporary serving station far from the dining area. The distance from the service area to the banquet room should be taken into consideration when the menu is proposed. In these situations, the hot food is normally dished out in the best-suited area or kitchen, placed in mobile cold or hot carts, and wheeled to the service area of the banquet room. Since the distance from the kitchen to the service area can be considerable, food is often dished out long before service time. When there is no freezer close by ice cream desserts must be delivered by freight elevator from a far away kitchen.

The distance from a kitchen or service pantry to the function room also has an impact on dishwashing and beverage service. If drinks are expected and there is no service bar in reasonable distance a portable bar must be provided with the service of a bartender. Delicate china and stemware are easily broken during transportation to the closest dish room.

Dinner Given at The Culinary Institute of America
by the
Great Women Chefs of America

Specialty Breads served throughout the Meal
Chef Nancy Silverton
****

Fresh Pea Soup with Spring Onions
Chef Debra Ponzek

1984 Simi Reserve Chardonnay
Zelma Long, Winemaker
****

Sautéed Catfish with Cajun Potato Crust
Crayfish Sauce
Chef Lyde Buchtenkirch-Biscardi, C.M.C.

Buena Vista Carneros Private Reserve
Pinot Noir 1987, Jill Davis, Winemaker
****

Roasted Veal Shank
Natural Sauce flavored with Rosemary
Chef Lidia Bastianich

Lungarotti Rubesco 1987
Dott. Teresa Lungarotti, Winemaker

Clos du Bois Briarcrest Cabernet Sauvignon 1986
Margaret Davenport, Winemaker
****

Seasonal Greens, Apple Blue Cheese Dressing
Black Pepper Cheese Sticks
Chef Caprial Pence

Pavillon Rouge du Château Margaux 1979
Corrine Mentzelopoulos, Winemaker
****

Lemon Crème
Chef Stacy Radin

Domaine Weinbach Gewûrztraminer 1983
Sèlection de Grains Nobles
Colette Faller, Winemaker

The dinner was given in April 1991. Responsible for the co-ordination between the chefs was
Certified Master Chef Richard Zack.

Cooked Food Storage

In normal industry practice, food is often plated, covered, and stacked ahead of time. Cold food is kept in mobile refrigerated trucks, on large shelf trucks called Queen Marys or plate trees, which are kept in roll-in refrigerators. In most cases, plated cold food, properly covered or wrapped in film, keeps well. Hot food is stacked in heaters. which should be equipped with devices to supply moisture when needed. If possible the heat is kept low during storage to keep drying out to a minimum, and then increased before service.

There are very sophisticated and ingenious heating devices equipped with timers on the market. Food can be plated cold and is gently heated directly on the plates. Meat and sauces are added at the last minute. Large banquet operations also have experimented with conveyors to speed up service.

Regardless of which systems are used, banquet food is mass-produced ahead of time. It is important for the *Banquet Sales Associates* to understand the holding characteristics of various foods.

- Scrambled eggs will keep well when stored in heavy china crocks. Thick china has low conductivity, and once hot, radiates slow and even heat that prevents the eggs from getting too hot and cooking further. Plated scrambled eggs dry out quickly. Metal conducts heat quickly and should not be used to keep eggs hot. In addition, cooked eggs will tarnish silver dishes. Plain poached eggs will keep under moderate moist heat.

- Fried eggs can be made ahead of time plated and covered. Some condensation can be expected and each plate must be inspected. Customers hate watery eggs.

- French toast will keep well. As a matter of fact, French toast can be made ahead of time and reheated.

- Corned beef hash keeps well in heaters either plated or on chafing dishes.

- Pancakes are a disaster (and very labor-intensive). They taste and look like shoe leather when made ahead of time. Frozen pancakes and waffles can get soggy in the heater.

- Breakfast sausages and ham keep better than bacon. Bacon requires dry heat, so it cannot be stored with food requiring moist heat.

- Fried food should be served while it is still crisp. Crispness is lost quickly when fried food is stored covered in heaters. Fried food should be served only when enough fryer capacity is available close to the banquet room and the food is made close to service time. This is for true for all fried food, such as fish, french fries, fried chicken, and fried onion rings. If fried food is requested and must be served, it should never be covered, and it should not be piled up during storage.

- Roasted poultry keeps well, and so does pot roast. Grilled chicken breasts can be pre-cooked and quickly finished at the moment of service.

- Food that is supposed to be served undercooked and sliced to order, such as roast beef and lamb, will lose color rapidly and should not be served unless it can be sliced at the moment of service.

- Steaks and Filet Mignon can be pre-cooked and finished at the last moment providing there are broilers in the vicinity. *Twin Tournedos* is a fancy name for small Filet Mignon. It takes much longer to dish them out, and they are more likely to get over-cooked.

- Food glazed with rich and heavy cream sauces keeps well, but these dishes are seldom ordered today.

- Plain poached fish, kept in moist heaters, holds rather well. Rich sauces, such as Hollandaise and Bèarnaise should be made as close to service time as possible to avoid contamination. Excessive heat will curdle these sauces.

- Scallops are difficult to serve to large groups. The customers expect the scallops undercooked and this is difficult to accomplish.

- Shrimp are rather sturdy and keep well. Obviously seafood should be cooked as close to service time as possible.

- Green vegetables do not stay green and crisp for a long time on covered plates in heated cabinets. Good alternatives are vegetable purées such as carrots, turnips, peas, and squash. Grilled tomatoes keep well. Snow peas are pretty, but unless dished out when hardly cooked, will quickly lose color and freshness.

- Hash brown potatoes will keep for some time, mashed potatoes will not. Old mashed potatoes are plain awful.

- Pasta is hard to keep plated in heaters, but covering them with toasted breadcrumbs will prolong their storage qualities.

- Couscous, rice varieties, and blends of legumes and grains keep rather well.

- Ice cream desserts should not be decorated with whipped cream if made ahead of time. The whipped cream will freeze solid and becomes inedible. An acceptable substitute is meringue. The service temperature is crucial; ice cream taken directly from holding freezers is too hard to be served immediately.

- Cakes covered with fondant icing must be stored in dry locations, because the moisture in refrigerators will melt the icing.

- Plated desserts are difficult to make ahead of time, because most are decorated with sauces, which could dry out. Ambitious pastry chefs plate desserts as close to service time as possible but this requires space and labor. 1,500 plates can take up a lot of space.

- The best desserts to serve in banquet rooms far away from kitchens are fruits, such as berries, with suitable sauces, whipped cream, and cookies passed out by the *Servers.*

- One logistic challenge could be coffee service. Occasionally coffee must be made in far away pantries, hours before service and kept in urns or air-voids. Obviously, the quality suffers.

Evaluating the Kitchen Equipment

Every piece of equipment has a certain capacity. This fixed capacity can be increased only by quicker turn around. This means cooking food ahead of time. Although the *Banquet Sales Associate* should not be overly concerned about logistics in the kitchen, good communication between the *Banquet Chef* and the *Catering Department* is necessary to avoid terrible mistakes. I remember a case when a large hotel opened and the opening dinner in the ballroom for a thousand invited guests was individual Filet Mignon. After the menu was printed, it was discovered that in the whole hotel was only one broiler, situated in the coffee shop three floors away!

The dinner was served, but it was not as good as it should have been. Thirty five Filet Mignons can be cooked on one sheet pan and with some juggling two pans can be cooked simultaneously between the broiler and the oven. It was the only oven installed by that time, heaters were also in short supply. It can be calculated easily how many times cooks were running up and down with trays of meat! In all fairness the menu was dictated by the eccentric owner who did not listen and refused to rent equipment.

Soup production is easy when the kitchen is equipped with steam-heated or electric kettles. It is a nightmare to prepare large quantities of soup on stoves, because it takes a long time to bring the liquid to a boil. This being the situation, soup on the menu should be avoided.

Space Considerations Both Back and Front of the House

The *Banquet Sales Associate* should consider the size and shape of the banquet room when booking a party. The room dimensions and configuration must be kept in mind. This is especially important when buffets are suggested. A major objective of buffet service is easy access. Lines should be avoided as much as possible. This is best accomplished by having numerous free-standing satellite buffets. At large parties, a number of them could be duplicated. Some types of buffets require *Servers* to slice meats or to prepare items to order. In these cases, the buffets could be U-shaped or have a hollow center where the *Servers* can safely stand.

The size of the required buffet tables must be calculated first. Then the best location of the buffet tables for guest circulation, and with easy access to the kitchen must be determined. One more challenge to keep in mind is the size, shape, and location of available back of the house space. This could be critical when the space is not normally used as banquet space. One should be imaginative and endeavor to book parties at locations most exciting for the client, but in some locations the quality of food and service could suffer for lack of back of the house space. Lack of space could also cause enormous breakage because drop-off bussing space is limited or nonexistent. I remember a garden party held in a country club far away from any kitchen or drop-off facility. On the way to the kitchen there was a sheltered lagoon, and some extra waiters dumped the soiled dishes in the water, because they did not want to walk so far, and no space for organized bussing was provided.

Selling Methods and Systems

There are a number of ways of selling banquets. This chapter deals with selling food. Selling beverages is covered in **Chapter 7.**

- Package deals include all charges for food, beverages, the use of the function room, gratuities, and taxes. The package may also include decorations, linen choices, and even the wedding cake. These packages are popular in operations with a large wedding business, and are also used in connection with convention and tour business.

- Full meals charged one price. All other charges such as beverages, decorations, taxes, and gratuities are extra.

- Food charged by units. This is often done when the exact number of guests attending a meeting or reception is difficult to control. For instance, coffee and other hot beverages for breaks could be charged by the gallon, soft drinks as consumed, or punch by the gallon. When the budget is tight, the *Banquet Sales Associate* could determine how much food the budget buys and order items by the piece, such as canapés, finger sandwiches, or pastries. When the food allocated in the budget runs out, the guests believe the caterer ran short, not the host.

- Lump sum pricing. This works best for large cakes, which are normally made ahead of time. If they are sold by the portion and the guarantee goes down when the cake is already finished, the house gets less money. Guarantees seldom go up. Large roasts for buffets should also be priced by the piece, and should not be affected by attendance changes.

Summary

Making banquet menus that meet guest expectations and the profit objectives of the operation is difficult and requires experience. By evaluating client expectations and by keeping the goal of the party in mind, the *Banquet Sales Associate* has information which will help to create a menu that will make the party successful. Most hosts have budgets in mind when booking a party. In some cases, the budget can be exceeded, and the *Banquet Sales Associate* can sell up. Alternatively, a restrained budget will make it necessary to get the chef involved to suggest dishes that will fit the budget. Most places have basic menus, called canned menus. They are normally less expensive than custom made menus.

The quality level expectations of both client and management should never be jeopardized on account of price. Menus must meet the profit expectations, and the *Banquet Sales Associate* is responsible for selling menus that are within the prescribed food, beverage and labor costs. Menus and service styles are also influenced by the staff capabilities, the seasons in focus, and by timing considerations. The distance from the kitchen to the dining room could influence the menu choices, because the holding capabilities of food varies. The proper assessment of the capabilities of cooking equipment also guides the *Banquet Sales Associate* in suggesting an appropriate menu. Space considerations in banquet rooms can dictate menu choices and service style.

Discussion Questions

- Why is it important to evaluate guest expectations?

- Should quality levels be lowered to meet a budget?

- When should the chef be involved in the menu making process?

- Explain the term canned menus. What are their advantages and disadvantages?

- Why is it important in menu making to keep the quality expectations of both guests and management in mind?

- Discuss controllable costs when making menus.

- Why is it important to consider the season when the party takes place?

- Why is timing a crucial factor in menu making?

- Is the distance from the kitchen to the dining room important when making menus?

- Explain selling by unit versus selling by the person.

Chapter Seven

BEVERAGE SALES AND SERVICE

California Wine Menu

RECEPTION

Tartare of Chilean Salmon with Ginger, Tamarind and Vegetable Crisps
Grandin Classic Brut

DINNER

Chilean Salmon Fillet, Roasted Brussels Sprouts, Pancetta
Pinot Noir Reduction
Les Grands Chef Chardonnay 1997, Limoaux AOC
Firesteed Pinot Noir 1997, Oregon
****

Chicken Ragout, Sweet and Sour Red Cabbage, Herbed Spaetzle
Miura Vineyards Chardonnay, 1998, Napa Valley
Ironstone Vineyards Merlot 1997, Sierra Foothills
M. Trinchero Merlot 1997, Coastal Selection, California
****

Venison and Pheasant Terrine
Warm Chestnut Fitters, Lingonberries
Rosemount Estate Shiraz 1999, Diamond Label, Australia
Lanzerac Cabernet Sauvignon 1996, Stellenbosch, South Africa
****

Butter Head Lettuce Salad, Red Burgundy Vinaigrette
****

Selection of Homestead Cheeses
Dunnewood Cabernet Sauvignon 1997, Barrel Select, North Coast
Rutherford Ranch Cabernet Sauvignon 1996, Napa Valley
Rodney Strong Vineyards Cabernet Sauvignon Reserve 1995, Sonoma
****

Mixed Berry Charlotte with Crème Fraîche, Raspberry and Passion Fruit Coulis
****

Coffee, Tea
Bowmore 17 Year Old Scotch
Don Yeygo Cigar Factory Torpedo Cigars

This menu shows much ambition and the desire of young chefs to break out of the established mold and create new menus. Salmon was served for the reception and as appetizer course. Brussels sprouts and pancetta (Italian bacon) could be a little too overwhelming for a dinner focused on wine.

Chicken ragout – in plain English chicken stew - looks messy on a plate. Cabbage is repeated because Brussels sprouts are also in the cabbage family. The aesthetic aspect should also be considered because the chicken stew and red cabbage could look rather awful on the plate.

Chapter Seven
BEVERAGE SALES AND SERVICE

Objectives

- To understand the profitability of alcoholic beverage sales.

- To learn about the responsibilities of the operator and staff.

- To comprehend the logistics of operating the Beverage Department.

- To comprehend the challenges of banquet wine service.

Introduction

Selling alcoholic beverages is potentially very profitable. However, beverage sales are dropping for many reasons. Awareness of the dangers of driving while under the influence of alcohol have affected beverage sales in banquet houses that depend on automobile travel to be reached. Health concerns have reduced alcohol consumption even at convention hotels, where guests stay in house.

Operators, their employees, and hosts have specific responsibilities concerning beverage service. These responsibilities must be kept in mind when beverages are sold. At corporate luncheons drinking is no longer acceptable. Mineral waters have taken the place of alcoholic beverages. They are potentially more profitable, but produce lower revenues. The challenge for the *Banquet Sales Associate* is to sell beverages, whether alcoholic or non-alcoholic. How to sell depends on the type of party, and guest expectations.

Final profitability also depends to a large degree on effective purchasing, storage, inventory turnover, and controls. Each of these will be examined in detail.

Profitability of Alcoholic Beverage Sales

Most catering operations have a liquor license that allows them to sell and serve alcoholic beverages on the premises. Selling alcoholic beverages is more profitable in percentages than selling food. In a well-run hotel, departmental beverage profit can be as high as 65% of sales. In other words, every dollar taken in for beverage sales adds up to 65 cents to the departmental bottom line. On every dollar taken in on food sales, between 20 to 25 cents become departmental profit. This fact underlines the importance of selling beverages.

Many *Banquet Sales Associates* put most of their selling skill into selling food. A high banquet food check is important because it brings in dollars to cover the overhead. A high banquet beverage check brings in the additional profit needed to stay in business.

New:
Selling bottled mineral waters, sodas, and juices can be more profitable in percentages than selling alcoholic beverages.

Off-Premise Caterers are not normally licensed to sell alcoholic beverages. Usually they serve alcoholic beverages provided by the host, and the caterer supplies the soft drinks, chasers, and labor. In some States caterers can obtain a day liquor license, also referred to as a traveling license, which allows selling and serving alcoholic beverages at a specific location for a specific time.

Beverage cost expectations vary. Bar drinks including beer should have a cost between 14% to 16%; wine cost could run from 20% to 35%. Comparing beverage cost percentages between different banquet houses could be misleading because they are dependent on the mix of business, local brand preferences and many other factors.

Wine sales have a higher cost than bar drinks and beer. Organizations selling wine will have a high beverage cost percentage, but important are the dollars taken to the bank and not the percentages. Soft drinks, sodas, and mineral waters are considered beverages and the revenue and cost are charged to the *Beverage Department*. Fruit juices and hot beverages are considered food.

The popularity of liquor brands and their varieties are changing constantly. Some beverage brands which were popular a short time ago are no longer fashionable today. When selling banquets, the *Banquet Sales Associate* should make as much effort as possible to find out the beverage preferences of the prospective group, and make sure that the right kind, type, and quantity is available. This requires flexibility from the *Purchasing Department*. After Prohibition the rights to control liquor laws were given to the individual States. These laws now vary greatly from State to State, from very restrictive to liberal interpretations affecting distribution.

When items not on the banquet liquor lists are requested the *Purchasing Department* must be given sufficient notice. Wholesalers adhere to strict delivery schedules, and some have exclusive marketing agreements and expect to sell other brands besides those specified by the client.

Most gatherings of people start with a reception because it is unlikely that all individuals attending a function will arrive at precisely at the same time. Beverage service is important at most receptions, making everybody feel comfortable, breaking the ice, and allowing the guests to mingle.

New:
It has become perfectly acceptable to serve mineral waters and sodas at luncheon receptions. Mineral water is popular, and the profit margin is high.

When the budget allows, an open bar should be provided at receptions, referred to as a hosted bar. During the meal service the bar could be kept open, as is the case at many social functions, or beverages such as wine or beer could be served at each table.

Legal Responsibilities of the Caterer

This section is not intended as legal advice and does not interpret the liquor laws of different States. It is strictly informative or suggestive in nature!

The federal liquor laws are quite specific: No persons under 21 can be served alcoholic beverages, not even at a party. Visibly intoxicated guests should not be served alcoholic beverages. Intoxicated persons should not be allowed to drive.

These laws are difficult to enforce at private parties. The caterer does not have the luxury of standing at the door and "proofing" or "carding" every arriving guest. Guests of all age groups, including children and teenagers, attend many parties, especially social parties. *Servers* should be instructed not to serve them any alcoholic beverages, even when in the company of their parents or when requested to do so by other adults. A sufficient variety and quantity of soft drinks should be readily available when minors are expected. Some guests allow under age persons to drink and it is almost impossible to prevent this without making a fuss.

It is also difficult to avoid serving alcoholic beverages to already intoxicated persons. At many parties, full bottles are placed on the tables. In other situations, different *Servers* pass drinks on trays, and they cannot be expected to remember which guests are drinking more than they should. It is important for the caterer to be able to prove that the *Servers* are fully aware of their responsibilities, and that they make every effort to obey the law.

When clearly intoxicated persons are trying to drive and the parking lot attendant hands them the car keys, the caterer and the employee could be liable. If the attendant has any doubts about the driving ability of the guest, the manager should be notified. The manager can do little more than try to reason with the intoxicated person, which is always difficult, and perhaps enlist the help of the hosts or friends of the individual. In any case, the situation could become most unpleasant. All efforts should be made to send the intoxicated person home with another driver or in a taxi. Fortunately, these situations do not happen very often in most catering facilities.

During conventions *Hospitality Suites* are popular. The clients rent suites and entertain prospective clients, friends, and employees. It is beneficial to the facility if the caterer insists that all alcoholic beverages be purchased from the hotel and served by hotel employees. This, however is very tricky with leftover liquor, which belongs to the client and therefore must be left in the room. There have been cases when both the hotel and host were sued when an intoxicated guest was involved in an accident.

The *Banquet Sales Associate* should not try to sell more alcoholic beverages than could be consumed. This is difficult when the sales personnel are sharing gratuities and the *Associate* is being urged to fill sales quotas. When discussing the banquet arrangements with the client, the beverage consumption and drinking expectations of the group should be realistically estimated.

The host shares the responsibility with the caterer of obeying the laws governing the sale and dispensation of alcoholic beverages. When beverage service is discussed with the client, the responsibility of the host under the law should be mentioned.

Different Ways of Selling

State laws govern the sale of alcoholic beverages. Certain ways of selling suggested in this chapter might not be legal in some states.

Single drink sales

- This way of selling is the most profitable way. The bartender, who could be located directly in the banquet room or in the service bar, makes drinks to order, which are picked up by the guests or served by *Servers*. The bartender keeps track of every drink consumed, and the client is charged by the drink. This method is often used at very small parties. The client may also be charged for the bartender labor.

Hosted bar with budget

- The client sets a budget, and the amount of liquor calculated at bottle prices is issued to the bars. When the supply of liquor is exhausted, additional supplies must be authorized in writing by the host. If a particular brand runs low, it could be substituted by another brand in the same price range. The host normally is charged for the bartender labor. The ratio of bartenders is 60-100 guests to one bartender. Non alcoholic beverages are sold by the unit.

Hosted bar with no budgets

- All bars are stocked, and the client is charged for the liquor consumed at bottle prices. As a rule, a bottle is charged for when opened. Theoretically, the host is entitled to any leftover liquor in open bottles, and in some cases wants the liquor sent to his suite or office after the party. The legality of sending liquor out varies from State to State. The client could be charged for bartender labor. The ratio of bartenders to guests is the same as above.

Full package sale

- This way of selling is popular for weddings. The client pays a flat fee for all liquor consumption. The package normally includes an open bar during the reception and during the dinner, wine or beer with the meal, and cordials after dinner. In the case of weddings, a champagne toast is included. Liquor consumption by person must be estimated when the price is negotiated but is on average much lower than originally assessed.

Full bottle sales

- This way of selling used to be popular at dances. The client would pay for one or two bottles of hard liquor, chasers, and ice, placed on every table. Guests normally would help themselves. The bottles would be exchangeable for other brands in the same price category. This package is not legal in some states and is therefore discontinued by many hotels.

Cash bars

- Guests pay for their own drinks. For large parties, cashiers are needed to sell drink tickets. The tickets should include all taxes and gratuities and all beverages should be priced the same. The cashiers should be visible, and located away from the bars in order to avoid congestion. There should be enough cashiers and bartenders to keep the lines small. At smaller parties, the bartenders could handle the money, but this is not advisable. When the bartenders handle money, it slows service and control is also very difficult. The client should be charged for labor of the cashiers and bartenders.

À la carte sales

- If the client does not want to pay for any beverages, the operator could suggest à la carte beverage service. Small wine and beverage lists are placed on each table and the *Servers* take drink orders. This process is time-consuming and should only be used as a last resort or when time permits. The client should pay for the labor of the cashiers and bartenders needed to service the function.

Off-premise catering service charges

- Caterers who do not supply the liquor served at a function are entitled to charge for bartender labor, and for any additional labor connected with beverage service. Ice and soft drinks should be charged separately.

Beverage Consumption Estimates

Champagne

- 1½ glasses per person prior to dinner and 1½ glasses with dessert.

- For weddings 2 glasses per person during the reception if no other beverages are served, and 1½ glasses for the bridal toast with the wedding cake.

The quantities will increase in the summer. One bottle of champagne will yield 5 – 6 glasses.

Wine Consumption

* 1½ glasses for lunch. 2½ glasses for reception serving wine only and lasting two hours.

* 2 to 3 glasses for dinner.

One 28 oz (750 milligram) bottle yields about 5 to 6 glasses.

Open Bar Receptions

* 2 drinks per person are consumed during the first hour, 1 drink during the next hour, and ½ drink per hour during the rest of the evening. This takes into consideration that some customers arrive late.

Bartender and *Server* Requirements

General guidelines:

* For 100 customers 1 *Bartender* and 2 *Servers* for food and bussing.

* 100-200 customers 2 single bars (2 *Bartenders*), 1 *Bar Helper*, 3 *Servers*.

* 200-300 customers 1 single bar and 1 double bar (3 *Bartenders*), 4 *Servers*.

Selling alcoholic beverages is a service that relies on trust. When the client wishes to use and pay for premium brands, lesser brands or house brands must never be substituted. Operators and their employees should never charge the client for more than was actually consumed. This can be tempting, because beverage consumption is hard to control. Although liquor requisitions and consumption sheets should be made for every party, the accuracy of these sheets is difficult to verify. It has happened that disputes about the amount of the beverages charged have delayed payment of the final bill, and have led to rebates. It behooves every caterer to be scrupulously honest with all liquor charges, and to make sure that all employees follow the same policy.

Corkage Policies

The client may like to serve beverages that were not purchased by the caterer. An example could be a rare wine to be used for a tasting or at a party of enophiles. It could also be wine that was given to the family of the host, to be served at a special occasion. In some States, on a licensed property, it is illegal to serve alcoholic beverages not purchased from the licensee. It should be made very clear that brown

146

bagging liquor is not permitted, and that all alcoholic beverages must be purchased from the caterer. If a specific wine is not on the standard wine list, an effort should be made to buy it for the client. However, there are always exceptions to rules. Only top management should approve these exceptions.

When the client is allowed to bring in wine the operator is entitled to a corkage fee and the employees entitled to gratuities. The amount of corkage charged is at the discretion of the operator, but it should cover the overhead cost connected with the service and the potential loss of beverage revenue. The gratuity is based on the estimated selling price, not on the number of bottles served. Some discretion is also necessary; if a group wants very rare and expensive wines, the *Servers* are not necessarily entitled to gratuities for the full value of the wine.

There are problems connected with serving wines sent in by the client. The wines must be shipped to the hotel ahead of time, and great care must be taken to see that the stock is kept separate, and not inadvertently taken to the wrong party. In large banquet operations, keeping track of special stock is cumbersome. Another problem is quantity. Sometimes not enough corkage wine is sent in, especially when the supply is tight and the party grows at the last minute. It can be embarrassing when the wine runs low. In such situations the *Servers* should be instructed to keep the portions small.

Only enough wine should be opened to cover the estimated requirements. Any wine left over must be securely stored, and should be picked up by the client within a reasonable time.

Selecting Liquor Brands

The variety of liquor brands is amazing, and even in controlled States hundreds of brands are available. In the catering industry, liquor brands are classified as:

- House or pouring brands

- Regular brands

- Premium brands

House brands or lesser-known brands are often custom labeled in large operations. They are usually less expensive than other brands. When brands are not specified in the banquet contract, house brands are used. Regular brands are known brands in specific product categories. Premium brands are the top brands.

Brand selection depends on local preferences. In some cases, operators can depend on liquor companies for major business. Obviously, their brands must be used. Most operators select house brands for their normal business. These brands should be known and accepted by the general public, because in many cases the client might ask what house brands are used. House brands should be purchased in reasonable quantities in order for the operator to take advantage when special sales, often referred to as post-off, are offered by purveyors. In most States, the law specifies the time span when liquor bills must be paid. A large purchase could adversely affect the cash flow of an operation.

Frequency of liquor deliveries varies among locations. As a rule, no more liquor than needed for the parties booked in the foreseeable future should be purchased. Liquor does not spoil, but inventory ties up money and should be kept to a minimum. Regular and premium brands should be purchased only when needed. Special brands could move very slowly, and often a full case might not sell in months. If the purveyor is not willing to break cases, and most are not, one or two bottles could be purchased at the local liquor store. Paying retail prices is still cheaper than having unwanted inventory around. The expected liquor room inventory turnover is about 1½ to 2 times per month in dollar value. Much depends on the amount of wine in storage. The turnover in operations with large wine cellars could be much smaller.

All liquor should be purchased in the same size bottles if possible. Obviously, the type of business the caterer books most frequently determines the most practical bottle sizes. In some operations, two bottle sizes must be available to take care of different kinds of business. When liquor is sold by the bottle, using fifths rather than quarts or liters is more profitable for the caterer. Liter or larger bottles are more profitable to use for bar service, because they are proportionally less expensive than smaller bottles, and also fewer bottles will be handled. If a catering operation specializes in complete beverage package plans, large size liquor bottles should be used at the bars. Beer should be offered in the smallest possible sizes. At parties customers often ask for beer and don't finish the whole bottle. Much of it is wasted. The smaller bottles save the operator money.

Wine served at the table should be served from the standard 750ml bottles, unless it is served from carafes. Wine served from bars should be purchased in 1½ liter bottles. If the bars are out of sight, wine could be purchased in cardboard containers and served from refrigerated dispensers, providing the wine quality meets expectation.

Selecting soda and mineral water brands is important. Large companies often sign exclusive agreements with the providers of major brands. Advertising and trends often affect the choice of brands. Some people will only drink a certain brand.

Service back bars should be equipped with soda guns. In all other locations, bottled sodas in plastic bottles, in quart or liter sizes, should be used. The brands should be well known. Very fine operations serve chasers in split bottles.

Management of the Liquor Storeroom

Hotels, restaurants, and clubs have beverage storerooms. They should be physically separated from the food storerooms if possible. In some States, the alcoholic beverage control laws stipulate that the liquor storeroom can only be used for liquor storage. All alcoholic beverages (where permitted by law) and bottled soft drinks are received, stored, and issued from the beverage storeroom to all outlets, including the banquet service bars. The beverage storerooms should be equipped with walk-in refrigerators for short time storage of wines and beer. If wines need to be stored for a long period of time, the storage space should be temperature controlled.

Alcoholic beverages must be tightly controlled at all times, whether in storage or in circulation. No beverage should be issued at any time without a requisition or authorized beverage slip.

The Organization of the Storeroom

The storeroom contains valuable inventory that is easily disposed of when stolen. Obviously, the room must be secure, and the keys controlled. The beverage storeroom should be entered only by a limited number of trusted employees. Rank and file employees should not be given the keys to the beverage room.

Liquor can be stored on shelves, or in the cases in which it was delivered. Much depends on the volume of liquor purchased and issued. Popular brands might be left in cases simply because this is probably the way they were issued. Slower moving brands could be stored on shelves. The goal should be to have the storeroom clean, well organized, and tidy.

Even a small operation could carry many different brands of liquor and wine. The best way to keep track of beverage inventory, issues, and purchases is the bin card system. It consists of using numbers to keep track of the movement of liquor bottles. A block of numbers is assigned to every type of liquor and wine. Sufficient spare numbers should be left between each group so new brands can be added and others deleted. All bin numbers should have three digits in order to have sufficient numbers to work with. For instance, all wines could be assigned bin numbers from 100 to 199. Bin numbers 100 to 120 could be reserved for sparkling wines, the numbers 121 to 140 for white wines, and so on. Scotches could be assigned the numbers 200 to 240. If the house carries 14 different scotches, it has 26 spare numbers to work with. Adding a prefix number could differentiate bottle sizes. For instance, Scotch in quarts could be 1200. A number without the prefix "1" automatically means liters.

Bin cards are normally cardboard cards, attached to the shelf or kept in a file. Every time there is a transaction of any sort, it is marked on the card. For instance, when liquor is received, the amount and date is marked on the card. When liquor is issued, the same is done. The bin card is a running inventory record, and the amount marked on the card as not issued should be in the storeroom. The system can easily be adapted for computers. It would be possible for the *Banquet Sales Associate* to get direct access to the beverage inventory. This would make selling beverages, especially wines, more efficient. The advantage of bin cards is that the amount on shelves or in cases is easily verified and checked against the amount noted on the card. Even when computerized, the old-fashioned bin cards have a place in the beverage storeroom.

New:
The beverage inventory is computerized in most large operations. To make the system work, tight control is required from the moment the merchandise is received until it is issued, and sometimes returned as not consumed. If the system is judiciously maintained, a *Banquet Sales Associate* has instant access to the beverage inventory and can sell wine in stock without first calling about availability.

Very large hotels with many public bars and function rooms use a bar code system. It is time consuming to implement but ultimately eliminates a lot of paperwork.

The Banquet Beverage Storeroom

At most parties, not all liquor issued to the banquet bars is consumed. To return this liquor to the general beverage storeroom is not practical. The returns could consist of opened bottles, and it would be difficult to take them back and keep track of this stock on bin cards. In addition, the beverage storerooms might not be open when the party is over. In some States it is against the law to store open bottles along with full bottles.

To overcome this problem, most establishments operate a banquet, or circulating beverage storeroom. When parties are over all beverages are returned to the circulating beverage storeroom and the consumption checked by a designated person.

In addition to the returned beverages, a reasonable liquor stock could be kept in the banquet beverage storeroom for reserves to be available when needed. The *Charge Captain, Beverage Manager or Charge Bartender* on duty should control access to the circulating storeroom. For accounting purposes, the stock in the banquet storeroom is considered issued and circulating inventory. As such, it is part of the month to date beverage cost of the operation. At the end of the month, the stock in the circulating storeroom should be inventoried, and the dollar amount added to the general beverage inventory.

Issuing Liquor

Liquor should be issued only with a requisition. The requisition should be on a custom printed form listing the most popular brands, their sizes and bin numbers. The *Charge Captain, Beverage Manager*, or *Charge Bartender* makes a requisition for each function based on the instructions on the *BEO*. The requisition is normally made in three copies. One copy remains in the *Beverage Storeroom*, the second is left in the circulating storeroom, and the third is given to the bartender in charge of the party.

When the beverages are returned the quantities are listed and verified by a designated person. The requisition becomes the beverage consumptions sheet and clients have the right to see it.

The requisition is filled from both the *General Beverage Storeroom* and the *Banquet Beverage Room*. The number of full bottles issued from the beverage storeroom is recorded on the bin cards. The rest of the order is filled with existing stock and open bottles stored in the circulating storeroom.

Note:
It is illegal to "marry" (pour together) the content of open bottles even with the same brands. Open bottles can be issued to banquet bars in most States.

Bottle Returns

Empty bottles should be treated with almost as much respect as full bottles. The empties should accompany the requisitions when possible. Due to the swings in volume in the catering business, this is not always possible. However, it should be the rule that empties are not disposed of with other garbage, but returned to the beverage room and broken. This measure helps to prevent pilferage. In some localities, empty bottles must be separated from garbage for environmental reasons. In other localities, empty soda bottles and cans carry a refund.

Logistics and Controls of Banquet Bars

Drink sizes

Drink sizes are decided on by management and not by individual employees. The sizes recommended by management are guidelines, of course. When there are open bars, the client often tells the bartender how big the drink should be. The situation is obviously different when drinks are sold à la carte. The normal drink size on package plans is ¾ oz. For à la carte service it is 1 oz. or more. Overpouring, especially on package deals, should be controlled.

Most banquet houses use pouring spouts when drinks are measured and free pour at open bars. Free pour is faster than using measuring devices. Service bars could benefit from automated liquor dispensing systems, which store the liquor at a remote location and dispense a precisely measured drink. The investment in these systems is high but is warranted in banquet houses with many à la carte parties.

Ice

The size and shape of ice has a definite impact on the apparent size of the drink (along with the glassware, to be discussed later). Smaller ice cubes occupy more space in the glass and make drinks look bigger. However, they melt faster than larger cubes and make the drink watery quickly. In warm locations, and when the party is a package deal, small cubes cost the operator extra money, because clients do not finish their drinks. Small cubes also melt faster when stored at the bars, and have to be replaced more often.

Pillow-shaped cubes seem to be the best compromise. They are available in different sizes. Many ice machines can be converted at a modest expense to make different size and shaped cubes. Tubular ice cubes are also popular. Ice machines should be away from traffic areas, but as close as possible to the most likely point of use. Many machines are noisy, and for this reason should not be too close to function rooms.

Many banquet operations store ice cubes in freezers. This way, the machines are used to their fullest capacity. Ice machines should always be equipped with metal or plastic scoops, secured by chains. When there are no scoops, employees are tempted to scoop out ice with plates or pitchers, which could have disastrous results.

Bar Fruits and Juices

Cutting bar fruits is the responsibility of the bartenders. Most banquet bartenders are extra employees. When they come to work and are asked to cut bar fruits, they often use any handy table knife for the job. The resulting fruit looks poor. The best policy is to provide the bartenders with small wooden cutting boards and serrated stainless steel knives, attached with chains. This way, the knife does not get lost so easily. Bar fruits cost money and only a reasonable amount should be cut at a time. Lemons, when their peels are removed for garnish, should be returned to the pantry for squeezing or for other purposes.

Fruit juices are purchased ready-made in most banquet operations. The same is true of other mixes. Juices and mixes can spoil, and open containers should be discarded after each party. The inventory should be rotated constantly, and the expiration dates watched. Dairy products for bars should be requisitioned from the food storeroom, and the unused portions returned to the kitchen. Off-premise caterers are normally responsible for the supply of all bar fruits, juices, and mixes.

Controls

Since liquor is such an easy commodity to dispose of, employees often pilfer it. Some employees even feel that they are entitled to leftover liquor, with the idea that the client paid for it all. In some cases, the host or even the guests reward *Servers* with opened liquor bottles. This is certainly the privilege of the host, who is now the owner of the liquor.

Company policy should be that no liquor is to be removed from the premises without written authorization. The authorization should be made on a printed stock form, easily obtainable under the name "package pass" from stationery stores. A duplicate should be kept in order to reconcile the inventory at the end of the party. Liquor given to employees should be removed at the end of the function and should not be stored in lockers. This policy is difficult to enforce all the time, but it is good to have a policy, and all *Servers* should be made aware of it. There have been cases when *Servers* hoarded liquor in their lockers, "married" bottles, and sold them to guests at dinner dances with à la carte liquor sales. It could be easy to get a check from the cashier, use it a number of times to collect from guests, and turn the check in to the cashier with the payment only once at the end of the day. Bootlegged liquor could also find its way into cash bars when bartenders are collecting the cash, depriving the house of income.

Employee lockers should be inspected periodically by management accompanied by an employee representative. Private padlocks should not be tolerated on company lockers.

Parties are generally fun occasions. The guests are in a festive mood, the hours are long, and the work is hard for the employees. The temptation to drink a little is great. A close inspection of banquet rooms, either during the party or afterward, could turn up empty glasses stashed away by drinking employees behind drapes, under tables, or in flower arrangements. In some cases, drinks or even full bottles are taken to the kitchen in exchange for food or other favors. If drinking is permitted, or even when it is only condoned, it can easily get out of hand. The best policy is that no drinking on the job is permitted.

Selling Wine

A genuine effort should be made to sell wine with every meal. Wine makes a meal more festive and more memorable. In order to sell wine, the *Banquet Sales Associate* must have a comprehensive wine list. This list should have a selection from each major grape variety and from every major grape growing area. Banquet wine lists should be short and in most cases should not list vintages.

It is expected to have white, blush, and red wine available by the glass on every bar. This wine should make a quality statement. It is often the first item a guest is given when arriving.

Selecting bar or house wine is an important, difficult and time-consuming process. Involving the *Executive Chef* in the process is a philosophical and practical issue. The chef is considered the culinary authority and is also expected to have a good knowledge of wines. To what extent the chef is familiar with current market conditions, customer's expectations, and vintages is questionable. Wine purchasing is a complicated matter and chain hotels have wine buyers and private labeling arrangements.

Spanish Formal Wine Dinner
to compliment Spanish Wines

LA MINUTA
Los Aperitivos

La Espuma de Endivia con Salsa de Queso Cabrales
(Endive Custard with Cabrales Blue Cheese)

Los Vinos: *Vega de la Reina Rueda Superior 1995*
****

El Pescado
Los Buòuelos de Raya a la Aroma de Alcaparras
(Skate Fritters with Caper Essence)

Viòa Tondonia Rioja Blanca Lopez Herida 1995
****

La Ensalada
Las Lechugas con la Vinagreta templada de Champinons
(Lettuce Salad with warm Mushroom Vinaigrette)

****

El Ave
El Faísan asado enrollado de Tocino ahumado con Moras
(Roast Pheasant wrapped in Blackberry smoked Bacon)

Contino Reserva Bodegas C. V. N. E., Rioja 1994
****

La Carne
El Filete de Ciervo marinado en Vino de Rioja con Arroz salvaje y Yames
(Filet of Venison marinated in Rioja Wine with wild Rice and Sweet Potatoes)

Marqués de Caceras Gran Reserva 1985
****

El Postre
La Tarta de Almendras con Compota de Frutas
(Almond Tart with fruit Compote)

Ferret Brut, Cavas Ferret Penedes
****

El Café o el Thé

Conde de Osborne, Puerto de Santa Maria
Osborne & Cia

Criteria for Selecting House Wines

- Good supply. This does not mean that the house wine cannot be changed from time to time. House wine should not however be leftover wine in the storeroom, or wine that the purveyor wants to sell off. The public is more wine-conscious than before, and can judge the quality level of the operation by the quality of the house wine.

- Generally accepted taste. The wine should not be too complex, and should be easy to drink. Although the trend of wine taste is toward drier wines, the white house wine should be slightly sweet or fruity to avoid complaints that the wine was sour. It is rather easy to pick a good white and blush house wine. Finding a good red is more difficult, because inexpensive red wines often have high tannin content. As a general observation, California reds are more rounded and smoother than inexpensive imports.

- Bottle sizes. Wine should be in 1½ liter bottles and larger, and in 750ml bottles for table service.

- Price. The price that management is willing to accept varies, but house wine should be a profit maker. The average portion size is 5 oz, and the cost should be no more than 25% of the selling price.

- Image. The price of jug wine brands can easily be checked at the local liquor store. The house wine should be a label which is less known, but has the reputation of being of high quality. This is especially important when selecting the sparkling wines used for weddings.

Making the Banquet Wine List

A major criteria for making a banquet wine list is availability. Banquets are booked months in advance, and it is difficult to get a commitment from purveyors that the wine will be available when the party takes place. Some purveyors suggest buying the wine when the party is booked, which leaves the caterer with inventory to carry and with the problem of estimating the quantity, because the function could grow or shrink dramatically.

Wines on banquet wine lists should be little known, but tasted to make sure they meet average taste expectations. The wines do not have to be complex. Vintages should not be mentioned, and banquet wines should be selected from countries with minor vintage variations, so there is no big difference in price and quality when one vintage runs out.

Guests are often dazzled by recognizable names. Generally known wine descriptions are wines with grape names, as is the case with many California wines, such as Cabernet Sauvignon or Chardonnay. Wines also have region names, such as Burgundy or Bordeaux, and country names, such as Italy, Australia, or Germany. Some countries, such as Argentina, Chile, and some Eastern European countries, have the reputation of producing cheap wines, although the products may be of excellent quality.

It is difficult to get the spelling of wine names right, and they should be checked against the label before the wine list is printed. The description should be as precise as possible. There are dozens of Niersteiner wines on the market, and most Burgundy wines are shipped from many different producers. However, when the description is precise, a secure supply is required. In some cases, the client asks the caterer to purchase a specific wine. Arrangements should be made with the purveyor to take any full cases back if consumption falls below the estimate.

For most banquet houses, investing in a wine cellar is not a good business move, although it could be a nice hobby for the operator. Banquet quantities vary so greatly that keeping the right amount of wine in stock in sufficient quantities can be very expensive. The exceptions are operations with very limited wine lists, specializing only in certain labels, or operations that have a small banquet room in connection with a busy restaurant. In these cases wine can be purchased when it is young and inexpensive, and sold at a good profit years later. The profit must be high, because the investment can be great.

Estimating Quantity

When selling wine, the quantities should be correctly estimated. A standard 750ml bottle of still wine yields about six glasses. Each table of ten customers needs about two bottles of wine. One case serves six tables. Sparkling wine glasses are slightly smaller than still wineglasses, so each bottle yields about seven glasses. Champagne toast for 100 guests requires fifteen bottles. One liter bottle of still wine yields about seven glasses.

Cost and Earnings Implications of Selling Wines

Wines carry a higher cost percentage than liquor. However, it would be a mistake to price wines by using anywhere near the same formula used in pricing liquor. There is no set formula for establishing wine prices.

Wine sales in banquet situations are additional sales, and add revenue and earnings to the bottom line. Wines do not need extra labor to serve; the *Servers* are already paid to do this. The only extra labor that may be needed would be for bringing the wines at the right temperature to the point of service. Normally *Bartenders* are not needed to open the bottles. This can be done by the *Servers* or the *Steward*. The other expense connected with wine sales is the use of glassware.

Some hotel chains expect the cost of wine to be on average 20% to 25% of the selling price. To achieve this cost, a bottle of wine costing $ 7.00 must be sold at $ 35.00. The single glass of wine would cost $ 6.00 per person before tax and gratuity charges. This is very high, and could discourage wine sales. Wine should be priced realistically in relation to cost and overhead. The cost of the wine is only one part of the calculation; low overhead connected with wine service is the other. Operations should establish a minimum price level that would be charged regardless of the cost of the wine. This charge would pay for the overhead and the profit for the operator. The rest of the charge can be flexible. When pricing wine, the cost per glass should be kept in mind. Wine served at the table should be less costly than the same wine sold by the glass at the bar.

It is better to serve two bottles of wine at each table than one or none. If wine is priced realistically revenue is increased with very little additional expense. Cost percentages cannot be taken to the bank. Dollars can.

Banquet Wine Service

Banquet wine service is slightly different from wine service practiced in restaurants or when wine is ordered à la carte.

Wine service is discussed in more detail in **Chapter 14.** It should be noted here that wine, like all beverages, should be served from the right. The label of the bottle should not be covered with a towel like a baby in bunting, the *Servers* should not act as if they are ashamed to show the label to the guests. The label should be turned to the guest while pouring.

Many *Servers* when handling wine fall broadly into three groups: one very timid; one who thinks they know all about the subject; and fortunately the majority who follow instructions. All they are expected to do is to go to the table and serve the wine to the customers. Wine is not a mystery drink and requires very little special handling.

If wine is chilled in ice, rubber bands should be used to prevent the label coming off in the water. The bottle should always be dry before it is brought to the table. When two bottles of wine are specified for each table, the *Server* should bring both to avoid having to go back to the pantry to get the second bottle. The glasses should be filled about half full, the space above the wine, in the proper shape glass, will allow the wine to breathe and to develop its aroma. In banquet service, the wine should always be opened in the back of the house. Letting one guest taste the wine is not necessary. If guests complain that a wine is spoiled, fresh glasses should be brought and the wine exchanged. Normally, fresh glasses are not provided when an additional bottle of wine is brought to a table.

Wine is always served before the food arrives at the table, but never before the guests are seated. Wine service should be swift, unobtrusive, and uncomplicated. It should be another pleasant part of the meal.

```
┌─────────────────────────────────────────────────────────┐
│                                                         │
│              HOLIDAY DINNER MENU                        │
│         FROM A NEW YORK CITY RESTAURANT                 │
│                                                         │
│         Hudson River Club Hors d'Oeuvres               │
│                                                         │
│                                                         │
│                  Four Champagnes:                       │
│              Bricout Blanc de Blanc NV                  │
│                   Bricout Brut                          │
│              Bricout Brut Elegance                      │
│           Piper Heidsieck Brut Sauvage, NV             │
│                    ********                             │
│                                                         │
│            Pumpkin and Apple Soup                       │
│                    ********                             │
│                                                         │
│         Pan seared Montauk Wild Striped Bass            │
│              West Park Chardonnay 1988                  │
│                    ********                             │
│                                                         │
│      Millbrook Farms Venison Chops with Chestnuts       │
│                Swiss Chard sauté                        │
│                  Potato Nest                            │
│              Côte Rôtie "Les Jumelles"                 │
│                    ********                             │
│                                                         │
│      Apple Pithivier with Cinnamon Caramel Sauce        │
│                      and                                │
│                Bourbon Ice Cream                        │
│              Château Suduiraut 1983                     │
│                    ********                             │
│                                                         │
│                  Petits Fours                           │
│                     Coffee                              │
│                                                         │
└─────────────────────────────────────────────────────────┘
```

The dinner was served around Christmas to a small group

Wine Service Temperatures

Most people know that white, blush, and sparkling wines should be served chilled. The temperature should be about 45 degrees. Red wines should be served at room temperature. Room temperature means that the wines should be only slightly warm, or at about 55 degrees. Wines that have been sitting in the back of the house or in kitchen areas could get too warm and not taste good. It is advisable to chill red wines slightly when they are to be served in hot, crowded ballrooms.

Choosing the Right Glassware

Beverage glassware in catering operations must reflect the quality image of the house, but should be highly functional. Thin stemmed glasses and expensive tumblers have no place in banquet operations. Banquet glasses should be open stock and readily available. Glasses that require a time to order are not suitable. The glass industry distinguishes between glasses with rolled rims, and with cut rims; rolled-rim glasses are sturdier and cheaper. Glasses with lead content are more expensive than glasses without lead.

It is the nature of the business that the employees and guests break much glassware. Glasses are left in unlikely places by guests, often taken to other banquet rooms, or even to guestrooms or to the parking lot. Back of the house space can become very congested when parties take place, and the *Servers* often leave glasses in corridors and staircases when drop off space is scarce.

It is important to have as few types of glasses in circulation as possible. Most banquet houses could operate with the following minimum variety:

- All-purpose rock glass, 6 to 8 oz capacity

- All-purpose highball glass, 8 to 12 oz capacity

- Water glass, 14 oz capacity

- All-purpose wine glass, 8 to 12 oz capacity

- Cocktail glass, 5 oz capacity

- Pony glass, 5 oz capacity

- Brandy glass or snifter, 6 to 12 oz capacity

All sizes are only suggested, and many more glass types and sizes could be purchased. Every additional type of glass in circulation creates another logistical problem.

The shape of glassware is important. Rock and highball glasses should have a heavy bottom. They feel better, and the drink looks better than in a thin glass. The inside should be curved, because this also makes the drink look larger. The glass should not be too wide, because people should be able to carry the glass around, often with a small plate with food. Plastic carriers, which clip to the plate, are available, but they accommodate only stemware. Stemware should not be too tall. High glasses look nice on the table, but take up too much space in storage racks. Wine glasses should be narrower at the mouth than at the middle to keep the bouquet of the wine inside and allow swirling.

Sparkling wines should be served in fluted or tulip shaped glasses only. The so-called champagne saucers, which are shallow bowls, should never be used. They make the wine go flat, and project an image of low sophistication.

The width of all glasses should not vary much in order to save space in glass racks. Glass racks should be color coded to keep the stemware separated. The stems of stemware should be octagonal or faceted, because this makes them easier to hold when wet. The foot of the glass should be faceted, because it sparkles under chandeliers. The glass, however, should always be clear and never tinted. Any kind of gold or silver rim on glasses will wash off before the glass is broken. And glasses must be crystal clear. They should be washed in a designated machine, or before the machine is used for washing plates.

Summary

Selling alcoholic beverages has a high profit potential, but it carries responsibilities for the host, the caterer, and its staff. There are different ways of selling liquor, each with advantages and disadvantages. Even when the host does not want to serve alcoholic beverages, mineral water could be sold.

Controlling the purchase, storage, issue, and final accounting for beverages is a complicated process. Selecting brands of liquor and wine takes experience and careful judgment, including selecting from the various bottle sizes on the market. Organizing the storeroom and keeping track of inventory and consumption are important tasks. Most large operations find it advantageous to operate two beverage storerooms, one for long-term storage, and one for bottle returns after parties. When the host provides beverages, corkage policies are needed.

Keeping a wine cellar in banquet operations sounds romantic but is seldom cost effective. It is important to select the proper glassware, and to serve the wines in an uncomplicated, efficient manner.

Discussion Questions

- What are the legal responsibilities for caterers?

- Why is controlling the service of alcoholic beverages to minors and intoxicated persons more difficult in a catering situation than in restaurants or bars?

- List different ways of selling beverages. Which ones are the best suited for which situation?

- What is corkage? When is a corkage policy needed?

- What is a bin card system?

- What is the purpose of the banquet beverage storeroom?

- How is the liquor issued and controlled?

- Explain the logistics and controls of banquet bars.

- Explain the ramifications of different ice cube shapes.

- What are the criteria for selecting house wines?

Chapter Eight
SERVICE

Les Amis d'Escoffier
Dinner Menu

Reception
Avant l'oeuvre il vous sera servi «Le Regal»
un assortiment d'amuse-bouches

Domaine Carneros Brut 1994

L'Escriteau
Première Assiette

Terrine de pâte de foie de canard en brioche
Duck Liver Terrine in Brioche

Château du Mayne, Graves 1996

Deuxième Assiette
La soup de tomates jaunes et coquilles St. Jacques
Oven dried yellow Tomato Soup with Bay Scallops

Troisième Assiette
Saumon grillé de la Bay de Fundi accompané
de jambon de Parme et petis pois à l'anglaise
Charred Bay of Fundi Salmon with Prosciutto and Peas

Santenay Clos de Malte blanc
Domaine Louis Jadot 1995

Intermède
Sorbet aux pommes Granny Smith

Quatrième Assiette
Selle d'agneau à l'Orloff farcie aux truffes noires
Stuffed Saddle of Lamb Orlof

Pernand-Vergelesses Clos de la Croix de Pierre
Domain des Heritiers Louis Jadot 1996

Issue de Table
Salade de l'asperges blanches et mâche
aux Croûtons Chavignol
Salad of white Asparagus and Lamb's Lettuce
St. Francis Reserve Zinfandel Pagani Vineyard, 1996
L'Apothéose
Les tartelettes aux fraises des bois avec sorbet de chocolate blanc
Wild Strawberry Tarts with white Chocolate Mousse

Fonseca Bin No. 27

Petits Fours, Café, Liqueurs

Chapter Eight
SERVICE

Objectives

- To explain different styles of service.

- To elaborate on the importance of service.

- To detail the operation of the service department.

- To learn how to motivate the service staff.

- To become familiar wih the gratuity distribution practices common in the industry.

- To learn about the *Diagram.*

Introduction

Friendliness is not always encountered in everyday life, and it is particularly difficult to practice it in commercial situations. One of the biggest challenges in all industries, but especially in the hospitality industry, is how to motivate employees to render cheerful service.

Operations are judged by the first impression. Usually banquet rooms are toured during the booking process and the prospective clients are likely to encounter employees at work. Well groomed, smiling employees in fitting, handsome spotlessly clean uniforms make a quality statement.

Service is not easy, and *Servers* have concerns which can directly affect their efficiency, and indirectly affect their attitude. The hospitality industry and especially the catering industry employ many part-time employees, and these employees, because of their more tenuous relationship with the caterer, can be especially hard to motivate. In spite of all this, the *Director of Service* must strive to present a pleasant, helpful staff to the client.

Hospitality

According to Webster's Dictionary, hospitality is defined as "The act, practice and quality of receiving and entertaining guests and strangers in a friendly and generous way". Hotels, restaurants, clubs, and catering houses are in the hospitality business. They must be profit-oriented to stay in business, but the true meaning of hospitality should never be forgotten.

In this book, references are often made to the items for which client should be charged. This is important, because only a business that charges enough to cover costs and make a profit will generate the funds to keep the operation in good repair and up to date. However, the client, once on the premises, should not be nickel and dimed to death. Generosity is a very important aspect of hospitality.

Motivating *Servers*

Banquet Servers are grouped basically in two categories, steady employees in large operations and extra employees working only when needed.

It is a challenge to motivate *Servers.* Many are extra employees and have different interests. They come to work to make money, and leave the catering facility as soon as the party is over. Other *Servers* are career *Servers;* many of them cheerful, but also some of them burned out, tired, and disillusioned with their lives. Most employees, however, can be motivated to give friendly, cheerful service.

Selection of employees is important. This is difficult in a tight labor market, but it can be done. Screening job applicants is not a priority in many operations. New employees are often put on the payroll with a brief interview and no checking of references. In large and small operations alike, pre-employment screening, however time consuming it might be, is very important. Some people are unfriendly by nature, or do not like to serve. These people can be spotted at the interview and weeded out. Time spent on interviewing is time and aggravation saved later.

The situation is altogether different in hotels with a collective bargaining agreement. The job of *Banquet Server* is lucrative and many union employees in other departments go on a waiting list to become *Banquet Servers.* The hotel and the union negotiate once a year the number of additional *Banquet Servers* to add to the steady payroll. This is a contested issue; the *Banquet Server's* union delegate normally does not want additional *Servers* because increasing the *Server* pool could reduce the number of jobs, and income, of the other *Servers.* The hotel in turn would like to increase the number of *Servers* if the business has increased, to provide better service and to reduce reliance on outside extra *Servers.*

Once the number of additional *Servers* is established it is very hard to select the most eligible person from the waiting list without provoking accusations of discrimination. Being on the waiting list does not automatically qualify the person to be a *Banquet Server.*

Training

Training is an important aspect of employee motivation. It demonstrates the commitment of the employer to the growth and development of the employee. Training can be classified as motivational training and craft training. Motivational training is

164

attitude training for all employees. Training is often part of the orientation program and training videotapes are available from professional organizations for this purpose. Employees should also be clearly informed of what to do in case of guest or employee accidents, and what steps to take in case of fires. All dining room employees should be trained in the *Heimlich Manoever* which is used when someone is choking.

Craft training is practical training in serving and clearing. In some operations, new employees are trained by trailing experienced *Servers* first, or they work as back *Servers,* also called kitchen runners. Other operations do not train at all. It is unadvisable to send new *Servers* onto the dining floor without specific training. Unfortunately experienced *Servers* could bring unacceptable habits and bad manners from previous places of employment, and without new training, it may be difficult to break them of those habits.

Management Attitudes

Information sharing does a lot not only for efficiency, but also for morale. There should be no secrets concerning the business at hand. Menus, diagrams, and menu and setup changes should be clearly posted. Business expectations for the foreseeable future should also be easily obtainable information, so employees can make plans and estimate their earnings. It is distressing how many catering establishments operate under a cloud of secrecy and mystery. Employees should know about renovation plans, about equipment on order, and about any other pertinent issues that might affect them directly. In general, being open with employees yields a double benefit: it directly increases efficiency and productivity, because better-informed employees tend to perform better; and it indirectly improves the smoothness and moral of the whole operation, because employees recognize and respond to a climate of openness and trust. Management must show respect at all times.

Behavior expectations should be clearly publicized. House rules should be explicit and conspicuously posted. The management expectation concerning dependability should be well known, and the consequences for not reporting for work or for lateness should be rigorously enforced. The procedures for calling in sick or for calling in when late should be clear and precise. Telephone calls are often made when the office is not yet open and are received by back of the house employees. A clear procedure must be established to record when the call was made and how to pass the information on to the right management person. It is not unusual that *Servers* call in and the information is not passed along.

Good treatment adds tremendously to keeping morale high. Of utmost importance is the friendliness of management when dealing with employees; fairness, and equal treatment of all employees; and attention to grievances. Clean lockers and toilets with showers should be provided. There are operations with elegant banquet rooms and the most deplorable back of the house areas. In some operations *Servers* change in makeshift locations and no lockers are provided. Female employees must have a secure place to lock up pocket books and other personal belongings. Organized staff meals should be provided. Some establishments do not provide staff meals, and expect *Servers* to snatch leftover food from buffet tables or dessert carts. *Servers* will not give cheerful service when their stomachs are empty, or when they have to worry about property left in the changing room.

English Lake Breakfast

Fresh Grapefruit Segments with Crème de Menthe

****

Porridge with Cream, Sugar and Whisky

****

Smoked Creamed Haddock in Puff Pastry Case
****

Deviled Kidney in Red Wine and Mushrooms

****

Hearty Lakeland Platter

****

**Homemade Marmalade and Baps
with Coffee and Tea**

Attitude Challenges

Many extra *Banquet Servers* are homemakers, college students, and in some locations aspiring artists, writers, and actors. They can be challenged to be dependable, friendly, and nice to people. Many of them are like that by nature and by life style. Good operators display their good character traits on the job. Most people are friendly, and like to be friendly when encouraged. It is harder to change the attitudes of some older employees. Some might have become burned out and grouchy. However most can be touched when the spirit of friendliness and service prevails in the operation.

Recognizing and developing the employees' strengths are important challenges for the manager.

Sample of a barbecue buffet menu with choices the client can select when booking the party.

Barbecue Buffet

(Choice of Four Hot Entrees)

**Whole Barbecued Pig
Corn Crusted Colorado Brook Trout
Grilled Mustard Flavored Chicken
Roast Sirloin of Beef, Wild Mushroom Sauce
Grilled Mountain Quail
Pan Fried Catfish
Barbecued Baby Back Spareribs
Grilled Leg of Lamb with Fresh Garlic and Rosemary**

To Complement Your Entrees:

(Choice of 6 items)

**Country Style Green Beans
Medley of Garden Vegetables
Whipped Red Skin Potatoes with Garlic and Roasted Corn
Country Skillet Spoon Bread
Chow Chow Relish
Oven Roasted Potato and Red Pepper Salad
Pepper Smoked Salmon and Penne Pasta Salad
Creamy Coleslaw
Tomato and Garden Vegetable Salad with Buffalo Mozzarella
Corn Bread   Country Rolls**

Dessert Buffet featuring:

(Choice of 6 items)

**Sliced Fruits and Berries in Season
Warm Berry Cobbler   Chocolate Fudge Cake   Apple Custard Flan
Pumpkin Whipped Cream Cake   Maple Cheesecake
Jack Daniels Pecan Pie   Apricot Bread Pudding with Vanilla Sauce**

Hot Beverages

Minimum attendance 75 guests

Discipline

House rules should be clear and to the point. Any infractions of the rules can be followed up in a three-step process. Every time the employee is disciplined, it should be recorded.

- The first step may be a verbal warning. This warning should be polite, to the point, and if possible given in private. Employees should never be reprimanded in front of guests. It makes both guests and employees very uncomfortable.

- The second warning is more formal and may be written. A printed form should be used. One copy is given to the employee, the department head keeps one, and the third is kept in the employee's record file. The incident should be described, and possible punishment, such as one day's suspension, should be marked down. The employee could ask to have another employee representative available. The employee should sign the warning notice. If the individual refuses to sign, this should be marked on the warning notice also.

- The third warning may lead to dismissal. It should always be in writing, in order for the operator to document why the employee was fired. The infraction should be explained, and the number of previous warning notices for the same infraction or other infractions should be noted. It is advisable for another employee to witness a dismissal.

In houses covered by a collective bargaining agreement, the warning steps and dismissal grounds are specified in detail.

Serious infractions such as theft, fighting, and use of controlled substances should provoke immediate dismissal. Lesser problems could be occasional rudeness to guests or to other workers, neglect of guests' needs, sloppy service habits leading to spills, leaving the floor when not authorized, arguments with other workers, and eating when not authorized. A warning should follow each of these infractions.

One diminishing problem is smoking. Some *Banquet Servers* are smokers, and it is difficult to ask them not to smoke for many hours. Smoking is a poor habit for *Servers* to have, because the smell of smoke lingers on them, and could be quite noticeable to guests.

New:
Smoking is not permitted in any public area in most states, but banquet rooms are exempt.

Servers should not be permitted to smoke in banquet rooms, storage rooms or in pantries. Tobacco smoke lingers on people and customers could take offence when the *Servers* smell of smoke. If absolutely necessary management might establish a small smoking area in a suitable spot. This area should be equipped with ashtrays, situated close to most service areas, and if possible, should be ventilated. *Servers* should inform their partners or the *Charge Captain* when leaving the floor.

Drug use could also be a potential problem, especially with employees who have not been screened thoroughly. The locker rooms should be patrolled occasionally, and managers should take all precautions at their disposal to prevent the prevalence of substance abuse by their personnel.

Service Styles

There are many different styles of banquet service. Most service styles have names, such as French service, Russian service and so forth. These historical names have little meaning today. In many cases, service styles during a party might vary. Some courses might be plated in the kitchen; others served from silver platters. The most important service styles are these:

Plate Service

This type of service is the most common. All food is plated and covered in the kitchen, stacked on large trays, and taken to the banquet room. In the banquet room the *Banquet Servers* use collapsible tray stands, also called tray horses, to put the trays on. The service is noisy, because the covers are removed in front of the guests. The plates are all alike, and if a guest would like an adjustment, such as having the meat cooked a little more, the *Server* would have to return to the kitchen with the plate. When food for large parties is dished out, the waiting time in the kitchen could be long if sufficient labor is not provided. Cooling and heating equipment is described in **Chapter 15.**

Silver service, also erroneously called French Service

All food is arranged on large silver platters, one for each table. The soup is put in tureens, the meat on platters, and the vegetables in dishes called Escoffier Dishes, the salads in bowls. *Servers* normally work in teams. They take the hot or cold plates to the tables, and return to the kitchen for the food. At the table the *Banquet Servers* dish out the food on to the plates. If a guest wants a slight modification of the food, such as a little more sauce or less vegetables, this can be easily arranged. This is important, because many guests are diet conscious, or allergic to certain foods. This type of service allows the guests a degree of choice when the food is brought to the table.

Silver service is fast, elegant, and efficient, but it requires a large investment in equipment and a skilled service staff. The food retains its quality better with silver service, because it is faster to dish out large platters in the kitchen than on individual plates, and this allows the food to be prepared and dished out closer to service time. The actual presentation of the food on the customer's plates may not be quite as professional unless the *Servers* are trained to dish the food out carefully.

New:
Silver service is being phased out in most operations. Many young chefs scorn silver service because they consider the plate presentation is lost when the *Servers* place the food on plates. This may be true and for small parties plate service may work. However, when a group numbers hundreds or more it is not practical to design each plate individually unless the food is plated well in advance and stored.

Buffet Service

Buffets are popular, because they allow the guests to choose. Buffets can be used for all meal periods. Many parties have a combination of service styles. The reception could be buffet service, the meal plate service, and the desserts buffet service again, often referred to as a Viennese table.

There are many logistical challenges connected with buffet service. It is important to have good circulation space to avoid lines; good re-supply of food as well as equipment such as plates and flatware, and good identification of the items on the buffets. Satellite buffets with distinct or duplicate foods are popular and practical if the space is available. Buffets are expensive, because a reasonable number of food choices have to be available until the last guests are served, which leads to inevitable waste. There can never be too many plates, napkins, and tableware.

Gueridon Service

The word gueridon is French for service cart or trolley. The food is placed on platters or heaters which are then placed on carts and wheeled to the table. In some cases, the meat is sliced at the gueridon in front of the guests. Gueridon service requires space for the mobile carts to be rolled around. It is also a little slower than other styles of service. Normally, one gueridon handles two or three tables at a time. This type of service is often used for weddings.

Butler Service

The term is used when food or beverages are passed on trays and the customers help themselves. Butler service is most often used at receptions. *Servers* circulate with drinks and bite-sized food. Plates and silverware, no matter how small, should not be used with butler service, but paper cocktail napkins provided instead.

The old definition of butler service was different and referred to food being passed on silver platters at the dinner table, the family members helping themselves. This style of service was practiced in households with servants.

Family Service

Food is put in bowls or platters and placed on the table, and guests help themselves. This informal style of service is used at picnics, summer camps, and sometimes for tour groups.

Good Grooming and Attitude

Good grooming is a cardinal rule for *Servers*, who are constantly in close contact with guests, and if they are not presentable, the reputation of the establishment suffers. The following is a general list of grooming points. Specific guidelines regarding makeup, jewelry, and other aspects of personal appearance should be made clear by management when the person is hired. Management may establish grooming standards if they are clearly communicated to the employee before they are hired, and so long as these standards apply equally to all employees, and are not changed. To avoid problems it may be advisable to take a photograph when the employee is hired and also on the first day on the job before being admitted to the floor.

Personal Hygiene

Servers should shower daily and use deodorant, cologne or perfume sparingly. The hair should be clean, groomed and styled away from the face. High tower hairstyles kept up with spray can be impractical when carrying trays.

New:
Our society has become more permissive and accepts any hairstyle as long as the hair is clean. It is not unusual today for male employees to wear their hair in "ponytail" fashion. However, many customers still frown upon beards and large moustaches.

Poise and Self Control

Good posture, an honest smile, and attentiveness are required at all times. Customers can be difficult occasionally, and *Banquet Servers* should exercise self-control at all times. They should never get into an argument with customers or with their fellow employees.

Jewelry

Besides a watch, minimal jewelry should be worn. Dangling earrings, nose rings, heavy bracelets, and rings besides the wedding band should not be worn.

Communication

Servers must be articulate and able to communicate clearly. Foreign born Servers should never converse in their language with each other in front of customers.

Attentiveness

Good Servers will practice observance, and pay attention to customers at all times to anticipate their needs. It is annoying and unprofessional when Servers walk by without noticing that they are needed.

Footwear

Banquet Servers spend most of their working time walking. Their footwear should be of excellent quality and meet the dress code established by management. In many places white sneakers are not permitted. Women should wear shoes with low heels.

Uniforms

Unless the house supplies uniforms, the normal dress code for Banquet Servers is as follows:

Males: Black pants, socks and shoes. White shirt, black bow tie.

Females: Black skirt, black hose, low heeled black shoes, white blouse.

Uniform Issues

The establishment could supplement the basic uniform with jackets, aprons, or other uniform parts. The uniforms should be good looking, projecting the quality image of the operation, and should fit properly. Some major hotels maintain large uniform storerooms and even have summer and winter uniforms. Since the sizes of the extra employees could vary greatly, a number of standard sizes must be kept in stock.

A great industry problem is uniform return and uniform abuse. In some establishments the Servers are not required to return the uniforms to the issuing point (e.g. the uniform storeroom or the Housekeeping Department) because it is often closed by the time the party is over. Employees should be instructed on how to return uniforms.

Catering houses often issue uniforms to their steady employees, embroidered with name labels. An exchange program requires that a new uniform be issued only against a soiled one. This system works well if the uniform room is open when needed. If it is closed, the soiled uniform can be kept in the employee's locker until it can be exchanged.

Some operations require employees to take their uniforms home for washing. This does not always work. Some employees have only limited access to laundry facilities; others have different expectations of cleanliness than their employer. It is in the interest of the caterer to have all employees dressed well, and be consistent in their appearance, and for this reason the operator should be responsible for uniform cleaning.

When uniforms are selected, a number of basic choices must be made. The first choice is care: should the uniforms be washable or suitable only for dry cleaning? Washable uniforms are cheaper to maintain, but the choice of materials is limited. The second choice is availability: should the uniform be a stock item or custom made? Local uniform stores carry a stock of ready-to-wear uniforms. Most uniforms in catalogs are made when ordered, and in the sizes specified. If the sizes are wrong there could be a considerable waste of money, plus it may take a while to get additional uniforms made.

Uniforms are made to work in. Man-made fabrics are often hotter than natural fibers. Badly cut or too elaborate uniforms could be impractical, hot, and uncomfortable. Sleeves should be short, especially for bartenders' jackets, because the bartenders work with water. Wide sleeves, long ties, and strings could become entangled or drop into food while serving.

Guests' impressions should be considered as well: bulky uniforms give the impression of slowness. Visibly uncomfortable uniforms make the guest pity the *Servers*. Uniforms should not stand out; they should blend with the theme of the establishment. Female uniforms should not be too *risqué*, not even for cocktail *Servers*.

Clients sometimes request that the *Servers* wear special uniforms at theme parties. These uniforms can be rented, and the client charged for the rental cost. Most *Servers* like to dress up like pirates or soldiers etc., and play the assigned roles with much enthusiasm. In some union houses, employees demand an extra uniform fee for wearing something other than the standard uniform. If these demands are not known and are not calculated into the cost, they could cut severely into the profit of the party.

Servers' Concerns

It is important to consider the problems, frustrations, and concerns that the *Servers* present. Managers often ignore the legitimate complaints and brushes them off as "gripes".

Happy employees give better service than unhappy ones!

Frequent Schedule Changes

Servers are entitled to a private life. Occasionally banquet attendance changes, and more or fewer employees are needed. Frequently asking employees to work or to stay home at short notice can by very irritating and disruptive.

Poor Working Conditions

Complaints can range from unsanitary locker rooms to slippery floors, and bad layout of work areas to dangerous practices.

Manipulation of Gratuities

There is often the suspicion that more gratuities were charged than were distributed, or that gratuities landed in the wrong hands. The gratuity distribution system should be explained to all employees.

Unco-operative Kitchen Help

Occasionally kitchens are badly organized and *Servers* are not helped when they need something. The cooks are busy, hardly look up, a supervisor is nowhere to be found and a request or question is often answered by a grunt or by: "find it yourself".

Weak Dining Room Management

When more than one party takes place at the same time some operations do not have sufficient floor management such as *Charge Captains* or *Assistant Dining Room Managers*. In family owned operations a relative without much knowledge or training is occasionally used to supervise a party. Banquet hotels schedule *Charge Captains* for each and every party to make sure the party runs smoothly. *Servers* resent having to work without direct supervision.

Insufficient Bussing Space

When tables are cleared many pieces of china accumulate in one spot. Management must make sure there is enough room to handle the volume. *Servers* are sometimes forced to place trays on landings, steps, or trash cans.

Unnecessary Trips to the Kitchen

Poor menu planning, timing, or lack of equipment can necessitate numerous trips. If the menu is too complicated it might take three or more trips to get all components on the table.

Tight Setups, Inaccessible Tables

This is difficult to avoid when the party grows or requires more space than was originally planned. Tight setups in banquet rooms increase the danger of spills and accidents.

Uncomfortable Uniforms

This mistake is often made when sales representatives of uniform companies sell a "look" rather than practicality.

Poorly Stacking China

This is a mistake that could be easily avoided. China must stack well and yet should not be too heavy. Banquet china is heavier than restaurant china but there are big weight differences between brands.

Some of these concerns cannot be corrected without major investments. Others need very little effort to change. The goal of the operator is to provide the friendliest, most efficient service. If employee concerns can be corrected, they should be.

Equipment Setup Expectations

Servers expect to get the equipment needed to serve a party. Equipment includes anything the *Servers* handle, from buffet props to linen, from table appointments to desserts carts. When the equipment is not available in the quantities needed, *Servers* have to scrounge around for it, sometimes take it from other *Servers,* or hoard it.

This behavior only aggravates the situation. I have known *Servers* who carried teaspoons in their pockets because they were in chronic short supply. In some houses, the *Servers* have to spend a lot of time rounding up equipment. This is often caused by poor planning by the *Kitchen Steward,* or by shortages because of budget problems or because equipment was ordered late. Custom decorated china for example can take many months to arrive.

Banquet equipment should always be abundant. This is an expensive practice, but about the only way to have a smooth running operation, especially when banquet rooms are located in many parts of the building and soiled equipment cannot be washed and recycled quickly.

Inspection of Equipment Responsibilities

It is the responsibility of the *Servers* to make sure that all equipment is inspected before it reaches the guests. There is no excuse for a cracked or chipped glass or plate on any table, or for using tablecloths with cigarette burns, or for folding stained napkins.

If any of the equipment is not in acceptable condition, the supervisor should be notified. Supervisors should never greet such news with annoyance. **Servers are the last and most important quality inspectors**. Their vigilance and eagerness in rejecting substandard equipment should be encouraged, not discouraged.

The Office of the *Director of Service*

All catering operations should have an office for the exclusive use of the *Director of Service*. The clerical responsibilities of this person are so important that quiet space and private office furniture are needed. Large operations have an office staffed with clerical help, but this is seldom needed in smaller operations. This office could be adjacent to the banquet sales office but should be a separate room. It should also be accessible from the back of the house.

New:
The office is usually computerized and equipped with a printer.

Typical clerical work performed in the office of the Director of Service:

- Scheduling of all *Servers, Bartenders, Housemen* and other front of the house employees.

- Preparing the payroll for these employees.

- Gratuities distribution paperwork.

- Receiving and temporary storing of programs, menus and other printed material for special parties and meetings.

- Co-ordination of audiovisual requirements.

- Co-ordination of carpentry and electrical work.

- Making diagrams and floor plans.

- Ordering linen from the *Housekeeping Department*.

- Co-ordination of other contractors, such as photographers, florists, and musicians.

- Co-ordination and documentation of all extra charges, and preparation of the final bill.

176

Interesting Classical Dinner Served
on February 11, 1899 in Bern, Switzerland
at the Hotel Bellevue

Attereaux d'huîtres à l'amèricaine

****

Consommé Czarèwitsch

Madère vieux

******

Suprême de Barbue à la Bernard

Dèzaley Clos des Abbayes 1895

******

Quartier de Marcassin
Sauce Cumberland

St. Estèphe

******

Bècasses à la Monte Carlo

Rauenthaler Pfaffenburg

******

Chaudfroid de Langouste à la Russe

******

Granit au Cliquot

******

Chapon à la Broche
Garnie d'Ortalans au Coulis d'Ananas

Chambertin 1877

******

Salade demi deuil

******

Timbale de Foie Gras
à la Bellevue

******

Beignets d'Artichauds
à la Vallière

******

Parfait à la Diplomate

Pommery & Greno
Moët & Chandon

******

Gateau Jamaique

******

Fruits et Dessert

Scheduling the Service Staff

Scheduling is based on the attendance numbers on the guarantee sheet and on the instructions on *BEOs*. The ratio of *Banquet Servers* to guests varies. In elegant hotels with a collective bargaining agreement the ratio is normally 1 *Server* for every 10 guests. In other houses, the ratio can be as high as 1 *Server* to 30 guests. When *Captains* are employed, the ratio is one *Captain* for every 6 to 8 tables (60 to 80 *customers*). Menu price, room setup and service style determine how many *Servers* to schedule; *Bartenders, Ushers, Housemen* and all other personnel are also scheduled accordingly.

Efficient scheduling of *Housemen* is difficult but often crucial to the profitability of the operation. When a room must be turned over quickly, enough *Housemen* should stand by to reset the furniture. Since rooms should be cleaned and reset after each party in busy operations, *Housemen* have to be scheduled until the parties are over. Often, the *Housemen* can clean and set up some function rooms as soon one party moves to another room.

Banquet Servers often work in teams. One *Server* is designated as front *Server*, the other as back *Server* or kitchen runner. The more experienced *Servers* should be scheduled as front *Servers*, the trainees as *Back Servers*.

The *Server's* schedule is normally based on rotation. Steady *Servers* are on the permanent payroll and their names are kept on a rotating list. The parties are staffed with the names taken from the top of the list. When there is no business on certain days and other days are very busy, *Servers* could be scheduled to serve two jobs on the same day in order to give them a reasonable income. Steady *Servers* can refuse to work a party. In this case, their names are put on the bottom on the list, and they have to wait until their names come up again. *Servers* working with steady partners are treated as one name on the rotation list.

Extra *Servers* are called *Roll Call Servers*. The list is maintained by the union and consists of unemployed or semi-retired union members. In busy banquet months the roll call list might become exhausted and *Servers* working in other food outlets in the hotel would be permitted to work at banquets. Since the catering business is highly seasonal and much heavier on weekends than weekdays, *Roll Call Servers* could work quite frequently during the busy season, but perhaps not at all when the establishment is not busy. They are on call. If they refuse to work their names are put on the bottom of the list. Some *Roll Call Banquet Servers* might not meet the appearance standards of management but there is little choice. Occasionally the union will send better-qualified *Servers* to the finer hotels.

Extra-extras are not on the rotation list. They are called only when the other lists are exhausted and when the party is unusually large. These employees come in for a specific function. They may never have worked in the specific job before, and these employees should only be used as *Back Servers* or *Kitchen Runners*. *Extra-extras* might work for other caterers or in restaurants. Others work in different fields completely, and enjoy working as *Servers* periodically for the extra income.

The purpose of the rotation list is to distribute the available work as fairly as possible. This can be difficult. *Servers* are paid gratuities for the parties they work. It can happen that, on account of rotation, some *Servers* could be scheduled for many rather low-priced breakfasts and luncheons, and others could work many profitable dinners. To avoid these inequities, some operations have rotation lists based on meal periods, or keep track of the type of meals for which *Servers* are scheduled.

The nature of the business requires that *Servers* are sometimes scheduled to work shifts close together. Sometimes *Servers* hardly have time to go home, wash up, and rest a little before they take off for work again. In some States, laws dictate the length of rest periods between shifts, but this does not take into consideration travel time. During very busy seasons, *Servers* have been known to sleep in locker rooms because they were scheduled so often. The life of *Banquet Servers* can be hard, with swings from idleness to frenzied activity.

Scheduling is based not only on the rotation list, but also the availability of the employees to work. Some employees have transportation problems. Other employees have school schedules, or have other jobs. Some employees have problems finding baby sitters. It is not enough to post a schedule and expect all employees to show up. Good knowledge of the employee's private lives and problems is needed to make schedules that work. Most computer programs can make schedules but it takes a lot of programming to include the times when *Servers* cannot work. The computer deals with names and not with people.

The *Servers'* Payroll

Making up the *Servers'* payroll can be time consuming and complicated. In most banquet houses *Servers* are paid by the shift, also called the job. The length of the job varies. The collective bargaining agreement specifies extra pay for setup *Servers* and for closing *Servers*. It also specifies extra pay for extra covers served, which are called splits. The usual ratio of *Server* to guests is 1 to 10. Up to 12 guests could be served for the same shift rate, but more than 12 covers would be considered a split. If a team of two *Servers* handles three tables, they would receive split pay in addition to their gratuity share. If a job goes over a specific time, *Servers* get overtime pay. The pay specifications vary, and all catering facilities do not pay according to the rules mentioned above.

In non-union operations the *Servers* are paid a flat rate for each job, and extra for setup and breakdown.

The hourly rate varies, but is usually very low. It could be as low as the minimum wage, less anticipated gratuity share. Taxes must be paid on all gratuities. The benefits of the steady employees are based on the yearly earnings.

Simple Dinner Menu

Scallop Mousse with Shrimp and Cilantro Dressing

****

Herb Roasted Filet of Beef
Ginger Sauce
Bouquetiere of Spring Vegetables
Medley of Wild Rice and Patna Rice

****

Baby Lettuce Salad with Vermont Cheddar
Walnut Dressing

****

Lemon Curd Tart and seasonal Berries

****

Colombian Coffee

Gratuity Distribution

Operations charge between 17% and 22% gratuity on all food and beverage charges. The distribution varies but the banquet contract must specify the percentage paid to hourly employees and to supervisory employees. All gratuities must be paid to employees. It is illegal to keep gratuities as general revenue.

Gratuities are paid for each party. Usually, the *Banquet Servers* get 12% of food and wine revenue. *Banquet Captains* get 1½% to 2% of the total charges. *Bartenders* get 1% of the alcoholic beverage charges. In some operations *Bartenders* get 1% of the total charges, to be divided by the back of the house bar staff. The remaining moneys are divided at the discretion of the house. The *Director of Service* often gets 1% of all parties. A small portion of this gratuity may be shared with the employees in the office. In some houses the *Executive Chef* and *Banquet Chef* are paid 1%.

The remaining share could go either as a commission to the *Banquet Sales Associates* or be posted to the sales office payroll account. The gratuity distribution should be printed on the banquet contract in order to avoid lawsuits from guests who believe that all gratuities are given to the employees.

Two common ways of paying gratuities to *Servers* are by pool or by cover. If the distribution is by pool, the whole sum is divided by the number of *Servers*. In some establishments, front *Servers* receive a slightly larger share than back *Servers*. When the gratuities are based on actual covers served, the diagram which indicates the number of covers on each table serves as payroll documentation. When *Servers* work with steady partners, their gratuity share is normally the same. Gratuity income can be very high. It is not unusual that the income of steady *Banquet Servers* in busy hotels is higher than the income of most executives.

Bartenders receive a share of the reception revenue.

Overtime Control Problems

The industry saying is that an operation without overtime is over-staffed. This may be true, but overtime can get out of hand easily if not controlled. Overtime caused because a party runs late is justifiable, and the charges are usually passed on to the client. Most overtime occurs when the starting and finishing times of parties are not well established by the *Banquet Sales Associates*. If the *BEO* does not state the correct starting times *Banquet Servers* might be scheduled too early or too late.

Diagram Responsibilities

Diagrams are floor plans, generally in ¼ inch scale on which all tables, platforms, and other furniture are indicated. The number of seats at each table is also indicated. Diagrams are made in the office of the *Director of Service*. In large banquet houses, one person specializes in making diagrams. Computer generated diagrams are usually limited by the size of printer in the office and are seldom large enough.

Diagrams serve a number of purposes. They allow the *Director of Service*, often in conjunction with the *Banquet Sales Associate*, to set up the room in the most efficient and practical manner. Diagrams confirm to the client the planned and ordered room setup. After the client has reviewed the diagram and indicated seating changes, the signed diagram is used as the guarantee. Once signed, the diagram is the work sheet used by *Housemen* to set the room, and as a worksheet for table assignment for the service staff.

Banquet Servers are assigned the tables for which they are responsible, *Banquet Captains* oversee the stations. If gratuities are based on the diagram, the number of covers each *Server* is assigned is indicated on the diagram. If additional seats are added, this is also marked on the diagram, and it is always reviewed before the final bill is made.

Diagrams are made on preprinted floor plans that show the configuration of the banquet room, doors, windows, platforms, and other architectural features. The person making the diagrams should be an employee who knows the property well, who remembers the location of outlets, the size of stages and dance floors, and can visualize the room when it is set up. Using rubber stamps or stencils, available in scale for all table sizes and shapes indicates the tables. In some cases, the client is shown a number of sample diagrams until the right setup and location for all other elements, such as the buffet tables, dance floor, and music stand have been determined.

New:

Diagrams can be computer generated with special software. The computer must be programmed with the exact dimension of each banquet room including all architectural features. The available tables, chairs, lecterns, and other furniture must be programmed for each room in the corresponding scale. The programming can take a number of weeks in large banquet houses. The room diagram can be brought on the screen and the furniture icons dragged into the picture. The diagram can be printed, most printers print 8½" x 11" sheets which must be enlarged. Computer generated diagrams may be adequate for simple small functions, but are generally too small for large ballrooms unless printed on a plotter.

Billing Responsibilities

The *Director of Service* is responsible for making the final bill. The bill is based on the actual attendance figures, which may be higher than the guarantee, additional liquor charges, overtime charges, and all other charges indicated on the *BEO*. The bill must be accompanied by documentation, such as the beverage consumption sheet if beverages are charged as consumed, the actual charges for miscellaneous labor, and other charges.

When to present the bill for signature or settlement is a question of house policy. As general practice, the bill should be presented for signature to the host at the end of the party. The host may authorize some extra gratuities to be added. The actual settlement normally takes place within a few days after the event.

All banquet bills for each day should be sent to the night auditor as soon as signed so they can be recorded as revenue for the day even when the bill is actually signed after midnight. In catering operations, the bill is sent the next day to the bookkeeper. The caterer does not pay invoices from outside contractors; these contractors bill the client directly.

Note:
Catering software handles billing but last minute charges must still be entered by the *Director of Catering*.

Summary

Friendly, efficient service is the essence of hospitality and the industry is facing many challenges in their efforts to provide consistent good service. Erratic work schedules, a hectic pace and occasionally poor working conditions make finding, training and retaining good *Servers* difficult.

Screening employees before hiring them is time well spent. Once hired *Banquet Servers* should be trained and motivated to develop good work habits and attitude. The *Director of Service* is responsible for operating the service department, and has many executive responsibilities, and in addition is in direct guest contact while the party takes place. The *Director of Service* is one of the key players in making the banquet event a success.

Discussion Questions

- Explain the meaning of the word *hospitality.*

- How can *Servers* be motivated by management?

- Why is employee selection and training important?

- List service styles and the most common situations in which one can be used.

- What is a gueridon? What are the advantages and disadvantages of its use?

- What factors effect decisions regarding employee uniforms?

- Name some of the *Servers'* common complaints?

- Describe the executive responsibilities of the *Director of Service.*

- What is a rotation list?

- What are *Roll Call Servers*?

- How are gratuities distributed?

Chapter Nine

THE CHEF AND THE STEWARD
TWO VITAL ROLES

Reception and Dinner
in
San Juan, Puerto Rico

NUEVO CRIOLLA APPETIZERS AT THE FANTASY POOL

Guanimes with Salt Cod
Fiambre Beef with Gooseberry Jam
Cassava Empanadas
Tostones with Land Crabs
Conch and Mongo Skewers

Louis Roederer NV Brut
****

SOUP ON THE VERANDA

Apio and Coconut Milk Potage
Chilled Papaya Gazpacho

DINNER IN THE BALLROOM

Roasted Seabass with Tomato Pastel
Beurre Blanc

Chassagne Montrachet
Marquise de Laguiche 1995
****

Pork Medaillon with Clove and Star Anise
Red Wine Sauce
White Rice with Pine Nuts

Bonnes Mares 1989
****

White Chocolate Passion Fruit Orangerie

Laurent Perrier
NV, Demi Sec
****

Puerto Rican Mountain Coffee
Tropical Delicacies

Note that the menu mixes three languages unnecessarily.

Chapter Nine
THE CHEF AND THE STEWARD
TWO VITAL ROLES

Objectives

- To understand the role of the *Executive Chef.*

- To appreciate the importance of clear and precise internal communication.

- To understand the administrative responsibilities of the *Executive Chef.*

- To get a short overview of kosher catering.

- To learn about the importance, responsibilities and duties of the *Steward's Department.*

Introduction

After the function has been sold, promises made, and the host has been assured that the event will be wonderful, unique, and memorable, it must be turned into reality. This involves two largely unseen departments, the *Chef's Department* and the *Steward's Department.* The skills of chefs are easily noticeable. Much less immediately noticeable is the crucial role of the *Steward's Department.* Unless the *Executive Chef* and the *Chief Steward* work closely together, a banquet will not be a success.

One of the most important attributes of the *Executive Chef* in a large banquet operation is the ability to organize and to delegate responsibility. Feeding large groups of people is complex and many things can go wrong. Experienced *Executive Chefs* plan for all contingencies, and are able to adjust quickly to unforeseen situations. Perhaps these attributes can be summarized as resourceful leadership.

Deservedly, chefs are recognized as skilled craft professionals. Chefs' organizations, culinary schools, gourmet societies, and to a large extent the media have given credit and publicity to certain chefs. Over the last few years many acclaimed chefs have appeared in the public eye. These highly talented professionals manage their publicity and resources to their advantage, opening restaurants, writing books, and appearing on TV. *Executive Chefs* in large hotels operate sizeable businesses with minimal publicity. Continuity and attention to detail, whether the party requires coffee and danish, or pheasant breasts, are expected.

Stewards have remained in the background and their contribution to the success of an operation is largely unknown. It is unfortunate for the industry that very few career

Stewards exist today. The *Steward's* position is often a stepping stone in the career path to *General Manager.* Stewarding is given only minor attention in most hospitality schools. There is no professional *Stewards'* organization, and certification is lacking.

The *Executive Chef's* Responsibilities

The responsibilities of the *Executive Chef* are constantly scrutinized and tailored to their specific operation. For many years the *Executive Chef* was the undisputed boss in all kitchens and in charge of all food production throughout the house, including all restaurants, room service and all banquet functions. As the administrative duties became more complex and time consuming and at the same time the customer's expectations increased, it became evident that one single individual could not perform all duties satisfactorily. A number of titles were redefined and the responsibilities divided.

New:
Some hotel companies treat each food outlet as an independent profit center and make the professional in charge directly responsible for profitability. This division, though perhaps beneficial in a managerial sense, may present logistical problems concerning allocation of expenses and resources.

In many large operations job titles and duties are:

- *Executive Chef.* The professional administrator who oversees the duties of food preparation and production personnel, and in some operations handles publicity. Attending meetings, solving personnel issues, and enforcing company policy are also time-consuming duties.

- *Chef de Cuisine.* This venerable French title normally refers to the culinary professional in the kitchen who is less involved in administration and who directly supervises food production.

- *Banquet Chef.* Assisted by a number of steady and extra cooks, the *Banquet Chef* is responsible for all banquet food. Originally the *Banquet Chef* reported directly to the *Executive Chef.*

New:
In some large operations the *Banquet Chef* now reports to the *Catering Director* and to the *Executive Chef*.

- *Pastry Chef.* The pastry department has always been semi-independent of the *Executive Chef* and often works directly in conjunction with the *Catering Director* and the *Banquet Chef* to create new desserts.

- *Restaurant Chefs.* Today's trend is to bring fine dining back into hotels. Some hotel restaurants have become independent operations, to a large extent self contained and sometimes operated by a well known chef.

- *Sous Chef.* This French title is often misused. *Sous* mean under and in large kitchens the *Sous Chef* was the second in command. There was never more than one Sous Chef. Chefs in charge of smaller kitchens were called *Floor Chefs* and chefs in charge of stations were called *Chefs de Partie.*

Responsibilities

The responsibilities listed below are in no specific order. They are divided and shared now by many foodservice professionals. The basic premise has not changed; the food must be ready when needed without any excuses and delays.

Kitchen Administration

Operating a large kitchen requires strong administrative skills and powerful leadership.

Food Production

The *Banquet Chef* and the *Pastry Chef* must have the food specified on the *BEO* ready when required, and prepared in a wholesome, tasty, and attractive fashion.

Food Cost Control

The *Executive Chef* is responsible for the cost percentage to sales of all food. This percentage is determined to a large degree by the selling price the *Banquet Sales Associate* achieves. The chef has to advise the *Banquet Sales Associates* about seasonal price fluctuations, and should work closely with the food control office or the bookkeeper to calculate the cost for each dish. The chef estimates the amount of food to prepare, and controls over-production and waste as much as possible.

Labor Cost Control

The *Executive Chef* is directly responsible for the labor cost of all kitchen employees, and in many cases of all back of the house employees.

Each labor dollar spent unnecessarily is a dollar lost.

Sanitation Enforcement

The *Executive Chef* is responsible for seeing that all food is safe to eat, and that the kitchen, food preparation areas, and cooking equipment are kept clean. This responsibility is a heavy one. Food can become contaminated easily, and it would be disastrous if food poisoning would occur as a result of food served at a party. It is expected that all food handlers wear head covering, use disposable gloves when handling food not to be cooked any further, observe personal hygiene, and maintain all food at the proper temperature.

Food safety is a major concern and the Food and Drug Administration in conjunction with other federal agencies support and recommend a 7-step system whose acronym is HACCP (Hazard Analysis Critical Control Point). This system was developed originally by The Pillsbury Company in conjunction with NASA for the astronauts in the 1970's NASA Space Program. It has evolved since then, and is now the food safety system of choice in many commercial and institutional foodservice operations throughout the world. It is definitely applicable to banquet operations. There are many resources available for learning and implementing this system.

Key control

This is an important responsibility. A large kitchen key ring should be established for each kitchen. The ring should be so large that it can be worn around the neck. On this ring are all refrigerator keys and keys to other kitchen areas, such as the china closet or bakeshop. Refrigerators should be keyed alike, to keep the number of keys to a minimum. The key to the chef's office and to all the storerooms should not be on this ring. The kitchen key ring should be kept overnight at the timekeeper's office in hotels, or in a secure place in smaller hotels and independent catering facilities.

The *Banquet Chef* and the *Chef de Cuisine* are the hands-on food production managers. They are required to be artistic, imaginative, resourceful and good cooks. Above all they are managers operating a vast and complicated food production plant. They have to be good administrators in order to manage a plant that turns out a wide variety of hot or cold food at the precise moment when ordered, often late at night, early in the morning, on weekends, and on holidays.

Regardless of whether the operation is large or small, it all comes down to the same simple routine: *Banquet Servers* file into a kitchen, a *Captain* yells "Pick up," and the food must go out, despite unforseen problems: a delivery not showing up on time; equipment awaiting repair; a pantry person who had to go home to attend to a sick child; and the special cake that was almost pushed over in the refrigerator. The show must go on when the curtain rises.

Staffing and Organization

Most kitchens, even in small operations, have stations preparing specific groups of dishes. Some cooks specialize in cold food preparation, others in pastry making, and others in cooking hot food. The challenge in banquet operations is to schedule the work force efficiently to match the requirements of each menu with the existing talent. Banquet menus vary, on some days parties might require more cold food than hot, on other days more cooked food than cold food. During some weeks many of the parties might order buffets, and some weeks most parties could be sit down dinners.

Many banquet cooks have limited expertise in all types of cooking and are not very flexible in their work. A good roast cook might not be much help when asked to make delicate canapés, and the pastry cook might not be productive dishing out steaks. When cooks are hired for banquet work, employees able and willing to work on all stations should be selected when possible. Scheduling is not only based on the availability of employees but it must also take their skills into consideration.

The *Banquet Chef* is in charge of all banquet food preparation. A number of banquet cooks are assigned to this chef for each party, the number contingent on the size of the party, menu and location of the banquet room. The cooks normally work in teams and are responsible for assembling and preparing the food. Depending on the specific organization of the kitchen, the meat or fish would be requisitioned ready to cook from the butcher shop, the soup or the soup stock would be prepared in the soup kitchen, and the buffet items or cold food dishes would be prepared in the cold kitchen under the supervision of the *Garde Manger Chef*, and all roasts needed for all parties cooked by one or two banquet cooks. In other places the banquet crew is completely independent and prepares all food from a wide array of components.

New:
The organization described above consisting of stations in the kitchen is increasingly challenged. In most large hotels the banquet kitchen crew is completely independent. This became possible with the use of semi-prepared and fully prepared food components.

At service time, each team takes the food to the specific banquet kitchen, where it is completed if necessary and dished out. Supervision is a challenge when many parties are scheduled in function rooms not adjacent to each other. The *Banquet Chef* cannot be at all parties at the same time and must put one responsible person in charge. Labor without supervision is wasted labor.

To spread production as evenly as possible over the whole week, it is very important that the *BEOs* arrive in the chef's office at least two weeks prior to the function. When this is the case food production can be planned efficiently, and some food can be prepared ahead of time. Ice carvings for a number of parties can be made by one chef and stored in the freezer, cookies can be made in large batches, and some sauces can be made ahead.

New:
Computerization allows the chef to access all banquet files and plan accordingly.

Preparing food ahead presents difficult choices of balancing freshness and quality with saving payroll, and taking into consideration equipment limitations. Almost all food can be made ahead and frozen, and some operations produce foods continuously, freeze it, and use it when needed. Other operations are very quality conscious, and would rather accept a higher payroll in exchange for serving only fresh food.

Scheduling kitchen employees is a difficult task. Large hotels normally have a steady banquet crew working under the direction of the *Banquet Chef*. These employees are flexible and can be scheduled when needed; however they are entitled to a full work week. When there is no banquet work the cooks can be sent to other departments in the kitchen. During the extremely busy banquet season many cooks work overtime. Usually this is less expensive than carrying more steady employees.

Since banquet volume varies greatly most catering kitchens also use extra employees. Many operations have a list of steady extra employees who are willing to come in and to work for one or two days a week. By having extra employees available when needed, much overtime can be avoided. These extra employees should be hired through the *Human Resource Department*, screened and treated like other employees. To what extent they must become union members and share in benefits and pension plans are issues to be resolved by the *Human Resource Department*. In some cases these employees are allowed to work only a limited number of hours a week.

Extra employees should not be hired through colleagues, allowed to work without insurance, and paid petty cash. Aliens should be properly documented.

Banquet cook schedules should be posted one week ahead on a designated bulletin board, adjacent to but separate from the banquet menus. The schedule blanks should be easy to read and contain the full name and payroll number of each employee. There should be a procedure in place indicating the person to notify when an employee wishes to change a shift. All changes should be approved and noted on the schedule accordingly.

Banquet schedules are liable to change. The task of calling the employees about schedule modifications falls to a *Sous Chef*, the *Banquet Chef*, or a clerical person in the chef's office. Computers play an important role in the kitchen, and most chefs' offices are equipped with PCs or with terminals connected to a main frame computer. The computer can store employee information such as addresses, telephone numbers, employment dates and other data. Most hotels require that schedules and payroll information be keyed into the computer.

Preparation

There is a historical progression in food preparation, from tending open fires to slaughtering animals on-premise to using semi-prepared food components. Only fifty years ago country inns in Austria were often combined with butcher shops and pigs were slaughtered every week and chicken delivered live to the kitchen.

Cooking today has become a process of assembling components available in a dizzying variety of quality levels, sizes, and conditions. These choices still offer opportunities for creativity and self expression and it would be foolish for any chef to turn the wheels backwards and insist on making all meals from scratch. The challenge for many chefs is to judicially select the right products and handle the logistics of getting them approved and delivered.

Vacuum packing is a practical method for preparing food ahead of time and storing it efficiently. It is rather a simple process and vacuum packed food has a longer shelf life under refrigeration and will not dry out easily. Counting is also more precise if the same amount is placed in each bag. Just about all items to be cooked later can be vacuum packed such as cleaned baby artichokes, fresh asparagus, fish fillets, cut meats and other foods.

Vacuum packing is not *Sous Vide*, which is a French developed process of placing cooked food under controlled conditions in vacuum bags. Many companies experimented with *Sous Vide* and the process is still under evaluation in the United States.

New:
Vacuum packing equipment is available in many sizes and is not expensive.

Chinese Dinner

Appetizer Platter

Roast Pig, Pickled Vegetables, Pig' Feet,
Ham, Chicken Jellyfish

Scallops with Broccoli

Fried Seafood Roll

Abalone, Chicken and Mushroom Soup

Abalon, Oyster Mushrooms and Shiitaki with Lettuce

Squab with red fermented Bean Curd Sauce

Sauteed Lobster

Steamed Pike

Shrimp Fried Rice

Lo Mein

Red Bean Soup

Fortune Cookies

Managing Paperwork

As soon as *BEOs* arrive in the chef's office, they are sorted as soon as possible and put on clipboards, one for each day. *BEOs* should never be left lying around, to be buried under other papers, or even lost. *Banquet Sales Associates* should never have to worry whether or not a *BEO* has been processed, and if the food will be actually prepared as ordered.

New:
Back of the house offices are widely being equipped with their own printers and can print their own *BEOs*. This being the case, there would no longer be the same need for distribution. This places the burden of distributing *BEOs* on the shoulders of the executing department heads.

BEOs are work orders and must be taken seriously. They are legal contracts between the hotel and the client and whatever is listed must be prepared. The *BEOs* should be posted, in an orderly fashion, in various parts of the kitchen and also in the food storeroom or in the receiving area for the same day and for the next day. *BEOs* can be lengthy because they contain all the information needed to service the party. Some of this information is not pertinent to the kitchen staff. The chef should highlight the important information on the menu, and post only the necessary portion of the *BEO*. Cooks should not have to waste time reading about the table decorations and the musician arrival time.

Note:
It is important to highlight the day and date when the function takes place. Most cooks remember the day of the week better than the date.

BEOs posted in the kitchen must be accessible and carefully managed. Sloppily posted *BEOs*, carelessly tacked to the wall, do not project the importance of these orders.

The portions of the *BEOs* pertinent to a specific department should be highlighted when necessary. For instance, the butcher shop is not very interested in the desserts, but could be interested in soups if their production requires lobster shells or meat bones. Managing the *BEOs* in a neat fashion adds much to the smooth and orderly operation of any department. Only authorized employees should be allowed to alter or remove any posted *BEOs*. They are important pieces of communication and should not be tampered with.

To verify annotations, it is a good idea for department heads to each select and use a different colored pen. Using this method, changes and additions can be traced for verification if necessary, without having to inquire who made the change.

Most catering software programs include the capability to store recipes and convert them to any number of covers. Some programs will also print the necessary food requisition. Stored recipes work only when all ingredients are carefully measured and the procedures are strictly followed. Many ingredients are difficult to measure, because the packages in which they are delivered are hard to divide. There are obvious seasonal differences in sizes, yields and quantities the computer cannot recognize. The computer also disregards how to dispose of unused material and leftovers.

As long as cooking is a craft and art standard recipes will be helpful but human judgment and experience is necessary to produce good meals.

Deciding Quantities

Before the *BEOs* (in the kitchen often referred to as "menus") can be posted, the chef has to mark on them the quantities that have to be prepared, unless the food is sold in units or there are computer generated recipes.

Deciding the quantities is a crucial step in controlling food cost and at the same time guarantees that the amount of food ordered is actually prepared. In many smaller operations, and in some large ones, it is pretty much left up to the cooks to decide by gut feeling and instinct how much to prepare. It is normally too much. This method is unacceptable. It is the responsibility of the *Executive Chef* to decide the quantities.

Deciding quantities is not an automatic process because the type of group, time of reception and type of dinner must be carefully evaluated to arrive at the right amounts. The computer cannot supply this type of information.

Note:
Many operations are fully computerized and calculate the number and quantities for every menu component. This quantity is then prepared regardless of past history and without human evaluation and judgment.

Quantities should always be given per person to be able to adjust the production when the attendance increases or decreases. For instance canapés could be marked as 4½ cold canapés per person. When the final guarantee sheet is issued the guaranteed number of guests attending would be multiplied by 4½ resulting in the number of canapés that must be made. To tell the *Banquet Chef* to make 16 gallons of soup might not be enough or too much. However when the soup on the menu is marked as x20, the cooks know that each gallon is for 20 servings and can adjust the amount according to the latest guarantee.

It is also absolutely essential that *Banquet Sales Associates* do not wander around the kitchen and tell cooks how much to make. Any comments and suggestions should be directed to the *Executive Chef* or *Banquet Chef.*

One of the most difficult tasks for any chef is to calculate quantities for buffets. Buffets are meant to provide a reasonable choice to all guests until the party is over. The chef has to decide how much of each food variety should be prepared, based on experience and menu price. Since chefs are responsible for food cost, and in some operations their bonuses are based on achieving a low food cost, they often try to skimp on expensive food. Many buffets are well supplied with macaroni salad and short on smoked salmon.

The interests of the house and the chef must be the same. In many operations, a standard buffet quantity list is used to determine the amount of food needed. The quantity list could be computer generated. The basic quantities per person are established and multiplied by the number of covers. Unfortunately, these lists do not take the eating habits of the groups into consideration. Some ethnic groups eat more than others do. Food quantities cannot be calculated by machine alone.

One difficult problem is the replenishing of buffets when they are not supervised directly by the *Banquet Chef* or the *Charge Captain*. Most *Servers* are eager to keep the buffet well stocked, and return frequently to the kitchen asking for more food, whether it is needed or not. Often, all food allocated for the specific party is already sent out, and arguments between *Servers* and cooks could ensue.

The replenishing of buffets should be co-ordinated and supervised by the *Charge Captain*. This professional should take into consideration the time frame of the party and the estimated number of guests yet to be served. When there are multiple buffets, some buffets could be closed as the party progresses, and the food consolidated on one or more buffets. The judgment of the *Charge Captain* must be respected, and the chef should always be ready to send out additional food when needed regardless of plan.

Customers should never be disappointed!

Purchasing

Large operations have purchasing contracts with full service companies, many of them associated with national companies. Some are gigantic and carry an inventory of 30,000 or more items. Most provide direct access to their office with free computer terminals containing the inventory and specifications. The person in charge of purchasing can communicate directly with the purveyor. Lengthy numbers and codes identify the food items. Just one typographical error can bring mop handles instead of chicken legs into the house.

There are clear advantages to dealing with large suppliers, from competitive pricing to having a single truck deliver a vast range of items, from wax paper to sirloin steaks. In many parts of the country certain large purveyors dominate the market. Billing is obviously simplified when dealing with only one supplier.

The downside is that the operation must conform to the ordering and delivery schedule of the purveyor. Orders typically must be sent before noon the day prior to delivery so the trucks can be loaded efficiently. In many cases daily deliveries are not available. Many purveyors have minimum orders and some provide drop off service only rather than inside delivery. This obviously is an inconvenience for operations with large fluctuating banquet business. Although an inventory of 30,000 items or more should satisfy just about every possible operation it does not fulfill the needs of all *Banquet Chefs*. The range of specialty items is often limited. In New York City there are still many local specialty purveyors, especially in the meat market.

New:
Many specialty items can be ordered nationwide from specialty purveyors thanks to Internet shopping and nationwide shipping companies.

Most large companies do not allow units to be ordered directly and require that all orders are placed by the purchasing office. The office selects approved purveyors based on pricing policies, discounts, credit arrangements and other factors. Purchasing offices charge a small fee for their service.

Salespeople are often not allowed to call directly on chefs. In most operations chefs are not allowed to order new items which they may have seen at restaurant shows, or by visiting colleagues, unless approved by the purchasing office. The purchasing office will occasionally introduce chefs to new products or inform chefs that certain brands have been dropped and substituted with other brands. There may be many reasons for this kind of decision, such as price increases or discontinued items. Foodservice supply is a very competitive business; food manufacturers will sometimes offer incentive bonuses to distributors to carry their products and to drop others.

Price is a major factor deciding when selecting food brands. Quality differences can be subtle and when chefs wish to buy better but also slightly more expensive products they have to justify their decision to the purchasing office.

The amount of food to be purchased is obviously based on the *BEOs*. First, the quantities needed for all the parties are established, and then the time when the food should be delivered is specified. When to get the food delivered could become a balancing act between the delivery schedule of the purveyor, storage capability, and labor on hand. Groceries, frozen foods, and dry goods can be ordered once a week or once a month providing there is sufficient storage. Produce, dairy products, fish, and poultry should be ordered as close as possible to the time needed. Red meat can be ordered a few days before the party takes place.

In high volume weeks, refrigerator space is often a premium. Storing unprocessed foods may conflict with storing food being prepared, and ingenuity and goodwill are needed to accommodate everyone's needs. Catering houses will sometimes rent refrigerated trailers and park them next to the kitchen for additional refrigeration space. Maintaining safe sanitary standards can become a difficult challenge during high volume periods.

In order to purchase food efficiently, specifications must be established. Almost all foods can be purchased in many different sizes and quality levels. Food yields also vary according to season. The *North American Meat Processors' Association* publishes a book detailing every wholesale and portion cut of meat. Each piece is precisely explained, often accompanied by pictures, weight ranges according to USDA grade are listed, and the permitted trim and fat cover is listed. Each piece has a number, and ordering 20 pieces #180, choice beef, Cryovac, 10-12lb is a precise order leaving little room for error. Specification and grades also exist for all other foods.

For many years printed market sheets were used to decide how much to buy. These sheets listed just about all food products needed in the operation and their specifications, and had columns for quantities on hand and quantities needed. These sheets were custom-made for each operation. When typed on a word processor adjustments for season and new menu items could be made quickly. These purchasing sheets, printed on legal-sized paper grouped by products and placed on clipboards were easy to carry into the refrigerators or storerooms when taking inventory before ordering took place.

Computerizing the food storeroom entails entering every purchase and subtracting every issue. This requires a large staff because food is taken from the storeroom all day, and often in different units than were delivered. Only when a rigid requisition system is in place can the storeroom be computerized with any degree of accuracy. Whether this is cost effective or not is difficult to assess.

When the food storeroom is computerized the chef can easily determine the stock on hand and orders are placed directly from the computer. This should not prevent the chefs and storeroom personnel from physically visiting the coolers and storerooms. Food is not a blimp on the screen, it must be looked at, touched, smelled and evaluated.

Once the food storeroom is fully computerized the food cost of every item on the menu can be calculated exactly. The reality of the catering business is that time is always short, parties constantly change, food prices change, and standard recipes are seldom rigidly adhered to. For these reasons, much work that theoretically should have been done by the computer is still done by hand or by "instinct".

Food Storeroom Inventory Turnover

Food storeroom inventory turnover is a good indicator of purchasing skill. A well managed food storeroom in a catering house should have a dollar merchandise turnover of at least 5 times a month based on the concept that food is purchased only as needed for the business booked. Special sales should be approached with caution. Caterers are not in the commodity business, and should not speculate on rising prices of certain products. However, they can take advantage of large drop shipments providing there is adequate safe storage. A banquet house using a large amount of shrimp could buy a truckload of shrimp at a very good price, providing there is enough freezer storage, or the purveyor is willing to store the product. Cash flow is obviously an issue when a large amount of expensive merchandise is purchased. It may take a number of months before the product is sold and the facility paid.

GALA DINNER SERVED TO WINE LOVERS
IN A PRIVATE HOME
December 4th, 1998

Bruschetta with crispy Focaccia
Spinach and Mushroom Beggar Purses
Shrimp Cremolata
Smoked Salmon Crepes with Caviar
Roquefort Beignets

Taittinger Champagne Reserve 1973
****

Lobster with Baby Greens and Hazelnuts
Hazelnut Oil Vinaigrette

Batard Montrachet 1982 Duport & Gaillot
Matanza Creek Winery Chardonnay 1995
****

Roasted Filet Mignon
Onion Jam, Mushrooms Bordelaise
Roasted Potatoes with Rosemary
Haricots verts

Château Lafit-Rotschild 1970
Château Cos d'Estournel in Magnum 1982
****

Cheeses with Fruits

Pavillon Rouge de Château Margaux 1982
Château Beychevelle 1982
****

Poached Pears in Cabernet

Erbacher Markebrunn Riesling TBA
Staatsweingüter Eltville, Rheingau
****

Coffee and Tea
Dessert Bars and Nuts

Bual Madeira 1864
Blandy's Madeira Ltd.
Funchal (Bottle #62 of 180 produced)

Comparing Prices

Purchasing offices should compare prices as often as possible. Accounts should be established with a number of reputable purveyors, and their prices should be compared. Unless precise specifications are used, price comparisons are useless. Lower priced products from one purveyor might not have the same quality, size, or yield as the products from other purveyors even when the specifications are the same. Quality is different to quantify. Some purveyors deal only in the very best merchandise and others specialize in offering the best prices. Service should also to be taken into consideration; purveyors offering low prices but not reliable service can cause havoc in catering operations.

Smaller operations should also compare prices. Few places do it consistently. Catering employees are often too busy and seldom take the time to compare prices. Most purveyors send weekly price sheets to steady customers. Operators should compare prices regularly and welcome new purveyors soliciting business.

The prices charged to the caterer depend on the credit rating and delivery cost. If a facility is slow in paying, higher prices may be charged, and the product quality may not be as good as that sent to other facilities.

Receiving

Proper receiving is an important aspect of purchasing. In many catering houses the food is dropped off, hardly inspected, and signed for by anybody who happens to be around. Food is seldom weighed, and many places have no dedicated receiving area. Receiving takes knowledge, and it stands to reason that unless food is checked carefully for quality, count and weight, the purveyor or the drivers will take advantage of the situation. For many years a receiving scale in the food storeroom was a prerequisite.

New:
Most food is packaged, the weight of the contents clearly indicated on the carton and there is little opportunity or need to check weights.

To check the quality of packaged meat is just about impossible. Meat is often packaged in Cryovac (heavy plastic) or netted. The quality cannot be judged until the product is unwrapped and defrosted. When the package is opened and the quality found not to be as high as expected, it may be too late to exchange the merchandise. The purveyor may say that it was the best on the market, and there is no way to prove him wrong.

Fruits, vegetables and fresh fish still can be inspected quite easily.

Buffets

Chefs in banquet houses are expected to be artistic. Most catering operations serve buffets frequently and the beauty of the food display is an important selling tool. Not all chefs, as excellent as they might be in other areas, are artistic. If they are not able to hire culinarians who can make artistic centerpieces, it is better to stay away from edible buffet centerpieces, and buy inedible decorations instead.

The trend is away from culinary showpieces although some clients still love cold whole salmon covered with egg white scales and shrimp riding in pineapple boats. Food is meant to be eaten, it should scream: "Eat me, eat me!" and not be molded, mashed, manipulated and played with. The public demands fresh, clean, wholesome food. It is important to be concerned about the possibility of food contamination. Food manipulated in the kitchen and then displayed on buffets for a long time could become contaminated.

Alas, it can take much diplomacy to change the culinary direction of a kitchen. On cruise ships and in many country clubs elaborate food displays are still much in demand.

Chefs should have a little storeroom to keep inedible buffet props. They could be attractive fruit crates, unusual carving boards, old copper pots or other antique kitchen equipment, seashells, nets, boats. etc. They might not be used at every buffet, but they come in handy when theme parties are scheduled. Risers, mirrors, flowers, flags, candelabras and lights can enhance buffets.

Carved ice pieces are attractive, popular and relatively inexpensive. They can be made ahead of time, and are easy to make with the help of templates and power tools. The most important decorating element is the equipment. Quality buffet equipment is costly, but it is a good investment. Food displayed in lavish chafing dishes, in beautiful bowls, and on elegant platters looks so much better. Since this equipment will be used many times if properly maintained, the cost could be amortized over a long period.

New Trend:
Buffet food presented on small platters that can be easily exchanged and refilled. Inedible buffet props provide attention centerpieces.

Small platters can be exchanged and refurbished quickly. Larger mirrors and huge platters look very attractive for the first customers but soon become unappetizing when half depleted. Often platters are too large to be easily removed.

Serving stations located throughout the room are popular. It is like the food court concept, giving the customer many choices and dispersing the crowd. There are logistical challenges concerning replenishment, such as how to control popular expensive items. There may also be payroll ramifications when cooks are working in the banquet room.

Getting the Food Out

If there is only one piece of advice I can give chefs, it is count, count and count again. Nothing is more frustrating, disruptive, and annoying for guests, *Banquet Servers*, and cooks than running out of food during service. There could be many reasons for this, but often it is just bad planning, and underordering of food. Banquet food quantities should always be generous and the portion sizes should be planned accordingly. A tray may be dropped; some *Servers* could take more food than needed, and by the time they have returned it, other *Servers* and their guests would have been kept waiting if there was no extra food.

When food is plated at the last moment for parties larger than 100 guests, at least two service lines in the kitchen are needed. More service lines obviously speed up service. It is frustrating for *Servers* to come to the kitchen and stand in line. Obviously silver service is much quicker; it takes less time to fill 10 platters with vegetables than put vegetables on 100 plates. With silver service I have seen the main course for parties of 1,200 guests dispatched from the kitchen in 20 minutes, the meat sliced to order at three stations. One culinary person should always be available to handle special requests, exchanges, and diet meals.

To avoid shortages and pilferage during production the portions must be counted carefully and as often as possible. This is easiest when the portions are precisely aligned on trays, such as 35 Filet Mignons on each sheet pan. Then the platters or plates and their covers must be counted out just before the food is plated. If there is a big discrepancy between the plate count and the cover count, a recount is necessary. It is not easy to count hundreds of plates or platters, especially while they are being set up and put in heaters.

It is obviously necessary to have the size of all pots, pans, and other utensils clearly marked to avoid guessing. This is especially true for pots used for soups, sauces, and dressings.

Shortages could develop when meat is sliced to order. Even when the written instructions made by the *Executive Chef* specify the number of portions yielded by each piece of roast, inexperienced or careless carvers may not produce the required number of slices. At large parties, one slice less per piece would result in a large shortage. Carving is especially difficult when the pieces are oddly shaped, like London Broil. Beef tenderloins normally yield seven portions (fourteen slices) each. If the meat is issued by weight only and not by weight **and** count, a lesser number of pieces are cooked and that could result in shortages if the cooks follow orders, regardless of the size.

The *Banquet Sales Associate* is responsible for providing the estimated service time, but the actual service time could vary greatly. The *Charge Captain* has to communicate frequently with the *Banquet Chef* to make sure the food will be ready on time. The *Charge Captain* has to inquire of the *Banquet Chef* how much time is needed for final preparation and plating. Occasionally menu components must be prepared at the last minute in a distant kitchen and transportation time must be taken into account.

Discipline in the kitchen is important, especially when parties are very long and late. Cooks waiting in the kitchen often get bored and start the final preparation steps if not properly supervised. Cooks can get nervous and "jump the gun" when they don't hear from the *Charge Captain* for a while, and start dishing out without authorization, perhaps encouraged by the *Servers*.

Occasionally cooks begin dishing out to get a head start, or simply to go home as soon as possible.

Keeping Up-to-Date

It is the responsibility of the *Executive Chef* and *Banquet Chef* to keep up to date on food trends. This can sometimes be difficult. Most chefs work evenings and seldom have the opportunity to attend other parties or even to go to restaurants. *Chefs* can easily become stale. Fortunately most chefs today have been trained at culinary schools and are open and even eager for suggestions and new ideas. *Banquet Sales*

Associates deal with the public, and should have first hand knowledge of food preferences. Food and trade magazines are also good sources of information. Food magazines show new trends, and clients often request the dishes featured.

New:
Many trade shows incorporate culinary competitions. They provide an excellent way to share ideas and learn new procedures.

Seminars, continuing education courses and food shows are excellent ways to keep up to date. New products become available all the time, and the salespeople are the best source of information about them. Equipment trade shows are excellent resources for keeping informed about new machinery.

New:
Chefs are expected to be computer literate or at least feel comfortable with the web, and with catering software selected by the hotel. Learning software can, however, be time consuming.

Kosher Parties

The term Kosher means clean or wholesome and Jewish dietary laws go back to the Old Testament. Basically, they prohibit the consumption of certain animals, and certain combination of foods. Generally no hot food can be prepared from sundown Friday until sundown Saturday.

For occasional kosher meal requests frozen meals can be purchased from certified kosher caterers or manufacturers. They must be served as is without any manipulation. Even transferring the food from the package to platters can invalidate that the food is kosher. There is no such thing as kosher style food, but there are Jewish traditional dishes often served at parties referred to as "kosher style".

Kosher dietary laws are complicated, based on biblical references, traditions and interpretations. For a meal to be legally kosher, it must be prepared by a kosher caterer under rabbinical supervision. Only kosher caterers have the kitchen equipment and expertise required. The rules are complex and finer points open for interpretation. The basic rules address:

- What animals are permitted.

- How the permitted animals must be slaughtered.

- Which cuts can be used.

- How the cuts are to be handled prior to cooking.

- How they should be cooked.

- What they can be served with. The most basic prohibition is serving any kind of dairy product with meat products during the same meal.

- How to clean and separate utensils that have been used for cooking and serving dairy and meat dishes.

- The term *parve* means neutral and refers to all grains, fruits, and vegetables. They can be eaten with meat or with dairy products.

Kosher social functions are often very elaborate. The caterer is selected by the client and establishes a menu. The client normally selects the hotel or catering hall and reserves the room. The kosher caterer is required to bring all food and cooking utensils affected by the dietary laws. The hotel or banquet house often supplies food that is neutral or "*parve*", usually fruit, salad, and hot beverages.

The menu price is usually split 50% between the Jewish caterer and the banquet house, although different arrangements are possible. The rabbinical supervision, often performed by a *Mashgiah* is charged extra. The caterer is assigned a kitchen area and equipment. The caterer normally kosherizes equipment such as stoves, broilers, and kettles by heat. Turning up the heat to the fullest level for a short time is usually considered sufficient, but some caterers send in a crew to clean stoves, or to burn stoves with a blowtorch. This practice could damage the stoves and should be done with great caution.

The kosher caterer will ask for refrigerated storage space before the party. If the party takes place on a Saturday evening, the caterer will deliver the food on Friday before sundown, in order not to violate the Sabbath. The caterer will bring all pots, pans, and cooking utensils. All tables will be covered with foil or Kraft paper. It can be trying at times to share the kitchens and refrigerators, but it must be done. Kosher social business is potentially very good business in many parts of the country, and the *Executive Chef* should make every effort to co-operate with the caterer.

Tableware used for kosher functions requires special treatment. Glass is considered parve (neutral), and can be used for both meat and dairy dishes. China, however, cannot be used interchangeably. In many cases the caterers will supply the china, which must be handled separately. Metal could be koshered by heat and the *Mashgiah* might require that all metal serving platters and flatware be dipped in boiling water. Solid metal flatware can be koshered, items with an inserted plastic handle cannot.

The Steward's Job

The *Steward* is the housekeeper in the back of the house. Hotels, restaurants, and catering operations are like gigantic households, and many tasks that must be done in order to keep the operation running are seldom acknowledged and noticed unless they are neglected. There is a saying in the industry: Nothing moves in the back of the house without the help of the *Steward*.

I was fortunate that I worked at The Waldorf Astoria Hotel with Frank Bogatay. He was a professional *Steward*, and when he retired, he was sorely missed. He commanded a work force of more than 130 employees, many of them with only rudimentary knowledge of English. His equipment replacement budget was immense, larger than the total revenue of some smaller hotels. Yet he was a hands on manager, in shirtsleeves or in a white *Steward's* coat. He knew only one answer: "Yes, we'll do it right away". And it was always done. He and other *Stewards* like him are every bit as deserving of praise and recognition as any chef. Yet *Stewards* are not often appreciated. Their job is not glamorous, and in many places they are taken for granted.

Purchasing Responsibilities

The *Chief Steward* or *Head Steward* is responsible for purchasing all inedible supplies such as:

- Tabletop equipment, china, glassware, flatware, chafing dishes.

- Food related paper goods, kraft paper, doilies, foil wrap, paper napkins, coasters, bar napkins, stirrers, cake liners, cake boxes, wrapping material.

- Candles, sparklers, ribbons.

- Cleaning chemicals, cleaning supplies.

- Canned fuel, buffet supplies, chafing dishes.

Other responsibilities Include:

- Arranging repair of silverware.

- Co-ordinating equipment repairs.

In smaller operations the *Steward* is responsible for purchasing linen, uniforms, and all small kitchenware. In large operations the housekeeping department handles linen and uniforms.

Tabletop Equipment Issues

Classified as tabletop equipment are:

- China, such as plates, platters, sauce boats.

- Glassware.

- Flatware such as knives, forks, and spoons.

- Hollow ware such as coffee and tea pots, made either from china or metal.

- Decorative items such as vases, candelabras and table lamps.

- Miscellaneous items such as wine coolers, salt and pepper shakers, and sugar bowls.

These items are highly visible and therefore most be carefully selected to correspond with the theme and decor of the dining room. China, glassware, flatware, and tabletop decorations are design issues and are frequently selected by architects or tabletop consultants, in conjunction with the owners and management.

Beside aesthetics, practicality should be a major concern. Input from the *Catering Director*, the *Director of Service*, the *Chief Steward* and the *Executive Chef* should be solicited. Replacement pieces or pattern changes should be carefully evaluated to fit existing dish racks, heaters, covers, and mobile equipment. China patterns and colors are of concern to the *Executive* and *Banquet Chefs*. Plates could look stunning when empty but unattractive with food. The plate rim should not be too wide because it reduces the useable area. Logos on plate rims are cumbersome because the staff must be trained to have the logo face the same direction.

One basic decision is whether to purchase custom decorated plates or open stock. When open stock is selected it is important that the pattern will be kept in stock for the foreseeable future. Delivery time and costs are major factors. The advice of a knowledgeable and reputable dealer should be sought.

Decorations placed over glaze will eventually wash off; most gold or silver decorations are over glaze, and will not last long. Banquet china gets abused and thin china could chip. Heavy china could be hard to handle. All china should be tested for high heat tolerance because plates are often put under the broiler. Banquet china and covers should stack neatly and securely.

Hotels with many restaurants might have different china patterns and distinguished china for special parties. A large operation could have many different china patterns, glasses, and also types of flatware.

Tabletop items are capitalized and charged against the department when issued. Anything ordered in large quantities, such as china, silver and glassware or requiring long lead-time is stored in a secure long-term storeroom. This storeroom may be off-premise if storage space on-premise is scarce. The inventory should be computerized which is easily accomplished since all items are purchased and issued in units. The person in charge of the long-term storeroom often reports directly to the accounting office.

It is conceivable that the operation would occasionally borrow equipment for a large banquet and return it the next day. For instance, if a large quantity of champagne glasses is needed on a specific day, the glasses could be taken out of the general storeroom with an IOU, and returned after the party.

In addition to the long-term storeroom, which could be off-premise, is a circulating storeroom. The *Steward* is in charge of this storeroom. It must be on the premises and is used to store items already issued and charged, but not always needed. Large swings in demand are normal in the banquet business, and it is prudent to store and lock up as much equipment as possible when it is not needed.

It is not practical to keep the circulating storeroom locked during the day. Employees should be able to remove and return equipment when needed. The storeroom should be policed by the *Steward*, kept clean and tidy and locked at night.

Paper doilies, candles, and related items are also kept in the circulating storeroom. To prevent abuse, these supplies should always be kept locked in a closet.

Equipment Responsibilities

The *Steward* is responsible for keeping all dining room equipment clean and ready and in sufficient quantities when needed. Depending on the type of operation and the configuration of the building, the equipment could be sent to a central location, or to a location close to each banquet room, such as a banquet pantry or banquet kitchen. It would not be practical in hotels with many banquet rooms to have *Banquet Servers* come to the main kitchen or wherever the equipment is stored to get it. In large hotels, the *Steward* to the nearest banquet pantry always delivers the equipment, or the *Steward* takes the equipment inside the banquet room, but this is usually not necessary.

In larger operations, a *Banquet Charge Steward* is assigned to each party or to a number of parties taking place on the same floor. This *Steward* receives an equipment list prepared by the *Chief Steward* for each party, collects the equipment, and sends it to the specific area. It is prudent to bring extra equipment because *Servers* are required to check all equipment for defects and cleanliness and some could be rejected. Last minute changes in setup requiring additional equipment are frequent, and the *Steward* has to get the supplies as often as needed.

ITALIAN DINNER MENU

RECEPTION

Canapés
Perrier-Jouet Champagne

MENU

Penne al Salmone e Malfatti del Ghiottone
1989 Chablis Premier Cru Montmains
1986 Domaine Michel Chardonnay

****

Scallopine alla Grappa e Funghi
1983 Le Meilleur du Chai Cabernet Rombauer
1984 Bin 398 Saouth Australian Cabernet/Shiraz Penfolds

****

Insalata Tricolore e Fromaggi
1966 Louis M. Martin Special Selection Pinot Noir
1969 Vosne Romanée Sichel & Fils Freres
****

Napoleone con Frutta
1971 Oppenheimer Sackträger Riesling Auslese Gutrum

Caffé

The dinner was given on March 26, 1991 to showcase wines but not one was Italian.

The *Banquet Chef* and *Banquet Charge Steward* co-ordinate the requirements for service equipment such as plates, covers, platters, bowls and buffet equipment.

Breakage prevention is a major responsibility and challenge. Most breakage occurs when the soiled equipment is brought back to the dish room. Sometimes the break down or bussing stations next to banquet rooms are makeshift or too small. It is amazing how much and how quickly soiled equipment accumulates in the back of the house. The *Steward* could provide rolling carts, folding tables, and enough personnel to receive, scrape and stack the equipment as quickly as possible. Sufficient glass racks in the proper sizes should be used when possible to prevent breakage. The *Banquet Servers* should be supervised, and should co-operate with the *Banquet Charge Steward.* Many *Banquet Servers* do not take the time and effort to wait until they can safely dispose of the soiled items.

Personnel Responsibilities

Scheduling *Steward* personnel can be difficult. Sometimes language barriers exist. Transportation must be solved if there is no public transportation to the location of the event, or none running at the time when the employees are required to work. Some banquet houses have to organize car pools to get employees to work, and others have built dorms nearby in order to have *Steward's* employees available.

Supervision can also be difficult. Most *Steward's* employees are decent, hard working people, but language barriers and lack of education could impair their judgement. Some catering houses employ handicapped people in the *Steward's Department* with excellent results.

Occasionally drinking is a problem when dishwashers wait for the half empty liquor glasses to come back from the dining room, and eagerly concoct their own mixed drinks, with disastrous results. Although drinking on the job should be against house rules, it is often hard to prevent in the dishwashing room. Washing dishes is hard work, noisy, wet, foul smelling and with few rewards.

Food Related Responsibilities

In some operations, the *Steward's Department* is responsible for the supply and preparation of certain food items. The items vary between different operations and are normally items that have not been cooked. The *Steward's Department* on ships and in clubs was in charge of all food service many years ago. It was also good management to let lower paid *Steward's* employees perform simple tasks. Why waste the time of a cook to make coffee or to squeeze orange juice.

New:
Food related responsibilities are taken from the *Steward's Department* and given to the *Chef's Department* where they belong.

Items formerly supplied by the Steward could be:

- Coffee and other hot beverages.

- Rolls and butter, toast.

- Jams and jellies.

- Fruit juices.

- Green salads.

- Fruit cups, melons, fruit platters.

- Bar food.

- Sugar and condiments.

- Ice distribution.

Years ago the department handled the *Oystermen*. They were allowed to open clams and oysters and made shrimp cocktail. The shrimp had to be cooked in the soup kitchen.

The *Steward* should work closely with the *Banquet Chef* to save clean, wrapped food items such as jams and jellies, crackers, butter, sugar and related items. Much is often returned and dumped, although it could be intercepted and saved.

Transportation

In larger operations, the *Steward* is responsible for transporting cold food. The concept is based on the premise that the *Steward*'s labor is less expensive than the chef's labor. Transportation can be very time consuming when banquet rooms are far away from kitchens, and accessible only by elevators. In addition, the *Steward's Department* controls the use of the mobile equipment, because it is also used to transport the table appointments. It makes sense to have the *Steward* transport all food as well, except for hot food prepared at the last minute. This works well in many operations, and *Stewards* bring items to the banquet rooms as diverse as ice carvings, buffet decorations, and all buffet food and reception food.

Banquet Servers should help to set up buffets, but they are often busy setting up the function room and are not available to bring the buffet food. In some houses, specific *Servers* are assigned to set up and break down buffets. *Stewards* also deliver butter, rolls, salads, snacks, and coffee to the nearest banquet pantry.

Sanitation Responsibilities

The *Chief Steward* is responsible for the cleanliness of all table equipment, for dishwashing and polishing silver and copper utensils. The *Steward* shares with the *Executive Chef* the responsibility for the cleanliness of all food preparation areas. In many cases, the *Steward* supplies the labor and supervision to wash pots, clean all stoves and other machinery and clean refrigerators and other kitchen areas. The *Steward's* staff cleans all back of the house areas, such as corridors, freight elevators, the loading dock, and storerooms. In smaller houses, the *Steward* is also responsible for cleaning the public spaces, including toilets, the sidewalk, and the parking lot. Garbage disposal, recycling and pest control also fall into the *Steward's* jurisdiction.

New:
***Stewards* are now responsible for re-cycling if that is a policy of the facility.**

211

In smaller houses, the *Steward's* office is located adjacent to or inside the food storeroom. The *Steward* works as receiving agent and as food storeroom manager. This make sense in smaller facilities, because many other items besides food must be received and stored, and some of them are ultimately used by the *Steward*.

Summary

The *Executive Chef* and the *Chief Steward* must work as a team to manage the back of the house efficiently. Both are faced with the challenge of staffing their departments due to wide swings in business. Both must be good administrators, and keep track of many banquets taking place in different locations.

The *Executive Chef* is responsible for food production, for the flavor, quality, look, and wholesomeness of the banquet food. He/she is also responsible for maintaining an acceptable food cost ratio. The *Executive Chef* should keep up to date with food trends and with equipment developments.

The *Chief Steward* is responsible for the availability of all table top items, for back of the house cleanliness, and for food transportation. In some operations, the *Steward* is in charge of supplying food items that do not require preparation. In smaller houses, the *Steward* is also in charge of the food storeroom.

Discussion Questions

- List the major responsibilities of the *Executive Chef*.

- Explain the specific staffing challenges in the kitchen.

- What does marking menus mean?

- List some inedible decorations.

- What is meant by the term Kosher?

- List three segments of Jewish dietary laws.

- What are the *Steward's* purchasing responsibilities?

- What are the *Steward's* equipment responsibilities?

- Elaborate on the sanitation responsibilities of the *Steward*.

Chapter Ten
BASIC RULES OF MENU CONSTRUCTION

DINNER MENU

RECEPTION

Hot and cold Hors d'Oeuvres
1983 Taittinger Brut

****

DINNER

Roasted Quail and Chicoree Salad
Verjus Vinaigrette

1987 Meursault Le Tillets, H. Bouzereau

****

Salmon Fillet with Tomato Confit
Fennel Coulis and Basil Chiffonade

1985 Santenay Les Cru Cravieres Prosper Mounfoux

****

Veal Medallions Flemish Style
Braised Endives and Market Vegetables

1991 Lynch Bages

****

Chocolate Passion
with
Raspberry and Vanilla
1976 Graacher Himmelreich Spätlese Von Kesselstatt
****
Coffee, Teas, Mignardises

The menu was planned as a wine tasting dinner and it is surprising that tomatoes and endives were served. Both are considered enemies of fine wine.

214

Chapter Ten
BASIC RULES OF MENU CONSTRUCTION

Learning Objectives

- The accepted sequence of courses on menus.

- The importance of varying raw material.

- The importance of varying texture and colors.

- The significance of flavor harmony.

- The influence of seasons.

- The differences between meals.

- The techniques of making menus.

- How to match wine with food.

- Common menu mistakes.

- The importance of eye appeal of printed menus.

Introduction

We have stressed that making the right menu for the occasion is one important ingredient for the success of the party. Menu making is an art, a talent, but also something that can be learned. The first step in successful menu making is a profound knowledge of food and of flavor harmony. The second ingredient is the ability to visualize food, how it will store, transport and, finally how it will look on the plate. Important also is a realistic assessment of the available technical and personal resources.

In this chapter we discuss the culinary aspect of menu making, the historical roots of our present menu construction, how to create harmony of colors and flavors, how to reflect seasons and holidays, and new trends in menu making.

Sequence of Dishes

The sequence in which the dishes appear on a menu has undergone many changes, because menus are a reflection of the life styles and dining conventions of the time. Up to the middle of the nineteenth century, banquet menus were very long; some contained as many as six soups, ten fish courses, and twelve roasts. Nobody could eat so much food, but since the guests were seated at long tables and each course was placed at the same time, they were served only what was within reach. The concept of shortening menus slowly gained acceptance, and then the idea took hold that all guests should be able to eat each course at the same time. But even these menus were long by our standard.

As the pace of life quickened, the menus were shortened even more. Already however, the basic sequence of dishes that is still accepted today was visible. There has been some experimentation during the last ten years in altering the menu structure but it has not taken hold.

Traditionally Constructed Menu

Cold Appetizer
Smoked Trout Fillet with Julienne of Celeriac

****

Hot Soup
Roasted Tomato Consommé

****

Main Course

Grilled Beef Medallions
Wild Mushrooms with Thyme

Vegetables
Mashed Yukon Gold Potatoes with fried Chinese Chives
Baby Bok Choy

****

Dessert
Lemon and Ginger Crème Brulée
Seasonal Blackberries

****

Coffee
****

The accepted rule is to serve the cold appetizer before the soup and the hot appetizer after the soup.

Sample of a more elaborate menu including a hot appetizer course.

Soup
Lobster Consommé with Lemongrass
Sesame Crisps

****

Hot Appetizer
Grilled Asparagus on Parmesan Polenta
Purée of Sweet Peas and Basil

****

Main Course
Roast Squab with Chanterelles
Sugar Snap Peas and Pancetta Julienne

****

Salad and Cheese
Local Chèvre Cheese with Roasted Pecans
Radichio, Watercress and Bib Lettuce
Balsamic Vinegar Dressing
Crisp French Baguettes

******

Dessert
Pear and Orange Sorbet with hot Apricot Flan
Almond Macaroons

****

Coffee

In the menu above, salad with cheese is served as a separate course. When salad is served without cheese, it is often considered an accompaniment to the main course and is listed as such. Sometimes, this could present a logistical problem, because the salad plates may not fit on the table together with the main course. Many banquet houses serve the salad before the main course and clear the plates, although the salad is listed on the menu after the main course and the vegetables.

On the above menu the first word of the menu item and all nouns are capitalized.

Rules for Making Appetizing and Interesting Menus

Attention to Raw Materials

The basic raw materials should not be repeated unless the dinner is a theme dinner, such as a game dinner in autumn. A dinner featuring roast beef tenderloin, as a main course should not start with a beef consommé; a creamy dessert should not follow a dish containing cream. A dinner starting with clam chowder should not continue with a fish dish garnished with mussels. Unfortunately this basic rule is often broken.

Flavor Harmony

Taste is very subjective, and bold culinarians are always experimenting with new flavors and flavor combinations. Some are very good, others are questionable. A banquet has to satisfy many people, and most people are very conservative in their food taste. It takes a long time for a new food idea to move from the pages of a gourmet magazine to the consciousness of the consumer. A banquet attended by many people is not the place to experiment with unusual food combinations. The banquet menu should be based on a common denominator.

The Intermezzo

During very long dinners a refreshing frozen drink is served between the hot appetizer and main course to clean the palate. The French call it *Trou du Milieu*, which loosely translated means *Hole in the Middle*. It is always a highly alcoholic, slightly acidic but never sweet slush drink. Unfortunately it often appears at the table as a scoop of fruit sherbet or Italian ice ruining the flavor harmony of the food and wine. Experimentation resulted in *Tomato and Basil Sorbet, Champagne and Thyme* and other bizarre combinations. They all miss the mark. The basic flavor must be a dry brandy such as Calvados, Framboise, Poire, Rum and others.

Contrast in Textures and Shapes

Textures and shapes should contrast from dish to dish, and also on the plate. Soft dishes should be followed by crisp food; food in a round shape followed by food in long strips. As an example, a warm salad could be sprinkled with croutons or with fried onion rings. A puréed vegetable could be sprinkled with tiny diced fried potatoes, or the ice cream could be served with crisp cookies.

A texture contrast can be subtle, yet it will add to the harmony of the menu. A good example is the combination of a dish made with crisp puff pastry and a soft filling, such as a patty shell filled with mushrooms, or the Napoleon Pastry, made with crisp puff pastry sheets filled at the moment of service with pastry cream. A modern adaptation of this idea is the Mille Feuille of Salmon, which is a fish Napoleon, served hot.

In traditional French cooking, poached fish dishes with creamy sauces are always served with a puff pastry half moon called Fleuron, because it added just a little bite of crispness. Another classical dish reflecting the same concept is *Sole Normande*, which is poached sole in a mussel cream sauce, garnished with tiny fried fish called *Goujon*. In modern cooking, the seared fish fillet with a crisp skin served with a sauce carries out the same idea.

Texture can also convey the season. Crisp vegetables communicate the feeling of spring, softer dishes indicate fall and winter. Mashed potatoes with different flavors and textures, and vegetable purees are really popular nowadays.

Pitfalls to Avoid

Some foods are more difficult to serve at banquets than others. *Seared* or *Rare Tuna*, so popular in trendy restaurants will invariably be cold when it reaches the table and not all customers like raw fish.

Lamb will not cool faster than other meats cooked medium rare but cold lamb fat will congeal quickly and is not appetizing.

Small pieces of meat have a very limited holding time. Serving two small *Filet Mignons*, poetically called *Tournedos,* will result in well done meat at a large party.

Cream soups are potentially more dangerous to serve than clear soups.

Meat with bones requires side dishes to get rid of the bones, and also requires more time to eat than boneless cuts. I remember a formal black tie dinner and the *Banquet Sales Associate* sold whole racks of New Zealand lamb, one to each customer. This dish made many people unhappy.

Whole asparagus belongs in the restaurant and not on banquet menus. They are hard to dish out and impossible to eat gracefully.

More than one sauce on the plate confuses the customer.

Roasted whole cornish hens still appear on menus. The bird is hard to tackle even when semi-boneless and too big for any plate.

Crustaceans in the shell are difficult to eat gracefully.

Color Harmony

Colors should vary from dish to dish and also on the plate. Visual appeal on the plate is very important, and the components of dishes should be chosen so their colors do not clash. A red beet salad with sliced tomatoes looks terrible on a plate. A menu starting with a *Tomato Consommé* should not be followed by a pink fish dish garnished with red pimento. Pot roast with chestnuts and brown rice will look dull on the plate.

Colors are also associated with seasons. Soft green, purple, and yellow are spring colors; bright red and strong green are summer colors; browns and dark greens represent fall and winter. Some chefs use flowers as garnishes, but flowers could overwhelm the colors of the food, or even clash with the food.

New:
Most banquet houses serve colorful plated desserts and credit must be given to the pastry chefs who started this trend.

Seasons

The season when the menu will be served should be taken into consideration. The season will affect not only the availability and price of food, but also the guests' reactions. Chestnuts and oranges convey the Christmas spirit. Green asparagus, herbs, pastel colors and tiny vegetables indicate spring. Edible flowers, berries, fruits, chilled soups, ice and light foods convey a summer feeling. Game, grapes, nuts, squash, and root vegetables reflect autumn.

Almost all food is available year round, because it can be imported when it is not in season. However, the quality, size, and price vary greatly. It is frustrating and expensive when banquet menus are made without regarding the availability of food. When the food must be ordered specially from far away, or is only available frozen at the particular time of year, then the menu was not well constructed. Customers today expect fresh ingredients, and this is only possible if season is taken into consideration when the menu is written.

The Difference Between Meals

There should be a difference between lunch and dinner menus. The perceived difference is often based on tradition, and might contradict healthy eating habits and common sense. In Germanic countries lunch was the main meal of the day and supper was always light. As a general rule, luncheon is perceived as being less expensive and lighter than dinner. Luncheons should also take less time than dinners, because most guests have to return to work or have appointments in the afternoon.

Business luncheons should not have more than three courses unless it is a festive event. The food should be light, and serving a cold main course salad is normally quite acceptable. Many luncheons have a specific purpose, such as a presentation, a speech, a fashion show, or an awards ceremony. Nobody wants to conduct a meeting with drowsy, overfed participants.

Luncheon buffets can be time consuming. Time can be saved if the first course is preset on the table. Even more time can be saved when the dessert and coffee cups are also preset on the table although this type of service is somewhat substandard.

IRISH INSPIRED DINNER MENU

Fluffy Pasty with
Jugged Venison in Claret Wine
****

Shannon River Salmon
Broiled with Prawn Butter
Chardonnay
****

Irish Mist Sorbet
****

Boneless Squab Stuffed with Paté
and Penny Loaves
Sauce flavored with Port
Tiny Sprouts
Merlot
****

Bibb Lettuce Salad
Normandy Brie Cheese
Jacob's Crackers
****

Hot Charlotte of Apples and Raisins
Whipped Ennis Cream
Laurent Perrier Champagne
****

Dried Fruits
****

Demi Tasse

Nutrition

Nutrition should play a role in constructing menus. The role of the hospitality industry is to satisfy the wishes of the customers. Today many people are conscious of nutritional values. This should be considered when the menu is made. If the dishes ordered by the client give few choices to nutritionally concerned guests attending the meal, this should be mentioned to the client. Healthy eating should be an important consideration and meals should be nutritionally balanced if possible. Despite all the publicity about nutrition, rich desserts are still much in demand.

The following pointers should be kept in mind when making a menu:

- Avoid animal fats.

- Avoid cream sauces.

- All menus should contain vegetables, fruits, and proteins.

- Grains and pulses are considered healthy.

- Olive oil is considered healthy.

- Butter cream cakes are out, but rich desserts are still loved.

- Margarine should be available as a butter substitute.

- Sauces can be thickened with vegetables to avoid starch.

- The term *Coulis* is French and means concentrated natural purée served as a light sauce.

- Grilled food, including grilled vegetables is considered healthy.

- Japanese food such as thin broth made with bonito flakes is widely accepted.

- In large metropolitan areas Japanese sushi and sashimi are accepted as reception food if there are additional choices. Japanese food requires specific skills and equipment it would be advisable to order these items from a Japanese restaurant.

The following menu is nutritionally unacceptable

> Patty Shell with Creamed Mushrooms
> *******
>
> Grilled Filet Mignon
> Bearnaise Sauce
> Three Vegetable Purees
> *******
>
> Salad with Brie Cheese
> ******
>
> Charlotte Russe with Whipped Cream

This menu was printed in the second edition of this book but there are still menus like that served today. It is loaded with high-cholesterol cream and egg yolks. The meat is served with a thick, rich sauce and with vegetable purees containing cream and butter. A fatty cheese accompanies the salad, and the dessert is made with cream and decorated with whipped cream.

Menu-Making Techniques

To simplify menu making divide a sheet of paper in as many sections as there will be courses. Then, using a pencil, establish the main course because it is the center around which all other courses must fit. It is a waste of time to start with a discussion of the appetizer or soup.

The main course anchors the meal, unless the client wants a specific appetizer or dessert. When the main course is established, and it might change many times which is the reason for using a pencil, the appetizer and other courses can be discussed. After the courses are chosen, the garnishes and accompaniments can be filled in. Menu making is like solving a puzzle. Each component should fit perfectly in order to create a complete picture.

New:

Custom menus can be made on the computer. Dishes, garnishes, and other menu components, along with their season, availability, and even suggested prices can be stored and recalled when needed.

Matching Wines with Food

Banquet wine lists are by necessity not normally the most interesting because the listed wines must be available when needed. This precludes listing boutique wines and in most cases even vintages. Most establishments discourage customers ordering special wines because there are the issues of how much to order, how to dispose of leftover wines and inventory control. Handling wines for special dinners is discussed in **Chapter 14.**

It would be impossible to even attempt to list the best matches of wine and food; there are simply too many factors to take into account. In addition, food writers repeatedly challenge the established, true and tried rules of matching wine with food. Today we see combinations reminiscent to the drinking habits of the 19th century. To what extent these matches will become popular remains to be seen.

The once ironclad rule that white wine should be served with fish and white meat, and that red wine be should be served with red meat and fatty fish, is being successfully challenged today.

Throughout this book are many menu samples with matching wines. Selecting wines is based on many factors, such as price and availability. Some menu samples in this book feature wine the author would not have selected. When choosing wines to accompany a meal, much depends on the preparation of the dish. The flavor of the sauces or spices often masks the original flavor of the main ingredient, and the wines should be selected accordingly. Generally speaking, guests still expect a dry, slightly fruity white wine with fish dishes, and a full bodied red wine with red meat. Fatty, dark meat fishes such as salmon, bluefish, mackerel, and tuna could be accompanied by light red wines. Lamb can be served with red or full bodied white wines, but red wines are generally preferred.

Veal dishes are pleasant with full bodied white wines, or slightly sweet Riesling wines. Oysters and other cold shellfish are best with dry white wines such as Chablis, or very dry Champagne. Foie gras matches well with sweet wines.

The wine market has become global and many rules concerning permitted grape varieties and expected flavors only hold true for some traditional wine regions in Europe. Other regions experiment freely and produce varieties in wide flavor ranges.

Desserts are difficult to match with wines. Traditionally, sparkling wines are served, which make a lot of sense because the wine is refreshing, but some champagne houses insist that serving it with dessert loses the delicate flavor of the wine. The same is true for sweet wines. They are often paired with dessert, but in many cases they are ruined by overpowering desserts.

Traditionally some foods are considered enemies of wine. Artichokes, Belgian endive, and asparagus fight wine. Acidic food, such as pineapples, tomatoes, and salad dressings also interfere with the subtle flavors of wine.

Refreshment Breaks

Eating habits are changing, and many people eat smaller meals more often than large meals at traditional hours. The rigid menu sequence is in many cases no longer appropriate. Guests enjoy snacks, or a succession of many smaller portions. The concept of grazing has also taken hold. It was a buzzword in the late eighties, and described the arranging of tiny portions of many different dishes on a large plate, and in some cases combining various courses.

Creating meals in conference centers for conventions lasting a number of days is a big challenge. Meetings are interrupted for refreshment breaks, and the food expectations have risen. Cookies in the morning and fruits and sandwiches in the afternoon are no longer sufficient. Many groups expect the refreshment food to vary by contents and look every day. The challenge is to serve interesting food without making the customers drowsy and spoiling their appetite when mealtime arrives.

Buffets

People love buffets. Buffets have one overriding goal, which is providing guests with choices. All other goals, such as ease of service, opportunity for social interaction and artistic food presentation are secondary to this goal. Buffets serve an important aspect of service. Many people are allergic to specific foods. A buffet gives the opportunity to these guests to avoid these foods.

People like the idea of being able to select. It is important that the food portions are small enough to allow for choosing as many items as possible, and as often as possible. When creating custom buffet menus *Banquet Sales Associates* should keep in mind:

- Portions must be small.

- Food must be easy to eat.

- There should be no bones or shells to dispose of.

- Food must be recognizable.

- Food should not be too hot or spicy. People hate surprises.

- Food should not be messy, dripping with fat or sauces.

- Too many choices confuse the guests. Some will still their appetite with items clearly accessible and then discover that there are choices they would have liked much better.

Operating good buffets is a logistical challenge to avoid lines and promote circulation. As a basic rule buffet tables should be accessible from all sides unless a hollow arrangement is used and *Servers* work from inside the buffet. It is best to have as many buffet tables as possible to stimulate circulation, to use round or oval tables when possible, and to have plates and flatware in as many locations as is practical. There should never be a place where long lines can form. For groups larger than 100 guests, duplicate buffet tables for every course should be provided, clearly marked with large signs, such as appetizers or main courses. This way, guests do not go to crowded tables, just to find out that they are at the wrong table. Properly set up buffets can be fun for both the guests and the operators.

Note:
Plates, flatware, and napkins should be small and abundantly available.

Popular ideas

- Pasta stations.

- Chefs slicing meats.

- Whole baked fish portioned at the buffet. The tail has the least amount of bones.

- Oyster and shrimp bars.

- Smoked meat and fish stations.

New:
Electric induction stoves eliminate potentially dangerous canned gas heaters.

Bars should also be scattered throughout the banquet room to avoid queuing. The selection should be limited if possible, but cocktails should always be made to order and not by the pitcher. One big challenge is to always keep enough glasses at hand.

Menu Eye Appeal

On more formal occasions the customers will get a printed menu. These menus could be incorporated into the dinner program or printed separately. At very formal and memorable events the menus are pieces of art, designed specifically for the occasion, and are meant to be taken home as a memento of the occasion. When this is the case, envelopes should be provided and available when the guests leave. Guests often take even less elaborate menus home, and it is important that they are attractive and well written. Even when the menu is not printed it should appear on the *BEOs* as a well written, balanced document.

When the host handles menu printing the *Banquet Sales Associate* should get involved and proof read the menu. Unfortunately most banquet menus I collected for this edition had spelling errors.

All menus should list the day and date and the name where the party took place.

New:
On many formal menus the names of the *Executive Chef*, *Banquet Chef*, *Pastry Chef* and *Director of Service* are listed.

The sizes of printed menus can vary widely. Menus of gourmet dinners are often very large, because there is much information to accommodate. Sometimes a guest list is included. At commercial dinners, the menus should not be larger than the pocket in a man's jacket. There is no way of making a menu in a size that would fit in most women's evening purses.

Regardless of size, the typeface should be easy to read. Menus are meant to communicate, and elaborate script is often difficult to read with the low light level in ballrooms. The menu can have various pages if necessary. Reception food and wines could be listed on one page and the opposite side could contain the food and wine of the main meal. Wines should be listed with the dishes with which will be served. The dishes should be clearly separated by asterisks, lines, or a suitable repeated motif.

Components of each dish, when served together should be listed together. It is nonsense to list the meat course and separate the vegetables and starches just to make the menu look bigger. If possible, the dishes should be shown proportional to their importance on the menu. If the main course is described in few words, the accompanying garnishes should not take up much more space. The main course could be in a different font size than the garnishes. The focus should always be on the main component of each course.

The sample menus listed throughout this book have been formatted to look aesthetically pleasing.

Establishing Meanings for Menu Terms

Menu terms are a technical language, like languages used in other trades. **Chapters 11 and 12** explain how to write menus in clear English and in other languages. Many menu terms are of French origin and their original meaning has often been lost. Living languages change constantly and terms are updated or often misused. Since banquet menus could be compared to written work orders. It is essential that the instructions given by the *Banquet Sales Associates* to the kitchen are clearly understood by all employees.

Banquet Sales Associates should not endeavor to create new menu terms, or give them new meanings. *BEOs* are sent to many departments and misunderstood terms can result in costly mistakes.

To prevent this, menu meetings should be attended by all *Banquet Sales Associates*, the *Executive Chef*, the *Banquet Chef,* and the purchasing staff. At these meetings, the exact meaning of each term should be discussed and established. Minutes should be kept, and copies sent to all sales personnel for future reference. The reality is that many banquet menus are poorly written with the belief that foreign phrases embellish the menu and impress the customers.

Summary

There are basic, established rules for constructing menus. Banquet menus must meet the customers' expectations. They should be fun, and should reflect the seasons and the occasion. Well-written menus harmonize flavors, colors, and textures. Menus differ by meal period. To accomplish these goals, a simple menu making technique can be employed.

Matching wines with food is a challenge, but simple rules exist that will satisfy the guests' expectations most of the time.

Menus are meant to communicate, but should also be visually pleasing. The menu language is a technical language, and should not be used without clear understanding. All employees must understand clearly all menu terms.

Discussion Questions

- List the accepted sequence of courses on menus.

- Why is it important to vary the ingredients?

- Why should colors and flavors harmonize?

- Explain why textures in a dish should vary.

- What is the significance of seasons? How can each of the four seasons be acknowledged or highlighted by certain foods?

- Explain the differences between lunch and dinner meals.

- Suggest wines for veal dishes, for lean fish, and for darker fattier fish.

- Why is eye appeal important on printed menus?

Chapter Eleven
WRITING MENUS IN ENGLISH

DINNER MENU

Napoleon of Baby Portabello Mushrooms and Artichokes
Sherry Vinaigrette

Domaine Thomas, Saint Veran 1998, Burgundy

****

Five Onion Cappuccino
Sprinkled with Crispy Shallots and Chives

****

Poached Dover Sole in White Wine Sauce
Crayfish Tails and Baby Leeks

Conundrum Caymus 1998, California

****

Grilled Filet of Black Angus Beef
Topped with seared Foie Gras
Roasted Kohlrabi and Parsnips

Lucente, Mondavi-Frescobaldi 1997, Tuscany, Italy

****

Assorted local and imported Cheeses
Melon, Belgium Endive and Hazelnut Relish

****

Warm Chocolate Tart
Vanilla Ice Cream and macerated Orange Segments

Graham's Ten Year Tawny Port

Jamaican Blue Mountain Coffee

Contemporary banquet menu written in simple but elegant English.

Chapter Eleven
WRITING MENUS IN ENGLISH

Objectives

- To understand how to write menus in proper English.

- To appreciate the significance of selecting words with care.

- To comprehend the importance of using correct grammar.

- To see the necessity of correctly spelling menu terms.

- To learn about geographical terms on menus.

- To understand the importance of using cooking terms correctly.

- To be aware of the truth on menu responsibilities.

Introduction

Menus are communication tools and serve two purposes. Internally, menus communicate the food and beverage arrangements to the kitchen, service staff, and other departments. To the customers menus communicate the selected food and beverage arrangements. A well-written menu not only conveys basic information, but also sends a quality message, raises the expectations of the guests, and adds immeasurably to the success of a party. The catering business is to a large extent an image business, and a beautiful, well-written menu sends an important message: We care, we know what we are doing, and we want you to get the very best.

A shoddily written menu makes a poor impression, regardless of how well the food is prepared and presented. Printed menus are often taken home as souvenirs, and looked at long after the party.

The Beauty of English

English is an incredibly rich language and lends itself very well to menu writing. Our culinary heritage is French, and some cooking terms are difficult to translate precisely into English, but when it comes to overall beauty and clarity, English rivals French. The following menu was written many years ago, as the wines indicate, but it is so beautifully written, that it can still serve as example of fine menu writing.

The Fare

**Persian Caviar
and the Fruits of the Seas and Lakes**
****

A Bisque of Oysters of the Atlantic
Fino Sherry
****

**Canadian Pacific Salmon
with a Nantua Sauce**
*Puligny Montrachet 1953
Estate bottled by Sauzet*
****

**Saddle of Spring Lamb
from the Salt Meadows of New Hampshire
Gratin of New England Marrow Squash
and Maryland Tomatoes
Small Roasted Potatoes**
*Musigny 1952
Estate bottled by Adrien*
****

Apple Brandy Sherbet
****

**Goose Liver with Truffles
as prepared in Strassburg
Filet of Long Island Duckling**
Château Petrus 1945
****

Brie Cheese of France
Château la Gaffeliere Naudes 1937
****

**A Charlotte of Mohawk Valley Apples
with its Garniture**
Château d'Yquem 1942
****

Haitian Coffee
*Château de Marsan Private Reserve
Armagnac Vielle Cure*

232

Menus are meant to communicate. What packaging does for the retail business, menus achieve for the banquet business. The way menus are written on the proposals, and how they read in the printed form, set the tone for the party. A menu written with flair and beauty establishes the quality expectations of the event.

The basic reason for writing a menu is to tell the guests what they will get to eat and drink. The style and tone of the menu language should be appropriate for the type of party and the client's expectations. If the meal is to be simple, the language should not be too elegant. If the event is luxurious, the language can be more sophisticated. Menu language should be poetic and even a little mysterious, but it should still communicate. Artful menu language adds excitement to the occasion, but the language should never be stilted. It should be precise enough to be understood by the guests, and if the same language is used for internal communication, by the kitchen and service staff.

Foreign words should be omitted on menus written in English if they are used to confuse the guests. Often foreign words are used thoughtlessly for the purpose of adding some meaningless language and making the menu sound fancy. This is confusing to the reader. Foreign words used out of context to make the menu more "elegant" have the opposite effect. There are enough words in English to describe any dish. Abbreviations should never be used. Too frequent use of the conjunction *and* can leave the reader breathless.

Selecting Words with Care

When writing menus, words should be selected carefully to express the intended meaning. Clichés should be avoided. For example, using the word "fresh" is tricky. All ingredients are supposed to be fresh, so why point out a specific ingredient as being fresh? How fresh is fresh? Are the string beans, picked in a far away field last week, still fresh? I recommend using the word "fresh" only when it indicates an item that is usually frozen but is seasonally available fresh, such as a specific fruit or vegetable. It could also be used to describe fish or seafood flown in from a distant place. Using the term "freshly squeezed" indiscriminately can be silly; freshly squeezed orange juice is available in some operations, but *freshly squeezed orange, tomato and apple juice* is not believable. The term *chilled* is also superfluous on many menus. It is expected that juices are chilled.

Menu language should be appetizing and can be poetic. It is easy to fall into traps. "Skewered" Tenderloin Tips does not sound appetizing because the term *skewered* has a connotation of pain. The same is true for the words "beaten", "scalded", and "burned".

Attention should be paid to descriptive words. Ambiguous and unintentionally comic phrases should be avoided, such as "Half broiled Chicken" (is it not cooked?), and "Beer battered Shrimp", which make me think of unhappy shrimp being bashed.

Some words often found on menus are legitimate, but old fashioned. Using the word "laced" in "Lobster Stew laced with Sherry" is correct, but no longer in today's usage. Making a noun out of a verb should be avoided. Some menu writers love terms like *Parsleyed Potatoes, Sherried Lobster Soup* or *Herbed scrambled Eggs*. Just as bad is *Herb scrambled Eggs* unless the name of the breakfast cook is Herb.

There is a distinct difference between sauce and gravy. A sauce can be made independently from the dish with which it is served, such as *Tomato Sauce* with pasta, or *Chocolate Sauce* served with ice cream. Gravy is always part of a specific cooking process. When meat is roasted or braised, the pan drippings or the braising liquid is thickened and becomes the gravy.

Local terms could be used effectively to add a little excitement to the menu, even if guests from out of town do not immediately understand these terms. As an example, in some parts of the country the term yams is used, in other parts the term sweet potatoes. Strictly speaking, they are slightly different, but this is seldom recognized in food service. There are many regional differences in food names, and they can also be used to brighten up a menu.

List of clichés and words to avoid:

au beurre	style	garni(e)
tossed	succulent	chopped sirloin
supreme	center cut	market fresh
home made	delicious	spring chicken

Silly wording culled from recent menus:

- Bread Display with Butter.
- Fresh roast Turkey Breast.
- Seasonal Greens drizzled with extra virgin Olive Oil.
- Sautéed in Wine (Not precise. The term sauté means tossed and cooked in butter or any other fat).
- Penne alla Vodka.
- Breast of Capon.
- Fresh Herbs (not dried?).
- Grilled French Breast of Chicken (imported from France?).
- Tarragon Chantilly (only a classical trained chef would know that Crème Chantilly means whipped cream).
- Aged Prosciutto is redundant. Italian law describes how long prosciutto must be aged.

- Jumbo Shrimp (there seems to be no size smaller than jumbo any more).
- Champagne Vinaigrette with a Gastrique of Balsamic?
- Almondine - the Anglicized French term *amandine*.
- Au jus.

Grammar and Spelling

Menus are always directed at the individual diner. This simple rule makes it easy to decide when to use plural or singular on the menu. It is proper to write *sliced beefsteak tomato*, because the diner gets only one tomato. The tomato salad could be sprinkled with *chives* (plural). Baked potato is listed normally singular because one potato is served to each person, but it would be proper to write *home fried potatoes*, because it takes several potatoes to make one serving. Ice cream is served with *strawberries*, because more than one berry is served per person. The same is true for *mushrooms* unless a single mushroom cap is served on top of a steak. For a number of words, such as "shrimp", "stew", "fried fish," and "salad," no differentiation is made between singular and plural.

Often confused are *filet* and *fillet.* When the term is used with meat it is spelled *filet*, but when used with fish it is spelled *fillet.*

The word *frenched* is a butcher term to describe when the meat is removed from rib bones such as from rack of lamb or veal.

Some poetic license is permissible in menu writing. In order to add interest and direct the attention of the reader to the main ingredient of a dish, nouns are usually capitalized. Descriptive words are in lower case. It is important to be consistent, and this can be difficult. It is also important to visualize how the words will look on the menu. *Pot Roast braised with tiny Vegetables* is acceptable, because the word tiny is an adjective. However, *Baskets of Tiny Vegetables* can also be correct, because tiny is in this case an accurate description of the type and quality of vegetables used.

Periods are normally not used on menus. The first word on a new line should be capitalized but there are also exceptions.

Chowder of Geoduck Clams
sprinkled with fresh Thyme

The word "sprinkled" is correctly in lowercase, because it is part of a sentence, although on a new line. The sentence should feature the main message. In the example above, the important message is that the course is chowder, so this is mentioned first. Then the ingredients are mentioned to make the menu more interesting.

The next menu uses uppercase letters only at the beginning of each sentence and for proprietary names. The spell checker did not like it.

The menu above is neither right nor wrong but rather the expression of a personal style. Important is consistency.

It may sound better when the adjective is used at the beginning of the sentence:

Live Crayfish from Louisiana
steamed over Seaweed

If the sentence were turned around, it would not read as well.

Geographical Terms

Geographical names, such as North Atlantic Halibut, Chesapeake Bay Shad and Roe, or Olympic Oysters add much interest to a menu. The use of geographical names should be as accurate as possible. Because it is difficult to establish exactly where the halibut was caught, it is permissible to say "North Atlantic Halibut" if the fish was caught off the East Coast. Olympic Oysters are a very specific kind of oysters, and the name identifies not only the location where the they came from, but also the type of oysters. Most crabmeat sold on the East Coast is marketed as *Maryland Crabmeat* but harvested in the coastal waters from New Jersey south and often not even processed in Maryland.

Many products with location names, such a Vidalia Onions, Gilroy Garlic and Indian River Grapefruits are better than the same products grown elsewhere, and the names are not interchangeable with products of the same kind grown elsewhere. Kona Coffee is grown in Hawaii only, Blue Mountain Coffee in Jamaica, both in very specific regions. Conversely, Colombian coffee could be grown anywhere in Colombia, and is not necessarily a guarantee of quality, although the term is often used on menus and in coffee advertising.

236

The term "locally" grown is tricky. No vegetables are grown in commercial quantities in New York City, however there are small producers in driving distance selling at Green Markets and directly to restaurants. When this is the case it is probably correct to use the term "locally grown". New Jersey tomatoes are not a special type of tomatoes but any tomatoes grown in New Jersey, where the combination of soil and climate produces succulent tomatoes.

A geographic name can also indicate a certain cut of meat or method of preparation. *New York Strip Steak* does not come from New York; it is a name for sirloin steak and the term is used outside New York City. The term *Rumanian Pastrami* indicates that the pastrami was cured as it was done in Rumania. It is not imported from Rumania. The same is true for Genoa Salami, which is a style of salami.

Using geographic names can be tricky. A good example is Virginia Ham. The genuine Virginia Ham is prepared from lean razorback hogs, and the hams are rubbed with salt, coated with coarse pepper and smoke dried for a number of weeks. This ham is often baked with molasses and brown sugar. Authentic Virginia Ham is different from other smoked hams. There is also a Virginia style Ham, which can be any ham baked with sugar, spices, and even fruit. It might be prudent to indicate "Genuine Virginia Ham" when the authentic ham is served.

Cooking Terms

Cooking terms can be used not only to make the menu more descriptive, but also to add interest. Words like "baked," "simmered", "poached", "marinated", "broiled", "boiled", "stir fried", and "steamed" are popular. Many people are on diets, and cooking terms help them to identify the dishes they can or cannot eat.

When using cooking terms, it is important that they mean the same thing to all people, especially when the menu is used for internal communication. The verb sauté is French and means to cook something quickly in a small amount of fat, if possible by gently tossing the product in the pan. You cannot sauté anything in Sherry wine or in sauce. However, the noun "Sauté" is used in French to describe a stew. To broil means to cook a portion-sized piece of meat, fish, poultry, or vegetable under a strong heat source. To grill means cooking food on a flat griddle plate, or on a perforated grill over an open flame.

The use of cooking terms can be tricky. I remember a menu that read: "Planked Chopped Steak broiled with Mashed Potatoes". I envisioned a chopped steak, smeared with mashed potatoes and broiled. A better wording would have been

Planked Broiled Chopped Steak
Mashed Potatoes

providing the chopped steak was cooked on a wood plank, which is unlikely. This menu item is very old fashioned and probably is no longer served; however it is a good example of careless writing.

Robert Burns Dinner

The Selkirk Grace:

Some Hae Meat And Canna Eat,
and Some Wad Eat That Want It.
But We Har Meat And We Can Eat,
And Sae The Lord Be Thanket.
Robert Burns

RECEPTION

Smoked Moray Firth Salmon
Finnan Haddie Mousse
Potted Shrimp
Pickled Leeks
Scotch Quail Eggs
Alloway Game Pie
Scotch: Glenmorangie
Hock: Rûdesheimer Bischofsberg Riesling Spätlese 1983

DINNER

Cock - A - Leekie Soup

Cod Fillet rolled in Oats
served with Pease Pudding
Graves: Château de Bellefont 1984

Kirkcudbright Haggis
served with bashed Neeps
Scotch: Glenlivet

Epigram of Lamb
served with Rumbledethumps
and smothered Kail
Claret: Les Forts de Latour 1973

Stilton Cheese with Ruby Port

Lemon Curd
and Walker's Shortbread
Hock: Niersteiner Orbel Auslese 1976

This menu was served one January 23rd in New York City and presented by The Wine and Food Society, Inc. of New York. Old-fashioned geographical names and old Scottish spelling were used to add interest to the menu. The smoked salmon was imported from Ireland.

Truth on Menus

Menus must be truthful. Special attention should be paid to meat grades and meat cuts. The meat grades established by the U.S. Department of Agriculture (USDA) are not interchangeable. "Prime Sirloin Steak" must be from meat graded Prime. Black Angus is a breed of cattle, and only meat from certified Black Angus animals can be labeled as such.

There is much confusion regarding the term *Prime Rib*. The term *prime* should indicate that the USDA classified the meat as prime. In industry practice, it is used to describe the standing rib roast from the 7th to the 13th rib, which is considered a prime cut but not necessarily of prime quality. Chops and cutlets must be solid pieces of meat, not ground. Chopped steak must be all meat, with no filler added.

There is a lot of confusion about the terms *Spring Lamb* and *Baby Lamb*. *Spring Lamb* is an animal born in spring, as late as April or May, in which case it might not reach the market until August or September. *Baby Lamb* is a very small lamb, not much heavier than 30 pounds with the pelt on, and it could be born anytime. It is not a good banquet item unless roasted whole, because it is so small. One enthusiastic *Banquet Sales Associate* sold *Baby Lamb Chops* without realizing how tiny these chops are.

Capon is a castrated male bird, which is especially fattened and therefore could be rather large. Roast capon could be a fine specialty in a restaurant, where the bird is served in portions. As banquet item capon breast is too large for a single serving.

Squab is a young pigeon with dark meat. A young chicken should not be called *Squab Chicken*, because it confuses the guests. *Shrimp* are crustaceans and come in all sizes. They have no legs to walk with. *Scampi* are crustaceans with long legs, resembling skinny lobsters. To write on the menu *Shrimp Scampi* is creating a new species. What the author of *Shrimp Scampi* really meant is the method by which the shrimp are prepared. They are large broiled shrimp with garlic; the way scampi are sometimes prepared. Incidentally, *shrimp* is spelled without the *s* whether singular or plural.

Rock Cornish hens are exactly what the name says, small Cornish chicken without any game flavor. Rabbits have white meat resembling chicken meat and hare has dark meat. *Hasenpfeffer* is the German name for a dark stew made with hare, and originally thickened with hare blood.

Trade Names

Many trade names have become household words, but they remain the property of companies. This should be kept in mind when writing menus. For example, *Roquefort* is a cheese made with ewe's milk in the town of Roquefort in Southern France, and the term cannot be used for any other blue cheese. *Maytag* is an

American made blue cheese. Brie cheese however originated in Normandy, France, but is now made in many countries including the United States. Veal is sold under a number of trade names; these names can be used only if the specific brand is served.

Historical Names

Years ago, chefs named their dishes after historical events, famous stars or good customers. Since the traditional menu language was French, and French cuisine used to be very structured, these terms were codified and became integral parts of classical menus. Many names had fascinating stories behind them. For instance, when the polar research vessel *Jeannette* became icebound in 1881, the British public was spellbound. Eventually, only two crew members survived and reached the coast of Siberia and were saved. In commemoration of this feat, Chef Escoffier created the cold chicken dish *Jeannette*, which was served on an ice block shaped like a vessel. Up to 1960, fine hotel restaurants in New York City put *Chicken Jeanette* on the menu every summer. These names do not mean anything to us, and should not be used.

Some names of people are still in use, such as *Newburgh, Delmonico, O'Brien,* and *Caesar.* These names have almost become generic, and are well understood by most guests. Menus are written to communicate, and classical terms popular only a short time ago, such as *Meunière, Boulangère, Jardinière, Argenteuil,* or *Bellevue* would not be understood by most of today's guests. However, if the menu is a theme menu, historical names have a place. Menus should be fun to read and convey the theme of the event.

Upgrading a Menu by Using Better Language

Here is an exact copy of the banquet menu served at a prestigious fund raising dinner in Washington. The menu is in bold and does not read well at all; it has spelling errors and makes no culinary sense. My comments and the revised version follow.

Creamy goat cheese medallion baked in a sun-dried tomato bread pudding with a salad of corn, asparagus and red peppers

Comments: The appetizer leaves the reader breathless and confused. What is it after all, a cheese dish, a pudding or a salad? There is no need to serve a second starch, corn, with a bread pudding. If possible the appetizer course should not appear larger than the main course on the menu.

Grilled tenderloin medallion in a sauce of port wine and roasted shallots

Comments: It can be assumed that the menu means beef tenderloin but other animals have tenderloins as well. A medallion is always round and rather thin; normally one portion consists of two pieces except when served as an appetizer. Probably one thick piece was served and if so the term *medallion* is wrong. Serving two pieces at a larger party is unlikely because the thin pieces would become well-done quickly. Is the medallion floating in the sauce and where do the shallots come into the picture?

Horseradish crusted filet of red snapper

Comments: It must be assumed that there is a choice between fish and meat. Fish fillet is spelled with two ls.

Kamut and colusari rices with wheatberry

Comments: The term rices is awkward and most diners would not know about kamut and colusari rice. Apparently one single wheatberry was served to each person.

Roasted Garlic broccolino
Glazed root vegetables

Comments: Garlic should be used with caution at large dinners, especially fund raising dinners where the purpose is to schmooze. The dinner was organized for a prominent Republican and it was well known that former President George Bush did not like broccoli; it shows little sensitivity to serve it. The glazed root vegetables are not very telling. The dinner took place in April, so why not serve spring vegetables?

Freshly baked rolls with sweet butter

Comments: It should be assumed that rolls served at a dinner are always fresh and not stale. There must be a specific reason that the butter was sweet. Normally salted butter is served in many parts of the country, so perhaps the host specified sweet butter. Rolls have names such as Soft Rolls, French Rolls, Pistolet Rolls, Onion Rolls, Sourdough Rolls and many more.

Orange meringue mirror cake
Orange segments and fresh berries

Comments: The term leaves the diner much to ponder about the mirror. Is it referring to the puddle of sauce in which the cake sits, or is the top of the cake shiny? It seams redundant to serve orange sections with an orange cake, and it should be given that berries served in April are fresh.

Demitasse
Micro-chocolates and tiny biscotti

Comments: The word micro is not a good food term. Tiny means the same as micro?

Revised Menu

Baked Goat Cheese Medallion
Bread Pudding with sun-dried Tomatoes
Asparagus and mild Pepper Salad
****

Grilled Filet Mignon (or Tenderloin Steak)
Roasted Shallots
Port Wine Sauce
- or -
Red Snapper Fillet
Horseradish Crust
****

Blended American Rice and Wheatberries
Asparagus, Carrots and Sugar Snap Peas
sprinkled with Chervil
****

Orange Mirror Cake with Grand Marnier Sauce
Chocolate dipped Stem Strawberries

Demi Tasse
Tiny Biscotti and Chocolate Morsels

Summary

English is one of the richest languages in the world. This is an advantage when writing menus but also an obligation and a challenge. It is easy to select the wrong terms. Poorly written menus can read awkwardly or do not properly communicate the exact description of the dishes.

Our culinary heritage is French. Many French terms have become part of the menu language, but these terms are often used unnecessarily or in the wrong context. It was considered elegant and sophisticated to thoughtlessly mingle French with English. The food industry has traditionally been one of immigrants whose knowledge of English was occasionally limited. Today the industry attracts educated American born men and women and there should be no reason for poorly written menus. However, the previous example demonstrates that menus are still carelessly written.

Discussion Questions

- Why is it easy to write menus in English?

- Explain why it is important to select the right words when writing a menu.

- What is the difference between a sauce and gravy?

- Explain when to use singular and when to use plural.

- What precautions should be used with geographical terms?

- Define why it is important to understand cooking terms.

Chapter Twelve

WRITING MENUS IN FRENCH
AND IN OTHER LANGUAGES

Classical French menu served in 1938 at the Hotel Pierre in New York City. It is very poetic and old fashioned but it demonstrates the beauty of the French language.

Assortiment de bonnes choses chaudes et froides
Servis en Antichambre avec les Aperitifs
****

MENU

Potage Bonne Femme
****

Mousse de Sole au Champagne
avec le Cardinal des Meres Polignac

Chablis Milly 1929
****

Poitrine de Volaille au Beurre Noisette
Petits Pois frais à l' Ètuvée
Pommes de Terre Chatelaine

Pommard Côte d'Or 1929
****

Parfeit de Foie Gras de Strasbourg
sur Jambon de Virginie à la Gelée Rosée
****

Il sera servi en même temps
Une bonne Salade d'Automne
Bien mèlangée avec Huile d'Olive de Provence
****

Biscuit glacé aux Perles de Lorraine
Fraises au Suc de Framboises
****

Milles Feuilles
****

Café
Cognac, Cigars, Cigarettes

Chapter Twelve
WRITING MENUS IN FRENCH
AND IN OTHER LANGUAGES

Objectives

- To explain the importance of writing menus in correct French.

- To stress the need to understand clearly French culinary terms.

- To explain by example basic French grammar rules.

- To know when to use articles on French menus.

- To learn important points about writing menus in other languages.

Introduction

As French culture gained more and more influence in Europe during the seventeenth and eighteenth centuries, French became the language of diplomacy, the language spoken at many European courts, and the language of educated people. It also became the menu language of choice at court, in fine private households and in hotels, because the distinguished guests universally understood it. French chefs and restaurateurs, such as Carême, Ritz, and Escoffier spread the fame and reputation of French cuisine, and French cooking terms were used around the world. An educated person was able to read the menus, and to communicate with the service staff anywhere. As late as at the beginning of this century, French was the accepted menu language.

In the United States, French was used routinely on menus in fine hotels and restaurants until a few years ago. When the author worked at the Hotel St. Regis in New York City in 1959, the menus were written in French, the orders were called out in French, and all the cooks were expected to be able to understand French, however rudimentary their knowledge of the language.

A menu given in honor of the German Kaiser Wilhelm II in Dresden on September 6, 1889 was still written in French in Germany.

For readers not fluent in French it is sufficient to say that the following menu is lengthy, heavy and was created for the German emperor who led Germany into war against France in 1914. Even excellent knowledge of French does not help much because some dishes are not well described.

Consommé à l'Imperiale
Madère
******

Petites Croustades
*****

Truites, sauce riche
Hochheimer
******

Aloyau à la portugaise
Château Margaux
****

Suprême de veau
******

Escalopes de foie gras à l'aspic
******

Perdraux, salade, compote
Grand Crèmant Imperiale
******

Pommes au riz meringuèes
******

Fromage, Glaces, Dessert
Muscat Lunel

Today, the traveling public no longer speaks French automatically. When menus are printed in a second language, they are most likely printed in English, which has become the most widely spoken language in the world. Outside France, French is used primarily on elegant banquet menus. It is a language of beauty and elegance, and many gourmet societies and hosts of fine dinners expect that the menu be written in French. Because this language is difficult, and is so often used poorly, this chapter is primarily concentrating on writing menus in French. Occasionally, menus written in other languages are required, and therefore the basic spelling and grammatical rules for Italian, German and Spanish are included.

The Importance of Writing French Correctly

It seems that nothing is more sacred to many French people than the French language, followed by French gastronomy and the accurate use of French gastronomic terms. Yet culinary French is so often abused outside France that it is the exception, not the rule, when menus written in French are correct. Even in newspaper articles about French gastronomy, in advertisements for French cuisine, and even in some cooking schools, French culinary terms are used inaccurately and words are often misspelled.

One of the main reasons for badly written menus in French is that it is a very complicated language. Often people with only a very rudimentary knowledge translate menus. When clients request to have menus written in French and there is no knowledgeable person on staff, a well-educated French chef or restaurateur should be consulted.

Even when a person with excellent French knowledge translates the menus there is no guarantee that the result is 100% correct. French is a very complicated language, and culinary French is a technical language that must be learned. Technical words used on menus cannot always be translated literally into another language. In addition, French grammar is quite different from English grammar. This chapter cannot detail how to write beautiful menus in French, but it will point out things to watch out for and show how to avoid common mistakes.

French is the most beautiful culinary language I know. In this chapter, and throughout this book, are several examples of well written menus in French. Some of these menus sound marvelously poetic in French, but could sound ridiculous if translated into English. This, of course, would be true of many translations. The exact names of foods change from country to country so much that translations done just by consulting a pocket dictionary, without a solid knowledge of the language, can easily become inaccurate, or even silly.

I remember one occasion when an American room service menu was translated into French. When the translator, whose knowledge of culinary terms was obviously limited, reached French Toast, it was translated with the help of a pocket dictionary to *Toast à la Française*. This was wrong, of course, because French toast in France is a dessert called *Pain Perdu* translated as *lost bread*. This example shows how important it is to know culinary French when making translations.

Culinary Terms

Obviously, culinary terms are best learned by working in France or in a French restaurant. I know of a prominent American-born chef who never worked overseas, but spoke French fluently because he worked in places where French was spoken on the job. For those who cannot work in a French operation, reading well-written menus and French culinary encyclopedias, such as the *Larousse Gastronomique* and *Repertoire de la Cuisine* are a great help. Still, basic knowledge of French is essential when making any attempt to translate a menu.

Like all living languages, French is constantly undergoing changes. As French cooking has changed during the last decade, and many traditional preparations have been replaced by different and modern versions, culinary French has also undergone changes. Culinary terms that precisely describe certain methods of preparation or dishes, are being used by some chefs today contrary to their true meaning, or out of context. However, these are exceptions rather than rules. France is a conservative country, and traditional culinary terms are widely used and accepted.

Garnishes and Names

It was customary to name dishes after celebrities, events, locations, and just about any name that came to the mind of the menu writer. This custom disappeared slowly by the middle of the last century but still appears occasionally on menus. These names are meaningless today. Menus years ago did not give any logical information at all. The diner just had to know that a dish with the name *Argenteul* contained asparagus, because it used to be grown in *Argenteul* outside Paris. *À la florentine* normally indicated that the dish was made with spinach, although nobody could explain the connection between the city Florence in Italy and spinach. *Steak Florentine* however had nothing to do with spinach, but rather indicated that the meat came from the famous *Chiania* cattle breed of Tuscany.

Dishes had garnishes, and each garnish had a specific sauce to accompany it. Who could remember that a dish garnished *à la Peruviénne* came with a *Sauce Demi Glace Tomatée*. If the hapless customer did not like tomatoes it was just too bad. Dishes were named after kings and queens, courtesans, wealthy patrons, racehorses or events. It is interesting to note that many now defunct garnishes were named after females. Apparently the French chefs knew who to please.

The famous composer Rossini was reputedly a gourmet and his name is appropriately associated with beef filet and *Paté de Foie Gras*. It is not known why the famous and rich tenor Enrico Caruso only got a dish of spaghetti and chicken livers named after him and the opera diva Tetrazzini lived on menus associated with chicken hash baked on a bed of noodles. *Marguery* was the name of a Parisian restaurant famous for a fish dish. There was a lot of confusion about these names. Diligent chefs tried to categorize the names and put them in dictionaries, but there was no authority who would definitely decide whether a dish called *Maréchal* contained small chicken dumplings, as listed in one book, or asparagus, peas and *Sauce Madeira* as listed in a competing book.

Old fashioned menu with terms that are meaningless today.

Consommé Bellevue
****

Truite Saumonèe Royale
****

Suprême de Selle d'Agneau Byron
****

Volaille de Bresse Vendôme
Salade My Lady
****

Coeur Alexandra
Friandises
****

Corbeilles de Fruits

A French speaking person would understand that the menu consists of salmon trout, lamb and chicken, the rest are surprises. It is important to remember that menus are communication tools and should not be cluttered with terms the customers will not understand.

Elegant modern French menu without the use of outdated names. It was served at the famous Auberge du Kochersberg in Alsace on September 13, 1986.

Mignon de lapereau
Escalope de ris de veau en salade tiède
1983 Lungarotti Chardonnay «I Palazzi» Torgiani
****

Filet de sole au thé de Ceylan et avocat caramélisé
1984 Puligny Montrachet 1er Cru Les Folatières Joseph Drouhan
****

Consommé aux ravioles de champignons
****

Suprêmes de caille, pigeon, et canard au jus de truffes
1984 Griotte-Chambertin Joseph Drouhin
****

Les fromages
1983 Calera Pinot Noir Jensen Vineyards
****

Feuilleté tiède aux poires, coulis de fraises
1983 Gewürztraminer Vendange Tardive Marc Kreidenweiss
****

Café
Vieux Kirsch F. Meyer
Eau-de-vie de céleri d'Alsace G. Miclo
Eau-de-vie de quetsch G. Miclo
Liqueur de framboise G. Miclo

Basic French Grammar

To write menus in french properly, an elementary knowledge of French grammar is necessary. In French, nouns have genders; they are either masculine or feminine. The gender of a noun is indicated by the preceding article, **le** for masculine, **la** for feminine words. It is essential to know the gender of a noun, because when used together, nouns, adjectives and verbs must be in agreement in gender and in number (plural or singular). Adding an additional **e** to the verb indicates feminine endings. Plural is indicated in most cases by adding an **s** to both the noun and the verb. In certain cases, the **s** will become an **x**. A feminine plural noun requires adjectives and verbs that have feminine plural endings, a masculine plural noun requires adjectives and verbs that have masculine plural endings.

249

As in English, French verbs must be in the proper tense. Since food when ready for service is already prepared, most verbs on menus are in the past tense. We say in English *grilled ham*, in French it would be *jambon grillé*. *Jambon* is masculine in French, and for this reason *grillé* has only one é at the end. That pesky accent indicates past tense. *Grilled trout* would be written *truite grillée*, because trout is feminine and the ending requires two e's.

Noun/Gender/Adjective Relationship

Here are some examples of how the noun/gender/adjective relationship works. In French, the word for butter is beurre and is masculine. Green butter, better written as *herb butter* is written *beurre vert*. Sauce in French is feminine, and *green sauce* often found on menus is written *sauce verte*. In translating green sauce, the letter **e** has been added to *vert*, because the adjective refers to the feminine noun. This rule is basic and not difficult to follow if the menu writer knows the gender of each noun.

Another example could be made with the word consommé. The term consommé is masculine. Le *consommé froid* is cold consommé; *la salade froide* requires the **e** because the noun is feminine.

To refer back to the difficulty of translating French culinary terms, we should look once more at *beurre vert*. It sounds well in French, but literally translated, *green butter*, does not sound appetizing in English. We would probably translate the item into *herb butter*.

Singular/Plural Agreement

As is mentioned above, plural is indicated in French by adding the letter "s" to most words (there are exceptions of course, which make learning languages so much fun). As in sentences with singular nouns, the adjective must be in agreement with the plural form of the noun. *Haricot* means bean, and one single bean is never served. For this reason the term *haricots* are automatically used on menus. String Beans are translated as *haricots verts*. The reader knows that the adjective verts reflect the plural of the noun. Since verts is written without an extra **e** it also indicates that the word haricots is masculine.

***Note: Haricots verts* and *petits fours* are some of the most frequently misspelled terms on menus.**

When singular nouns start with a vowel or with an "h" which is silent, the article preceding them is replaced by a single l'. This makes it difficult to tell whether the noun is masculine or feminine. In our example, one single bean would be written *l'haricot*.

The article for all plural nouns, regardless of whether they are masculine or feminine, is **les**. This gives no clue to the gender. The endings of the adverbs however, correspond with their noun in gender. *Les pommes de terre persillées* are potatoes sprinkled with parsley. The potato, pomme de terre in French is feminine, the adverbs are spelled with an additional e. One single potato sprinkled with parsley would be *la pomme persillée*. Since more than one potato is normally served, The **s** is added to both the noun *pommes* and to *persillées*.

Things still get a little more complicated. There are many exceptions to the rules, especially when the noun is considered a quantity without plural such as *le café*. We recognize right away that the noun is masculine, however the verb is not written in plural. *Café froid* would translate as cold coffee. More elegant would be *café glacé* meaning frozen coffee, but that could also mean iced coffee.

The Pesky Accents

French has three types of accents and all of them can be placed over vowels. They are **à, á, â, è, é, ê, ì, í, î, ò, ó, ô.** Knowing where to place them requires much study. Generally speaking **é** indicates past tense, all the others pop up at unexpected places. If the menu writer is unwilling to look up each word in the dictionary it is acceptable to omit them in uppercase letters. It is a tidy way out for the inexperienced menu writer. However, a menu written in uppercase looks awkward.

Verb Tenses

Menus are written normally in the past tense, because the food has been prepared when it is brought to the table. As usual, there are exceptions to this rule in any language. We say in English *Broiled Fillet of Sole*, but we also normally say *Roast Chicken. Roasted Chicken* would sound stilted.

In French, the past tense is expressed in the verb by adding an **é.** This accent is called *aigu*, and is not limited to the last **e** in any word. When it is, it means that the **e** is pronounced (not silent), and the verb is in the past tense. There are two more accents, but this book is not a French grammar book.

Gateau doré means cake baked to a golden brown. Cake, *le gateau*, is masculine as the article *le* indicates. Therefore *doré*, the masculine form is required. The fish sole is feminine in French and *la sole dorée* is a golden brown sole and requires one **é** because it is in the past tense and a second **e** because the noun is feminine. Complicated but this is the way it is. The infinitive of the verb for is *dorer*, which means in culinary French to brown or to make golden.

When the noun is used as plural, the adjective and verb must also agree. For example the French word for mushroom is *champignon*, and it is masculine. Many mushrooms are normally used for each serving, and they would be written as *les champignons*. If they were grilled, the menu would read *champignons grillés*. As we have seen already, potatoes are feminine and almost always used in the plural, because more than one potato is used in a serving, except when serving baked potato.

It would be called *pomme au four.* Please note that *four,* the oven, is masculine. The *pomme,* although feminine, is baked and there is no reference made to the gender of the item baked. Fried puffed potatoes would be called *pommes soufflées* to correspond to the gender, plural and past tense.

The word *four* meaning oven is often used on menus to describe little cookies called *petits fours.* The term is always used in plural as the endings **s** indicates but it can be argued that the little cookies came out of one oven and not several. This is one of the peculiarities of the language with which one has to live.

Other Grammar Rules

Most of the grammar lesson is over, but a little more must be explained. When one item is served with another, the word linking the two must correspond in gender and number with the noun. A good example is roast beef, called *boeuf rôti.* When it is served with its own juice, it is called *boeuf rôti au jus,* meaning in its juice. *Le jus* simply means juice whether it is orange jus or beef juice. The word is masculine, and the connecting word is therefore masculine, which is *au* in the singular form. Incidentally, many chefs misuse the term au jus, when they mean the roast beef juice. If the chef had decided to make the roast beef in his very own fashion, he could have called it *boeuf rôti à la mode,* or in fashion. Mode is feminine, so the connecting word is à la.

The term *à la* appears often on menus because French chefs gallantly gave many garnishes female names such as *à la boulangère,* the baker's wife, *à la meunière,* and so forth. On English menus the term still floats around as *à la carte* meaning from the menu.

When the noun is plural, the connecting word is always *aux* regardless of gender of the following noun. For instance, *sole aux amands* means sole with many almonds; *salade aux crevettes* means salad with more than one shrimp, which we would translate as shrimp salad. Certain words have no plural form, and in these cases the singular form is used. A good example is cream. *La crème* is feminine and is always used singular, and therefore the connecting word is *à la* at all times, regardless of how much is involved. *Café à la crème* is a good example, and also shows how accents can point right and left. Milk in French is *le lait* and coffee served with milk would be *cafe au lait.*

Another, perhaps less confusing example, would be *purée de marrons,* the French term for chestnut purée. In this case, the word *de* is meaning "made of". The word for chestnuts must be plural, because many chestnuts were used to make the puree, but only one purée was made, to which the word *de* refers. We say *corbeille de fruit,* which means fruit basket in very general terms. *Corbeilles des fruits* refers to many baskets filled specifically with many different fruits. *Plateau de fromage* is the tray from which cheese is served. When the tray is filled with many cheeses, it is called *plateau des fromages,* but it can also be written as *plateau de fromages,* which we would translate simply as "cheese tray". When the *Steward* cleans the trays at the end of the evening, he is cleaning *plateaux de fromage,* or many cheese trays. The plural form of plateau is indicated with an **x.**

There are still other grammatical rules of importance such as the use of the word *de*. It means for all practical purposes "from" or "of". *Filet de boeuf* means beef tenderloin. However, there is a grammatical catch. *Filets de sole* means many fish fillets of sole, which is considered an unknown quantity. If we know that many fillets were cut from many fishes, the correct way of writing would be *les filets de soles*.

One more important rule concerns the use of the words *du* and *de la*. *Du* is the masculine form; *de la* is the feminine form. *Potage du jour* is the soup of the day, jour meaning day being masculine. The house specialty is *specialité de la maison*, because maison meaning house is feminine.

Use of Articles

Whether or not to use articles on menus is a matter of personal taste. Some menu writers feel that articles add flair and elegance to a menu, others feel they clutter up the copy. In some cases, the article is used only at the beginning of each sentence, such as:

La sole dorée aux concombres étuvés

Consistency is important. If the article is used in one sentence, it should be used in all. The article may be used only to enhance the main courses. If the noun is plural, the article must be plural of course, as in:

Les crevettes frits, sauce remoulade

In both menu examples, the nouns are written in lower case, but could have been written in upper case as well.

Example of a luncheon menu using articles served at the famous *Auberge de l'Il* in Alsace, France.

La salade de laperau, vinaigrette aux truffes
Friuli Pinot Grigio Collio 1985, Collavini
******

Le saumon soufflé AUBERGE DE L'ILL
Chablis Fourchaume 1er Cru 1981, Albert Pic
****

Le filet de chevreuil aux champignons des bois
Knepfla au fromage blanc
Château Haute-Sarpe, St. Emilion Garnd Cru 1976
****

Les fromages
Cabernet Sauvignon Réserve 1978 Mondavi
****

Le café
LE 15 SEPTEMBRE 1986

Mixing Languages

If at all possible menus should be written in one language only and not become a stew of languages. It still happens frequently that the menu writer runs out of words and creates a jumble of menu terms.

**Example of a menu with a mixed bag of languages and misspelled words.
There is no consistency in capitalization.**

Amuse Bouche

****

**Lobster Bouillon with Brunoise de legumes
Crème Fraîche and Osetra**

****

**Sautéed Foie gras in a nest of Potato "Alumettes"
with Grapefruit Segments and Ginger sauce**

****

**Seared Ahi Tuna with potato scales served
on Artichoke Ratatouille with Pernod Sauce**

****

**Roasted Duck Breast and Green Olive Sauce with glacé
Pearl Onions and baby vegetables in a Basket**

****

**Marbled Chocolate Mille Feuilles and Raspberries
with Bitter Orange and sauce vin rouge**

Menu Writing in Other Languages

Occasionally, at the request of the client, menus are written in other languages than French or English. In some hotels, the room service, and even some restaurant menus are available in a number of languages for the convenience of the foreign traveler.

Banquet menus are seldom translated for the benefit of foreigners attending, unless they are for tour groups or emphasizing a theme. In all cases, subtitles in English should be provided.

Basic spelling pointers

- In German all nouns are capitalized.

- German uses letters called *Umlaut*. They are Ä Ö Ü ä ö ü and are used in upper and lower case. They can be spelled also **ae**, **oe**, and **ue**.

- German grammar uses three genders, **der** is masculine, **die** is feminine, and **das** is neuter. In plural only **die** is used.

- Spanish has only two double letters, **rr** and **ll**, but there is a new letter **ò**.

- The two articles in Spanish are **el** and **la**; the plurals are **los** and **las**.

- Plural nouns usually end with **s.**

- Italian uses two genders, **il** for masculine words and **la** for feminine words.

- Italian masculine nouns ending **o** change to **i** and feminine nouns change to **e** when plural. Nouns ending with **e** also change to **i.** There are other endings for composed words.

Whatever language is used the goal should be to communicate with the guests in the most pleasant and appealing way. The ultimate test should be: Does the menu communicate? Does the menu sound appetizing?

Summary

Writing menus in French is not easy. The language is beautiful, but complicated. Culinary French is a trade language and translating literally English terms into French or French terms into English can result in ridiculous sentences. For this reason, it is important that menus, when required to be written in French, are composed by a competent person, and checked if possible for grammar and the correct use of culinary terms. There is a traditional interpretation of these terms, which is prevailing in the industry, but modern interpretations are also being used. French menu grammar allows in some instances for nuances and interpretations. Articles can be used to make the menu sound more elegant.

Banquet menus are written in other languages mostly for theme parties. Occasionally, banquet menus are translated into a foreign language for the benefit of travel groups.

Discussion Questions

- Why is writing menus in French difficult?

- Why is the gender of the noun important?

- In what tense are menus normally written?

Chapter Thirteen
OFF-PREMISE CATERING

CALIFORNIA CATERED PICNIC BRUNCHEON

Marinated and Grilled Lamb Riblets
Beef Tri-tip with a brown Sugar and Poblano Crust
Grilled Jumbo Shrimp and Walnesto on Croutons
Grilled Vegetables
Forni-Brown Napa Greens and Bartlett Pear Salad
with Balsamic Vinaigrette
Boneless Quail Breast and Grilled Mushroom Sandwich
on Acme Bread
Wine cured San Francisco Dry Salami, Prosciutto
and Sonoma Cheddar on Baguette
Stem on Napa Strawberries with a Key Lime Crème Anglaise
Assorted Cookies

Wine and other beverages passed butler style.

The menu was copied as written and uses purveyor names and geographical terms.

Chapter Thirteen
OFF-PREMISE CATERING

Objectives

- To understand the differences between on-premise and off-premise catering.

- To appreciate the opportunities that exist in off-premise catering.

- To find out about the competition from hotels, catering halls, restaurants, and other caterers.

- To realize the economics that make off-premise catering potentially very profitable.

- To make menus that can be produced successfully off-premise.

- To learn about the unique challenges of off-premise catering.

Introduction

The term catering is very broad. Some catering companies are very large, and provide food service at factories, office buildings, exploration sites, plants, and executive dining rooms. Some companies provide janitorial and laundry services, others specialize in catering at ballparks and other sport facilities. Some catering companies operate restaurants and dining rooms and there are caterers specializing in servicing vending machines. Caterers provide food for transportation companies such as airlines, railroads, ship lines, and bus terminals. There are caterers specializing in trade fairs and others in expeditions. These companies are called contract feeders and often referred to as vendors.

The definition of catering off-premise is to provide food, beverages and related services at locations away from the commissary where the food is prepared. This book focuses on banquet catering. It can be best defined as providing food service for a single event. However, single events can stretch over a number of days. A good example would be a wedding requiring a number of meals.

The requirements and quality expectations vary greatly, and so do the capabilities, experience, professionalism, and integrity of caterers. Many caterers specialize in specific events, some are more skilled in managing elegant social functions, others specialize in barbecues, and some are very experienced in catering office parties. However, the business is very competitive, and most caterers bid, and take on, any job they think they can handle.

A specialized group is kosher caterers. Since their commissary is under rabbinical supervision while food is prepared and always under scrutiny, these caterers seldom, if ever, handle non-kosher parties. Kosher caterers often have working arrangements with temples and can use their kitchens as commissaries. In cities with large Jewish populations some caterers have specialized in non-kosher Jewish social parties. These parties require understanding of the particulars and expectations of the market and the caterers are usually Jewish.

There are many catering opportunities, and the field attracts many small operators who handle a few parties with minimal equipment, little experience and much luck. Often, they have no product liability insurance and do not stay not in business. They are more interested in making a profit today, and less concerned about building a long-term reputation. Other small operators are very conscientious. They handle a limited number of parties, most of them annuals, and provide a valued service.

Off-premise catering has become big business. Some parties traditionally held in hotel ballrooms have moved elsewhere as new facilities became available, such as museums, restored mansions, parks, and libraries. For some non profit organizations, the rental income derived from using the facilities for outside parties has become an important revenue source.

The Competition

Competition for business is fierce. The term "caterer" is loosely employed, and the business often poorly regulated by health authorities. In some localities homemakers, a group of students or unemployed restaurant workers start a catering business. Some of them work out of their homes or apartments, and often with scarcely any equipment. Delicatessen shops, food stores, and supermarkets also offer catering services. Hotels, restaurants, and clubs, as well as banquet halls, seeing their catering markets eroding, now also feature off-premise catering.

Marketing

The off-premise catering business is very diversified and consists of:

- Corporate meetings

- Office parties

- Weddings, christenings and bar and bas mitzvahs

- Birthdays, anniversaries, and other social parties

- State visits, government parties

- Inaugurations

260

- Commencement exercises

- Fairs

- Parties in houses of worship

- Charitable functions, fund raisers

Much of what has been said about selling banquets in hotels and catering halls also applies to off-premise caterers. The reputation of the caterer is the most effective selling tool. Parties are attended by potential future clients or by existing clients. If the party goes well, the word will spread. If something noticeable goes wrong, word about it will also get around very quickly. The off-premise catering business is a business of trust, and when confidence in the caterer is lost, it is hard to regain.

But in many cases, reputation and trust are not enough to get the account. Price could be a factor. Charitable functions are especially price sensitive. Normally, caterers bid for events. The bids are submitted in writing, and are often followed by personal visits and sample dinners. Sample dinners are important selling tools for some caterers, and can also be a considerable marketing expense. If the dinner is held in the commissary or in a conference room at the place of business of the caterer, clients may expect to be transported by limousine.

The menu for many catered functions, especially fund-raisers, is often selected by committees. It is not easy to deal with committees. Some members may have romantic ideas about a little dinner held in a charming bistro, and would like the food duplicated for a large party. Other committee members are just quarrelsome and fight every attempt to agree on the menu or on other aspects of the party. Selling can become very time consuming.

There is a high anxiety level on the part of the host and hostess at almost all parties. They might worry about the wear and tear on their property, damage to heirloom china and silver, guests not getting the food and service as expected, parking problems and keeping the rest-rooms clean. The caterer must have unending patience, remain calm and reassuring, and direct the staff as needed. Flexibility is essential because the best thought out plans might need sudden change.

Profitability

Despite the time spent on selling and potential commissary down time, the off-premise catering business can be highly profitable. The caterer has no direct expenses connected with the space where the party is held. If rental fees are charged, the client pays them. Utility costs connected with the function space are borne by the client. If the party takes place in a rented hall the utility costs are included in the rental fee.

Like most businesses, caterers charge what the market will bear and prestige caterers charge as much, or even more than hotels. The caterer has the advantage of knowing the exact number of guests in advance, and buys only the food needed for the event. The deposit paid by the client usually covers the food purchases.

A major cost factor is insurance. Off-premise caterers should have product liability insurance, insurance against accidents and all other insurance prudent to have when operating a business.

Challenges

Off-premise catering can be compared to operating a circus. The show takes place at different locations every day, and every location presents different challenges. The work is strenuous, very hectic at times, and the hours long. Because the caterer has no control over the condition and layout of the function space, the setup is improvised.

Access to the facilities where the banquet takes place could be a problem. The place where the banquet is held may be far away from the loading dock, often reachable only by freight elevators and traversing long corridors. Sometimes, access to the building is policed by security guards, and all staff members must show passes to get in. Extra help could even get lost in a large buildings, such as museums, before finding the room where they are supposed to work. When I worked for a catering company in Bogota, Colombia, we catered many functions at the Palacio San Carlos, the residence of the President of the Republic. Just getting through the checkpoints in front of the building, and gaining access to the private quarters, where many of the parties were held, was a lengthy and frustrating process.

Often, the kitchen facilities at the party venue are not adequate to handle the demand. Occasionally there is no kitchen, and the caterer has to work with portable stoves and heaters. Getting water may even be a problem. The banquet room could be far from the assigned work space, making it difficult to serve food hot. If food runs out, for whatever reason, it is difficult to get additional supplies. The commissary might be too far away. In such a situation the caterer might have to shop at the local supermarket.

I remember from my experience in the off-premise catering field in Bogota, Colombia that I always had some cans of apple juice in the station wagon, because the president was known to ask unexpectedly for apple juice. I also had a large can of ham, in case a party was larger than expected, and there was no way of getting more supplies from the commissary. Caterers should always bring extra food along.

One basic rule of the business is to leave the catering facility at least as clean as it was found. Enough help must be hired to keep all equipment constantly clean, to store equipment as soon as it is no longer used, and to keep the work space as tidy as possible. It is a challenge to work in tight and makeshift quarters and good organization helps make the party a success. A cluttered space is difficult to work in.

A special challenge is to dispose of garbage and conform to recycling requirements.

Operational Issues

Professional off-premise catering requires expertise and an investment in basic equipment and staff. Professional caterers maintain a commissary for food production and equipment storage. A commissary resembles a banquet kitchen. It is equipped with heavy cooking equipment, and plenty of table space. It has ample walk in refrigeration and freezer space. It also has storage space for non-perishable food and for small equipment. It should have loading bays, or at least a convenient space to park and load a number of trucks and vans simultaneously. If the caterer supplies tabletop equipment, such as plates, glasses and flatware, dish washing facilities are necessary. Many caterers find it also practical to wash in-house soiled kitchen uniforms, towels and related items. Because the business is highly seasonal, the commissary can be under-utilized if the business is not promoted vigorously.

Inspection of the Facilities

No party should be confirmed before the facility is inspected. The costs and problems of serving a party cannot be assessed without visiting the building first, including the assigned work space. The delivery entrance should be inspected, and the corridors where the food and equipment must pass should be walked. The experienced caterer will notice the width of doors and hallways, any ramps, and the size of the freight elevators. The freight elevator schedule should be checked. In many office buildings freight elevators shut down at the end of the business day, and the cabs remaining in service are occupied and controlled by cleaners, garbage collection workers, or by maintenance workers.

When catering in a private residence, parking for the caterer's truck and staff cars should be discussed with the host/hostess. In case a number of deliveries are necessary for logistical reasons, access to the service entrance after the guests have arrived should be checked out. I remember one party when the caterer's truck making the crucial second delivery could not even get close to the mansion on account of parked vehicles.

Nothing should be left to chance. If the caterer is planning to use electric equipment, the number and location of power outlets should be noted. The location and sensitivity of smoke alarms should be evaluated. In some buildings, the slightest trace of smoke could set off the fire alarm, with the potential to cause panic among the guests. In private homes pets might be present and become a problem. A very sensitive issue concerns using the available equipment. The hostess might insist on using her personal platters and dishes, but often this equipment is household quality and not designed for heavy duty use. A cook might inadvertently put an heirloom platter in the oven and it will crack, or scratch a priceless silver tray when slicing the roast.

It takes diplomacy to discuss with the hostess possible damage to irreplaceable tablecloths and tableware. At larger parties in private homes the guests often cause damage. It would be wise to remove heirloom furniture and fragile decorations before the event.

Walk Through Checklist

- Where can guests and staff park?

- In office buildings is the location of the party clearly indicated?

- Will the lobby be staffed with a knowledgeable person to direct the guests?

- Who will receive and direct the guests when they emerge from the elevator?

- Is there space for a control or committee table?

- How will coats be handled?

- If a reception line is planned, where will it be?

- Is the space large enough to provide bars and buffets or must all service be butler style?

- Where will guests put down soiled glasses and plates?

- Are the restrooms adequate and who will maintain them?

- Do all electrical and microphone outlets work?

- Is there a plan in case it rains?

Creativity and Imagination

Caterers have to work in locations which are usually not used for parties. They might be too big, too bright, too industrial, or just too plain and uninteresting. Successful caterers can turn these locations into settings, which make the events memorable. If the caterer is lacking this talent, then an imaginative and resourceful decorator can be employed. Often it does not take much money to make a space hospitable and inviting. Props can be rented and florists are usually able to rent potted plants, space dividers, and often stunning tablecloths, matching napkins and chair covers. Small personal touches can change the atmosphere of the space. For large parties elaborate decorations can be rented such as laser light shows, fountains, torches, and even portable lounges. There is no limit to the imagination if the budget is big enough.

Making the Menu

With rented equipment and space, just about any kind of food can be prepared off-premise. Usually food is semi-prepared in the commissary and assembled, finished and heated at the last minute. Sanitation is a major issue, since semi-prepared food can potentially be very dangerous if not properly chilled and kept refrigerated.

New:

Blast chillers have come on the market in many different sizes and price ranges. Even small units can chill food in hotel pans in a short time and therefore reduce the danger of contamination.

The menu should fit the occasion and the food should never taste as though it was prepared under makeshift conditions. It is not wise to promise more than can be delivered. The menu should reflect the season and the theme of the party.

Most private homes are not equipped with strong exhaust fans, as are commercial operations. Even a slight cooking smell can drift through the whole house and can be very unpleasant. Garlic should be used sparingly or not at all, strong oriental spices such as curries can also become difficult to control. In office buildings smoke alarms are very sensitive and can be set off even with steam.

Menu items to be avoided in most off-premise locations:

- Fried food is difficult, dangerous, and smelly. It is not advisable to fry food in off-premise locations, unless a properly vented professional fryer is available. Food fried at the commissary and reheated does not taste good.

- Thick hot soups are difficult to reheat, because they might scorch. Thick soups can also be a potential hazard during handling and service.

- Roasted lamb should be served medium rare, and very hot. Both are difficult to accomplish in off-premise catering.

- Roast duckling or geese. The skin should be crisp, which is hard to achieve unless a powerful stove or broiler is available.

- It is not efficient to transport whole poultry. From the standpoint of space available, it makes more sense to transport roast turkey breasts than whole turkeys.

- Stews are difficult to heat and to keep warm.

- Home fried potatoes taste good when made fresh, which is difficult at most locations. Hash brown potatoes keep better.

- Mashed potatoes are hard to keep hot.

- Gelatin desserts and delicate cold creams in the summer.

- Fish cooked on premise. The smell is impossible to get rid of.

Food choices that work well:

- Baked hot hors d'oeuvres.

- Cold canapés. They should be transported on covered trays or in boxes and plated on site.

- Items sliced in the dining room, such as smoked salmon, whole fish, and meats.

- Buffets, salads, shrimp bowls.

- Preplated cold appetizers.

- Cold soups.

- Clear hot soups providing they can be heated.

- Salads.

- Steaks (that have been pre-cooked and heated).

- Roast veal or pork, pre-cooked scaloppini.

- Poached or grilled poultry, boneless and in portion size.

- Casseroles than can be delivered while still hot and kept in the oven.

- Steamed vegetables (pre-cooked and heated at the last moment).

- Ice cream (kept frozen with dry ice).

- Fruit salads, fruit displays.

To meet the competition, the attitude of the caterer should always be positive. If a specific menu item is difficult to produce, perhaps a suitable substitute can be suggested to the host. For instance, since fried food is hard to handle, a breaded baked item may be satisfactory. Caterers must be resourceful. They should never say no before all possible methods of preparation are considered.

Equipment Rental

Most equipment is rented. Because of the large inventory needed, it is more advantageous for a caterer to rent equipment than to own it. The client normally pays the rental charges. In most places, almost anything can be rented: furniture; linen; tabletop items; buffet equipment; cooking stoves and grills; dance floors; and even temperature controlled tents with chandeliers, carpets, and spotlights.

Many caterers own trucks and additional trucks can be rented when needed. A large refrigerated truck could serve as a cold pantry where food is dished out. Noise from the compressor could be a problem. It is important to have good knowledge of the equipment available in the rental market, and to anticipate the demand during certain times. Trying to rent champagne buckets at 5 P.M. on New Years Eve might present a problem!

The rental company, or a number of different rental companies, may operate as independent contractors, and deal directly with the host. Tents, furniture and tabletop items are often rented directly to the client. This relieves the caterer of a financial burden and responsibility. Alternatively, the host or hostess will leave all party arrangements to the caterer. Regardless of who rents the equipment, the caterer has a vested interest in getting the right equipment for the party, and should work closely with the host.

Transportation

Transportation can be a big headache. One of the biggest nightmares for caterers is the possibility of being late. The driver of the catering truck should leave the commissary early, anticipating possible traffic delays or any other situation. Being late is embarrassing and unprofessional and should be avoided. Even if the caterer is not actually late when serving the party, it is very awkward unloading the truck after the first guests have arrived. Access to the loading door may be blocked by parked cars, and unloading the caterer's truck is delayed even more. The host should not be put in the position of having to frantically call the caterer.

Just about everywhere traffic patterns have become unpredictable and usually

Servers are scheduled to report directly to the place where the party is held. When travel time is not paid for *Servers* might cut travel time as close as possible. Usually the rental company will set up the tables and chairs and *Servers* set the tables. Florists usually place the centerpieces on the table as long as the tablecloths are on.

Kitchen and other personnel have to be scheduled well ahead of time to set up the kitchen. In some instances, access to the back of the house is restricted, and kitchen personnel, food, and equipment must be on site very early, producing overtime labor.

I remember an incident in Bogota when we served a luncheon attended by the President of the Republic at the Air Force Academy. We were late, and when approaching the Academy gates I could see in my rear view mirror the flashing lights, and hear the sirens of the approaching motorcade. I had no choice but to speed up, and reached the gates when the cadets where already standing at attention at the parade ground. We rattled past them to the kitchen door, and served the luncheon just in time.

Logistics

Getting the right food and equipment to the proper party can be a challenge in large catering houses that handle many functions on the same day. Computer catering programs can generate complete equipment lists, calculate recipes and quantities needed. However it is wise to be able to fall back on written records because computers do crash. The machine will suddenly display: "One Window's program has stopped responding and will shut down". Programmers get away with it, we cannot tell our customers that the party will not be served the main course because the computer did not order the meat and also lost the recipe.

It is good practice to color code every function. A color is assigned when the function is booked. In the commissary, the components of each function are slowly assembled according to the computer-generated work sheet. Every component and piece of equipment is identified with a piece of colored masking tape. Some equipment and certain food items, such as dressings and cookies, could be assembled days before the party takes place. Every day components are added, until the party is ready to be shipped on the assigned day and time. This system is very effective, but requires sufficient dry storage and refrigerated space to work well.

The off-premise caterer should bring all necessary equipment, and leave nothing to chance. I remember once serving a small dinner in a private residence. The menu called for hot soufflé as dessert. I timed the soufflé so that a few minutes before the main course was scheduled to be served I would have to start whipping the egg whites. Then I discovered that I had forgotten the whisk! A search of the kitchen turned up no whisk and no electric beater. It was too late to go back to the commissary; it was even too late to call the commissary. I had no choice but to use three table forks for beating the egg whites. It worked, but not very well.

At some locations, freezer space is not available to store ice cream dessert. In this situation, the ice cream should to be stored in coolers with dry ice, or an employee of the caterer has to stand by at the commissary to bring the ice cream when called. Depending on traffic conditions, this could work, or it could be a disaster.

When speed is important, good driving skills and caution are necessary. The food and equipment being transported must be secured to prevent damage caused by sudden braking or sharp turns. Even the best drivers may have to brake suddenly, and I have seen beautiful wedding cakes arriving at the party in rather poor condition. The chef in charge of the party should always be prepared to make minor repairs to cakes and other decorated foods. It is always preferable to assemble food at the last moment, such as cakes, canapé trays, and other buffet items that could be damaged in transit.

The caterer should offer to remove the garbage generated by the party. At least, the caterer should bring enough garbage bags to dispose of all refuse efficiently and according to local recycling regulations.

Checklist

Many caterers use a computer generate equipment checklist. The list below is additional:

- Garbage bags
- Plastic garbage cans
- Portable microwave oven
- Folding tables
- Carts
- Cutting boards and sheet pans
- Plastic wrap
- Strong plastic sheets to protect furniture
- Kraft paper
- Plastic pot cleaning pads
- Paper towels
- Soap and hand towels
- Head covers
- Extra aprons
- Extra kitchen towels
- Broom and dustpan
- Mop and bucket
- Kitchen tools
- Scissors

```
┌─────────────────────────────────────────────┐
│                                             │
│           INFORMAL SUMMER MENU              │
│       Iberian Tapas with Spanish Ham        │
│   Marinated Squid, roasted Peppers and Melon│
│      Manzanilla Olives and Caperberries     │
│        Crusty Country Bread Loaves          │
│                ********                     │
│                                             │
│            Cold Cucumber Soup               │
│        With Dill and seedless Grapes        │
│                ********                     │
│                                             │
│          Grilled Swordfish Medallion        │
│          Brushed with Fennel Butter         │
│          Orzo with Basil, Orange Salad      │
│                ********                     │
│                                             │
│              Almond Custard                 │
│     Pitchers of Red and White Spanish Wines │
│               Mineral Waters                │
│                                             │
└─────────────────────────────────────────────┘
```

This menu was produced in an open air kitchen and fish smell was not a problem.

Beverages

If the host or hostess is supplying the alcoholic beverages and hiring bartenders, the caterer should find out who is responsible for supplying ice for bar drinks, and for chilling wine and beer. It is important to know who will order glassware, soft drinks, bar fruits, and supply large tubs to chill the beverages, and it should be determined who is responsible for washing and packing glassware.

In some communities, caterers can get a one-day alcoholic beverage license, which allows them to purchase and serve liquor at a specific party. The host or hostess may then leave the supplying of alcoholic beverages up to the caterer. Even if the caterers are not supplying alcoholic beverages, they should advise the host about popular brands, wine selection, and estimate quantities needed. The caterer should also co-operate with the bartenders to assure a smooth running party.

The caterer should discuss the responsibilities of the host with regard to serving alcoholic beverages to minors or to intoxicated guests. Caterers could be sued if an intoxicated guest is involved in an accident. The best defense is to have a meeting with the service staff before every party to stress alcoholic liability.

Dealing with Employees

It is the nature of the off-premise catering business that most employees are classified as casual help, meaning they work only part time. The caterer must have a resource of dependable and knowledgeable employees who can handle a party.

The caterer is expected to supervise every function. When many parties take place at the same time, some parties can only be visited for a short time to check on the arrangements and to reassure the host or hostess that all is going as planned, and that the party is in capable hands. The employee in charge should be introduced to the host/hostess. As soon as the truck has left the commissary, this employee is like the captain of a ship, and makes all decisions regarding the final co-ordination of the party. The lead employee is often the chef, but it could also be a dining room employee.

Important: The employee in charge must have a mobile phone.

The dining room help normally reports, in uniform, directly to the place where the party will be held. Kitchen help travels with the truck from the commissary. Help is needed to load and unload the truck, and everybody is expected to pitch in. Caterers should bring porters to handle miscellaneous work.

New:
In some large cities independent companies supply the service staff. They will guarantee that the number of *Servers* will be available when contracted and even provide bus transportation for them.

Employees are entitled to meals. The caterer has to make provisions to feed the employees. A staff meal may be brought from the commissary and served before the function takes place. The second meal is a snack meal and could consist of leftover party food. Drinking of alcoholic beverages should not be tolerated. This is difficult to control, because many employees are extras, get swept away by the party spirit, and feel that the beverages belong to the host. The caterer should provide non-alcoholic beverages for the staff.

Billing

The same credit and billing policies that apply in hotels also apply to off-premise caterers. The caterer normally pays for all extra help and bills the client. The host should not have to pay the *Servers* at the end of the party. Gratuities above the contracted gratuities are often given, but should never be solicited. It is important that a contract is made that contains all arrangements discussed and agreed upon: all firm and estimated charges; down payment information; information about taxes and gratuities; information about gratuity distribution; and information about the limit of liability of the caterer. It is industry practice that a sizable down payment is retained when the contract is signed, and all charges are paid in full before the party.

The pricing policy of off-premise caterers differs from hotel and restaurant pricing. Hotel/restaurant pricing is often dictated by the law of supply and demand, because they are supplying the space. Pricing of off-premise caterers is dictated more by cost and competition. A profit and loss statement should be prepared for every party before a price is quoted. The cost of food, beverages and labor can be easily calculated.

Social functions are usually once in a lifetime occasions and the host/hostess could be very anxious to make sure the party is perfectly executed. A caterer with a good reputation can get a high menu price.

Summary

Off-premise banquet caterers handle only specially scheduled meals at different locations. They compete directly with hotels, catering halls, restaurants, and clubs. Since the off-premise caterers have no banquet space expenses, purchase only the food that is needed for a specific party, have low labor costs, and often operate with the money that is paid as security deposit on parties, their operation can be very profitable. However, there is plenty of competition from small operators with low fixed costs.

There are challenges. One of them is to create a menu that can be produced successfully off-premise, under difficult working conditions. Another challenge is working with extra employees. Other aspects of off-premise catering which require special attention are equipment availability, transportation, and working in different locations.

Discussion Questions

- Why is off-premise catering potentially profitable?

- List some potential problems when catering a party off-premise.

- List food that should be avoided, and explain why it should be avoided.

- List food that can be served successfully.

- Explain a good method of keeping track of many parties during the setup.

- Mention some transportation challenges.

- Elaborate on the service of alcoholic beverages.

- Make a list of equipment that can be rented.

- What is the accepted billing policy?

Chapter Fourteen
HOW TO ORGANIZE GOURMET DINNERS

Classical Gourmet Dinner

LA RÉCEPTION

Sélection de Fruits de Mer
Terrine de Faisan, Sauce Cumberland
Melon au Porto
Dry Sack Sherry Williams & Humbert
Tio Pepe Gonzales Byass
Hans Korbell Extra Dry
****

LE DÎNER

Potage Sénégalese au Noix de Coco

****

Gâteau de Filet de Sole Bonne Hostess
Sauce Homard
Chablis Grand Cru 77 Vaudesir
Albert Pic & Fils

****

Soufflé de Veau Prince Orloff
Epinards en Timbale
Courgettes Farcies
Le Bâtard Montrachet 1971

****

Sorbet de Cassis

****

Caille Rôti au Nid
Salade de la Saison
Rosé of Cabernet Sauvignon, Simi Vineyards

****

Les Fromages de la Belle France
Château Brane-Cantenac 1974
Château Margaux 1974

****

Poires à l'Impératrice
Friandises
Piper Heidsieck Demi Sec 1973

Chapter Fourteen
HOW TO ORGANIZE GOURMET DINNERS

Objectives

- To be able to evaluate the economic ramifications, benefits and challenges of serving a gourmet dinner.

- To learn the basic rules concerning food and service.

- Understand the role and rules concerning decorations.

- To learn classical menu construction.

- New trends in gourmet dining.

- To know the rules concerning serving rare wines.

- To learn how to organize wine tastings.

Introduction

A gourmet dinner is a happy marriage between wine and food and an ambiance befitting the occasion. There can be gourmet luncheons and even gourmet picnics, but if the epitome of gastronomy is desired, only a dinner will do it justice. Throughout this book are sample menus from gourmet dinners.

There is increased interest in gastronomy today and gourmet dinners are held frequently throughout the country. They may be organized by the local chapters of large gourmet societies, or by private groups who gather to taste wines or to taste unusual foods. There is a dinner menu accompanied with rare wine given in a private home in **Chapter 9.**

The best known gourmet societies in the USA

Confrerie de la Chaîne des Rôtisseurs. This organization is based in Paris, and the national headquarters called Baillage is in New York. It is an international society with chapters in many cities around the world. The emphasis is on elegant, black tie dinners. The organization started in Medieval times when the position of *Rôtisseur* - Roast Cook in English — was important and highly esteemed at the court. The organization was revived in Paris to foster understanding between the customers and the industry. The members wear colorful ribbons which designate their rank.

The International Wine and Food Society. This group is headquartered in London, with branches in many English-speaking countries. The largest chapters are in New York City and California. The emphasis is on educational wine tasting, seminars, and dinners. It holds an international convention every three years, each time in a different city.

Les Dames de Escoffier. Female gourmet organization, headquartered in New York City.

Escoffier Society. This gourmet group gives donations for scholarships at hospitality colleges.

Chevaliers du Taste de Vin. Burgundian wine brotherhood. The U.S. branch is headquartered in New York City. The group organizes elegant dinners.

Commanderie de Bordeaux. Another wine brotherhood. The U.S. branch is headquartered in New York City.

Lucullus Cercle. This small and exclusive gourmet group was founded by the late Claude Philippe of The Waldorf-Astoria.

There are numerous more gourmet clubs, many of them regional. Most functions are for members only. Guests are admitted on a space available basis and only when invited by a member. Some gourmet societies have wine cellars and new members must buy shares of the wine inventory to be admitted.

Evaluating the Function

Gourmet dinners are never profitable. When booking these dinners the questions to ask are:

Can We Afford It?

This is a philosophical issue. One famous but short sighted hotel manager once said: Show me how many additional sleeping rooms I sold because you organized a gourmet dinner. He was obviously right, few additional rooms if any are rented because a gourmet dinner is held. The benefits are intangible, gourmet dinners boost employee morale, create publicity and goodwill.

Expenses can easily get out of hand and a budget for the event should be made and approved. There has to be a commitment by top management to pull all stops, to provide the very best the house can muster. When there is only lukewarm support from management, and the department heads are concerned that they will be criticized after the dinner even though they provided an excellent event, the house should not book gourmet dinners. There are enlightened hotel owners who appreciate the efforts of the staff and the publicity a successful gourmet dinner can bring, and there are others who worry only about the daily bottom line.

Rule one: Management must wholeheartedly support the effort.

Can We Do It?

This question is serious and requires careful consideration. The expectations at gourmet dinners are very high. Both the kitchen staff and the service staff must be well schooled. The equipment must meet expectation. If the entire operation is not of high quality, it is difficult to pull off a successful gourmet dinner. Inviting a guest chef to cook the dinner is not enough. The raw material, the equipment, and kitchen help must all be first rate.

I remember a gourmet dinner I was asked to cook at a country club out of town. The menu was selected beforehand, and I arrived the evening before the dinner. The menu called for turbot (fish), stuffed with fish mousse. When I started preparing the fish, there was no grinder with a fine blade to be found anywhere to grind the fish for the mousse. There was no blender in the house, nor was there a buffalo chopper. Making a fine fish mousse was just about impossible.

The main course called for venison saddles. The animals were hunted by members and delivered to the club. Upon inspecting them, I found them to be of different sizes; some from young, others from rather old animals. There was no meat saw to cut them to an even size. To cook them properly was a challenge. One kitchen helper was not used to handling stocks and poured out the carefully made lobster stock thinking it was dirty water. Finally, the bake oven used for the soufflé had a broken thermostat. It was not a glorious dinner. They should not have booked it.

Rule two: The kitchen must be well equipped and staffed with trained culinarians.

Should We Do It?

Gourmet dinners bring publicity although some gourmet groups shy away from that, enhance the image of the operation, provide an educational experience for the staff, and give all the feeling of having done something to perpetuate gastronomy.

Gourmet dinners should not be too large. How large they can be is a question of logistics. To feed thousands of people at a gourmet dinner is not realistic, but I have served dinners as large as 80 with success, and have provided Chaîne des

Rôtisseur dinners for over 300 guests. The latter figure meant straining staff and the capacity of the equipment. When serving a gourmet dinner, both kitchen staff and service staff must strive for perfection, and that is difficult for very large groups.

Rule three: The necessary kitchen equipment must be available and the banquet kitchen should be close to the function room.

Do We Have The Trained Service Staff?

Service at gourmet dinners is very demanding and complicated. It is difficult to accomplish with casual employees even with much enthusiasm and good will. At least a mock dinner should be organized and the service of every course demonstrated.

Rule four: A trained service staff is essential to the success of the dinner.

Is The Tableware Up To expectation?

Gourmet dinners require elegant china, silver, glassware and linen. Rare old wines cannot be served in cheap glasses. It might be possible to rent or borrow some equipment.

Rule five: Fine table appointments are expected.

Basic Rules for Food and Service

A number of rules are observed by most gourmet societies, although not all gourmet societies obey them completely.

- There is never any hard liquor served before dinner.

- No bread and butter is served, and there are no bread and butter plates.

- No salt and pepper shakers are placed on the table. The food is supposed to be seasoned perfectly.

- There are no water glasses. Water is served on request, and when served it should be neutral bottled water.

- Guests are allowed to start eating as soon as the food is served, without waiting for the others to be served.

- Business and politics should not be discussed.

- Guests are encouraged to tie the napkin around their neck although few do it.

- There are no speeches during the meal. Food and wine comments take place at the end of the meal.

- It is customary to give an accolade to the *Executive Chef* and the *Director of Service* after the meal. A *Server* should stand by and have champagne ready for a toast.

A very important aspect of any gourmet dinner is timing. The meal is supposed to be leisurely. Sufficient time should be allowed for the careful preparation of each dish and for eating each course. However, the meal should not be dragged out needlessly. A dinner lasting more than three hours is too long. Service should be swift and continuous.

Service should be formal, but that does not mean it should not friendly. Employees often get very stiff when serving a gourmet dinner. They are lectured about the importance of the dinner, all the rules they have to follow, and how complicated the menu is. The result is very nervous *Servers*. Make them relax, and the dinner will run smoothly.

The Setting

The setting should be lavish and elegant. The best china, glassware, and linen the house can muster should be used. There is, however, a fine line between lavishness and conspicuous consumption. The purpose of gourmet dinners is to enjoy the best of gastronomy, and not to mount a theatrical production.

Some hosts, and some caterers spend an exorbitant amount of money and effort on decorations. This is not essential for the success of the dinner. The banquet rooms should not look like a funeral parlor loaded with floral displays. Fountains could add sparkle and glitter with little expense. *Servers* could be dressed in fancy costumes but it is not important. Courses could be carried in on stretchers and ceremoniously dished out but it is more important that the food is served at the proper temperature. At a dinner held at *Delmonico's Restaurant* in New York at the turn of the century, all the men dined sitting on horse back, with attendants standing behind each horse to scoop up the droppings.

Some dinners have been held in flooded ballrooms to create a feeling of Venice, others in Oriental tents erected in the ballroom. There is nothing wrong with theme parties and with creating a wonderful setting. We are here to please the guests, and whatever they request should be provided if possible. However, a gourmet party does not need a setting which is too lavish or distracting. The emphasis is on excellent food, rare wines, and perfect service.

The decoration of the reception room should set the mood for the party. If a specific theme for the party is selected, such as a season or a geographic area, this could be expressed in the setting. When wine is the focus of the meal, winemaking paraphernalia could be part of the decoration. If a country or region is the theme of the party, their colors could be reflected in the table skirting or in the flowers. Ice carvings are always attractive and well received. They are clean looking, and convey a sparkling, fresh feeling.

The menu should always be printed and should be collectible. It is often a major expense. Some gourmet societies may have their own menu stock and printing on it is not terribly expensive. When custom menus are designed, the cost could be considerable and could easily add a number of dollars to the cost of each cover. The client or host group should always pay for menu printing. If possible, extra menus should be printed to keep on file as promotional material, and to give to some key employees. These menus often contain a list of attending members and their titles.

Menu language must be carefully considered. Many gourmet party menus are printed in French, even when few attending guests understand it. This could be tradition or snobbery. Menus should communicate and if many guests cannot read them they are out of place. Great care must be taken to see that they are grammatically correct. Since these menus are often printed some time ahead, the content, especially in regard to food and vintages of wine, must be carefully checked. The final proof of the menu should always be signed off by the *Executive Chef* and the person in charge of wines.

The menu should always list the name of the *Executive Chef*, the *Director of Banquet Service*, and the *Maitre d'Hôtel* in charge of the party. If top management is actively involved in the food operation, the name of the *General Manager* should also be included. It is a nice gesture to have the people who directly supervise the party autograph each menu.

New:
Pastry Chefs are frequently listed on the menus.

The table setup can vary. If the group is not too large, the preferred setup is one large table, either double width, or horseshoe shaped. The inside of the horse shoe should not be used for seating, but could be used for a low display of flowers or ice carvings.

The flowers placed on the table should not have a smell strong enough to interfere with the subtle aromas of wine. It is worthwhile to mention in this connection that lady members should not use strong perfume for the same reason. The flowers could be either very low, or put into thin, high vases. Guests should be able to see across the table. Fruits and nuts could be appropriate decorations. The lighting should be subtle, but since the focus is on food and wine, there should be enough light to let the guests see what they are eating and drinking. Candles are always welcome at elegant dinners, because they add a very soft atmosphere to the setting.

The temperature of the banquet room should be carefully controlled. Ladies in evening gowns get cold easily, and men in formal attire can get too warm. It is always better to take care of the ladies.

Music during gourmet dinners is optional. Since the focus is on food and wine, a musical interlude could distract from the purpose of the dinner, and waste time. Soft live background music is acceptable. There should never be dancing.

How the table is set depends on the menu. As a rule, there should not be more than six wine glasses and more than three sets of flatware at the table. When more is needed, the items should be brought by the *Servers.* The flatware is set in the sequence it will be used starting on the outside. Flatware is removed after every course even if it was not used. In most cases it will be necessary to bring additional flatware. It should be brought to the room on trays covered with napkins and again placed in the proper sequence it will be used. It is a nice gesture to bring fresh napkins for the dessert course.

Menu Construction and New Trends in Dining

Dining is subject to trends and fashions. A gourmet menu served at the turn of the century would not be served today. Many menus in this book are based on the classical format, which was established to allow a logical progression of wine service. White wines were served first in ascending order of substance; red bordeaux wines followed; and then burgundy wines were served. Champagne was often served with the desserts. This sequence was adhered to most of the time, unless a group was drinking only wine from one specific region.

Like all established customs, the classical menu sequence is challenged by both chefs and wine makers. Occasionally the dishes are arranged in a seemingly wrong fashion. But gastronomy is a personal, subjective experience, and therefore there is no right and wrong way. The menu below was published in the second edition of this book but is so daring and interesting that it is repeated here. It places the soup in the middle, it disregards that supposedly asparagus and artichokes are enemies of wine, and it uses menu terms few people besides the chef would understand.

Important Rule:
Cheese is always served before the dessert because it is served almost always with red wine. Desserts are served with Champagne or sweet wine. If the cheese would be served after the dessert it would be unacceptable to go back to a red wine.

Special menu created to compliment the wines of Château d'Yquem

---

MENU

Les Amuse Bouches
«Y» 1979
****

Chaud Froid de Foie de Canard au Navets
Château d'Yquem 1979
****

Tresse de Sole aux Quartre Oignons
Sauce Ciboulette
Château d'Yquem 1980

Queue de Homard de Maine au Céleri Rave
En son Fumé de Cabernet Sauvignon
Château de Fargues 1978
****

Consommé de Canard aux Asperges
Riz Sauvage
Médaillons de Veau aux Artichauts
Château Gruaud Larose 1976
****

Le Roquefort de Gabriel Coulet
Pain de Noix
****

Tarte chaude de Pommes et Maïs
Servie avec la Glace de Coqueliot
Château d'Yquem 1975

Château d'Yquem is the highest rated sweet Sauterne wine and very expensive.

Gourmet food is not necessarily expensive food. It should be the best food of the season, prepared in the most enjoyable fashion. Some chefs think a gourmet dinner must contain truffles, lobster and goose liver or food from exotic places. Excellent gourmet dinners can be prepared with locally produced fish, fowl, and produce. Often there is pressure to put expensive ingredients on the menu because the organizing committee feels that the clientele expects it. Truffles can add a disproportional expense without much benefit unless the truffles are fresh and served in noticeable quantities. Vinaigrette with truffles is nonsense and a waste of money.

Important: Portions must be small.

Many exotic ingredients have come on the market and some chefs feel that they have to demonstrate that they are familiar with them. They must be chosen with great care because they could overwhelm the aroma of fine wine.

Not too long ago, gourmet dinners were served from silver platters. Today plate service is primarily used. Too much emphasis can be put on plate presentations, and each plate is laboriously arranged. When edible flowers, sauces swirled in designs, carefully selected baby vegetables, and fish or meat stuffed with colorful fillings are used to create very artistic compositions, the flavor could be sacrificed for beauty.

New:
Simplicity in plate presentation has replaced elaborate designs. The emphasis is on flavor, taste, texture and clean look.

Reception food should always be simple and elegant. The reception at gourmet dinners serves as an opportunity for the guests to gather and socialize. The food should be very light and not filling. At some dinners, the reception is a veritable smorgasbord, and leaves little room to enjoy the many courses which are to follow. There should never be an open bar at the reception. Acceptable libations could be dry champagne, mineral water or white wine passed butler style.

Mystery and controversy surround the service of *intermezzo*. When menus were excessively long, a sorbet course was served to cleanse the palate for the courses to follow. This sorbet was always very alcoholic, aromatic, slightly acidic, and never sweet. The consistency was grainy, and semi liquid, almost like slush. Sorbet presented this way made sense. Many chefs and hosts feel that no gourmet dinner is complete without a sorbet. In most cases it is a dessert like concoction, much too sweet to cleanse the palate, and often served stuffed needlessly in the shell of a fruit. Sometimes, the sorbet is based on herbs, and this generally ruins the palate.

Desserts at gourmet dinners should be stunning. By the time the dessert arrives, the guests are tired from eating and drinking all evening. The dessert should jolt them. The beauty and cleverness of the dessert presentation is often remembered. Plated combination desserts are popular. Coffee is almost always served demitasse. Tiny cookies, candied orange peel, or chocolate truffles could be passed in sugar baskets.

Gourmet parties can have many themes. I mentioned parties based on geographic regions and on seasons. Gourmet dinners could also center on a food idea. I remember a party based on veal, and between the appetizers and the successive courses, all parts of the animal were served. It was fun for guests and cooks alike.

Wine Service

Wine service is an important aspect of all gourmet parties. The glasses should be scrupulously clean. It is advisable to steam each glass over boiling bottled water and dry it with a lint-free cloth to remove any detergent or chlorine smell that could be left after washing the glasses in the machine.

There must be one glass for each wine. The glasses should have the proper shapes: red Burgundy wine glasses should be different from red Bordeaux glasses; white Burgundy wine glasses for Rhine wine, and dessert wine glasses. Tests have shown that the shape of the glass can influence the taste of wine. The glasses have to be aligned exactly according to the sample place setting posted in the *Server's* pantry. The sample place setting should note which wine is served in which glass. *Servers* must be instructed to serve the right wines in the proper glasses.

Wine is always served before the course is served. The *Servers* should show the label to each guest, and pour the amount of wine as they were instructed by the *Director of Service*. Normally, one bottle serves eight guests at gourmet dinners. Wine glasses are not removed between courses, unless so many wines are on the menu that additional glasses must be provided. In that case, all glasses but the glass with the last wine served are removed. Occasionally guests like to keep one or more wine glasses on the table to check how the wine will react later in the evening. This is inconvenient to the *Servers* because the next flight of glasses might not fit properly on the designated place. There is nothing that can be done about it.

The wines are usually selected by the host. In many cases, the host would like a sample dinner to assess the match of wines and the food. In many cases, the operator charges for the sample dinner. Sample dinners are useful but controversial. When they are held long before the party, the food might not yet be in season. Preparing a small number of portions for a sample dinner is different from preparing a dinner for a larger group. However, sample dinners have been served to better match wine with food, and in adjusting some dishes to better suit the occasion.

Handling Rare Wines

At many dinners, very old or rare wines are served. These wines must be treated with the greatest respect and caution, because in most cases they are irreplaceable. The wines should be brought to the service pantry at least one day ahead of time, but they must be well secured to avoid losses. White wines should be refrigerated and not chilled in ice, because the label could be damaged by ice. Red wines should be left standing upright at least 48 hours before service in a cool but not refrigerated place.

One knowledgeable person should be put in charge of guarding and opening wines in the back of the house. When to open the wines should be discussed carefully and for every wine separately, with the host. The basic concept is that red wines should be opened before service to let them breathe. It stands to reason that the rather small surface of the wine exposed to the inrush of air cannot be harmful, and most red wines benefit from being opened for some time, even one hour, ahead. Very old wines could collapse as soon as they are opened, doing irreplaceable damage.

Old red wines and old Port wines develop a sediment. This sediment settles to the bottom of the bottle. *Servers* should be instructed to handle the wine very carefully, to pour slowly and to stop pouring when the sediment is reached. In some cases it is better to decant the wine before service. Decanting means pouring the wine gingerly from the bottle into a glass carafe, separating the sediment from the wine. It is most often done in front of a light source, to be able to see precisely when to stop pouring. When wine is decanted it is exposed to air, and this could lead to loss of bouquet and nose. The host should be consulted and permission obtained before any wine is decanted. It is a nice gesture to show empty bottles to the guests before or while the wine is poured, to alert them to which wine will be poured from the carafes.

At some parties, wine is served from magnums (double bottles), and even from double magnums, holding four regular bottles. Serving wine from heavy magnums is uncomfortable, but possible. Serving wine from double magnums is beyond the strength and expertise of most *Servers*. These wines should be decanted, providing the host gives the permission. It would be foolish to risk a spilling accident at a gourmet dinner.

The question of charging corkage and gratuities has been touched on in other chapters. For gourmet dinners, the caterer should waive all corkage charges, and the gratuities could not be based on the value of the wine because it is just about impossible to attach a wholesale value to rare wines. A fair gratuity should be applied.

Niceties

Some touches make a party special:

- The checkroom should always be hosted. If the reception takes place in a banquet room on a different floor from where the dinner takes place, coats should be moved to the closest checkroom.

- Seating list is provided by the host committee. A seating diagram should be available at the entrance to the banquet room, in order to spare the guests having to look for their seats.

- Place cards should be provided. They help guests to find their seats and to introduce them to their fellow diners.

- Guests that do not show up, their place settings, including chairs, should be removed as discreetly as possible after the first course has been served.

- Menus are usually placed on the chair. If the menus are intended to be taken home it is a nice gesture to have envelopes available on the way out.

- Napkins should be large, and only lightly starched. Napkins as stiff as cardboard fold well, but are most uncomfortable to use. It is a nice gesture to collect the soiled napkins during the dinner and replace them with fresh napkins, presented opened.

- *Servers* should wear white gloves. Gloves should be changed when soiled. Wine *Servers* might wet their gloves to grip the bottles better. When extra flatware or glasses are needed, they should be brought out on silver trays covered with napkins to keep the noise level to a minimum.

- *Servers* should not stay in the room while the guests are eating. This could be distracting to the guests. The *Charge Captain* times the service, and gives the signal when to serve and when to clear off.

- At some dinners, finger bowls are given to guests to clean their fingers. They can add a nice touch, but are not really necessary at gourmet dinners, because all food should be easy to eat.

- Souvenirs and gifts add a nice touch. They should be given on the way out, always in a little attractive bag.

Wine Tastings

Wine tastings are held by many different groups. Normally, between 10 to 14 wines are tasted. In most cases, wine tastings are not connected with full meal service.

Rules for Sit Down Tastings

At sit down tastings, one glass for each wine must be supplied. The glasses are placed beforehand on a placemat with circles indicating the name of the wine and consecutively numbered in the sequence the wines will be tasted (see example next page). The same care described for the gourmet dinners should be used when cleaning the glasses for wine tasting. Seldom more than ten wines are tasted.

If the operation cannot supply the needed number of glasses (and this could amount to 600 glasses or more for a group of 60 guests), a jar of water and a bucket should be placed on each table, to allow the guests to rinse their glasses. Some oenophiles claim that wine glasses should be rinsed with wine, not with water. The tables should always be set with water carafes to rinse the mouth between wines, and a bucket that can be used as spittoon.

Most tastings require a lectern for the guest speaker. The program will list the wines to be served, and usually includes space for annotations. In some cases, a description of the winery is also included. It is always supplied by the host. The wines are usually kept on a table or sideboard in the room, the white wines and champagnes in ice tubs. The host or speaker decides when the wines will be opened. The bottles are never opened at each the table. When the speaker, who is often the wine maker, asks that the wine, or the flight of wine be served, the *Servers* go to the table and get one bottle for each table. At some tastings, one volunteer from each table serves the wine. A serving is about 2 oz. One bottle serves at least ten glasses, and some wine should be left for second tasting. The numbered glass sheets help to keep track in which glass the wine should be poured. Glasses are not removed until the tasting is over.

The food served at these tastings, if any, is normally diced cheese and French bread.

Place Mat Signed by Christian Moueix.

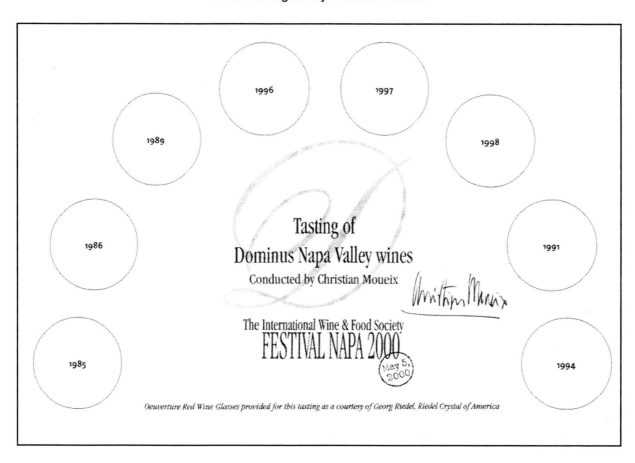

Stand Up Tastings

Stand up tastings are wine buffets. The wines are clearly identified and arranged on buffet tables. No more than two or three wine varieties should be displayed on each table. The guests go from table to table and taste the wines. Often, a representative of the winery is behind the table to give information about the wines. Water and spittoons should be provided at each station and often trays of glasses are placed near the entrance. The guests are expected to take a glass and go from table to table and rinse the glass when needed. It is advisable to provide extra glasses and water at tables throughout the rooms; and empty tables to drop off the soiled glasses. *Servers* should continuouslly collect the dirty glasses, and bring fresh ones.

Good circulation is important. The tables should be nicely spaced apart, and the aisle space should be wide. Trays with finger food, such as cheese, breads and pate, should be placed at different locations throughout the room. At buffet wine tastings the guests have access to unlimited amounts of wine, at sit down tastings the amount of wine served is controlled.

Summary

Arranging gourmet dinners is fun and a challenge. Gourmet dinners add excitement to the daily routine, give the staff an opportunity to learn or to practice different skills, and they generate enthusiasm with clients and employees. Gourmet dinners are not normally very profitable, if at all. In many cases, they generate a loss because the cost of food and labor are high. The size of the deficit is also dependent upon the cost of decorations, and equipment rental. Unless the hotel is willing to underwrite the costs, the dinner should not be booked.

Gourmet dinners are the epitome of fine food and service. There are rules concerning the food, service and how the guests are expected to behave. Most gourmet dinners follow the classical sequence of food and wine, but there is experimentation with new trends in dining. Most gourmet dinners include a number of wines, in some cases very rare wines. They must be handled carefully before and during service. Many small niceties can help to make the dinner a success.

Many groups organize wine tastings. Some tastings are formal sit down tastings, with guest speakers and tasting sheets. Others are stand up wine buffets. In all cases, special attention must be paid to the cleanliness and quantity of glassware.

Discussion questions

- What are the benefits of booking gourmet events?

- Are gourmet dinners profitable?

- Why should the decision to book a gourmet function be carefully evaluated? List factors that should be considered.

- List rules concerning food and service.

- How should glassware be treated?

- When are wines served during the dinner?

- What is meant by the term "decanting"?

- Describe how are sit down wine tastings are organized.

- Describe how stand-up wine tastings are organized.

Chapter Fifteen
KITCHEN EQUIPMENT AND LAYOUT

CORPORATE DINNER
Served in a New York City Hotel for 1,800 Guests

MENU

Bouillabaisse sous Crôute

****

Roast Loin of Veal with a Scent of Ginger
Natural Juice
Medley of Oriental Mushrooms
Baked Pasta Medallion
Carrots, Fennel and Sugar Snap Peas

****

Beggar's Purse filled with Berries
Accompanied by
Sacher Torte Slice

****

Coffee

The dinner had to be served in 1 hour to accommodate the speaker schedule. The banquet kitchen was equipped with roll-in Combi ovens. The Bouillabaisse was prepared in the early afternoon, put in individual soup tureens, chilled and covered in the pastry shop with purchased puff paste circles. It took about one hour to bake the soup.

The main course was served from silver platters. The dessert was served on decorated individual plates. The Sacher Torte was pre-plated; the Beggar's Purses were baked off after the soup was baked and served while still warm on the same plate.

Chapter Fifteen
KITCHEN EQUIPMENT AND LAYOUT

Objectives

- To learn about the kitchen design process.

- To know how to select a kitchen designer.

- To understand the basic concepts of banquet kitchen design.

- To learn the names and functions of banquet kitchen equipment.

- To understand the importance of proper installation.

- To be aware of sanitation requirements.

Introduction

Kitchens are food production plants. They should be designed like factories, with maximum efficiency as the goal. The configuration of the building may not allow for the most efficient kitchen location and layout. Ducts, elevator shafts, electrical feed lines, plumbing risers, and other mechanical items could put restrictions on the placement of the kitchen equipment. In many older hotels banquet rooms are not adjacent to the kitchen.

The Design Process

Architects design buildings and they are judged aesthetically. Architects hire specialists such as mechanical engineers, structural engineers, and other professionals to design special components of the building. For kitchen design they hire *Food Facility Consultants*.

When a building is designed one of the issues is space allocation and adjacent room requirements. During the design process spaces change many times as the building takes shape on paper. These changes might be necessary to accommodate mechanical requirements, revisions desired by the owners, code requirements and other considerations. Food service and support areas are just one component and are often considered more flexible than public spaces. Even with the best intention it is sometimes impossible to give food service the space desired. Other priorities get in the way and kitchens more often than not get the space left over. Precisely calculating the square footage of kitchens and storerooms is very difficult because it depends on many operational factors not known when the building is designed. In order to design the most efficient kitchens a detailed *Food Service Program* should be commissioned.

The Food Service Program

Good kitchen design requires consideration of many factors and should be based on a *Food Service Program* written by a competent consultant. A well-designed kitchen could easily save the fee of the consultant. By its nature the *Food Service Program* is based on assumptions. The program should address all anticipated aspects of the operation in detail such as:

- The type of operation because every facility has specific requirements.

- How the food is received.

- How and where the food is stored.

- The type of ingredients that will be used such as the proportion of frozen food versus fresh ingredients. Storing one bag of flour takes less space than storing 30 cases of frozen croissants.

- Anticipated volume.

- Anticipated frequency of deliveries.

- How the food is issued.

- The type of menus.

- The quality level of food to be served.

- The type of service.

- Garbage removal and recycling requirements.

- The location in relation to restaurants and function rooms.

After the *Food Service Program* has been approved by the owners it becomes the basis for space allocations and adjacencies to conform with the building design. The next step is to hire a *Food Facility Consultant* or *Kitchen Designer*. They fall broadly into following groups:

Architects care about efficiency and flow, but are also interested in getting technical information on time and in a useable format. The design standard today is computer generated with a CAD program. Architects need the utility schedule early in the design process to calculate the utility loads; a plumbing layout to establish the location of drains; the ventilation requirements to establish the location and sizes of ducts; and the equipment schedule. Often the *Kitchen Designer* is selected because the architect is comfortable with the technical expertise and adherence to schedules rather than with the ultimate efficiency of the kitchen.

When kitchens are designed without a *Food Service Program* operational problems could surface. Many kitchen designers have no operational experience and are guided mostly by budget and experience, filling the assigned space with equipment without understanding the requirements of the operation. Often new kitchens filled with shiny equipment function poorly.

Kitchen equipment dealers frequently offer to design kitchens free of charge. Obviously they are in the business of selling equipment; specifically the brands they represent and the equipment they have in stock. The fee of a *Kitchen Designer* is easily saved by selecting the equipment more expediently.

Poorly designed and equipped kitchens are often encountered in the industry. They could cause unnecessary labor turnover, high labor costs, low food quality and food waste. Yet many of these kitchens function, their shortcomings being less costly than the expense of renovating them.

The Bidding Process

After the kitchen has been designed and the equipment selected, the job should go out for bid to at least three or more kitchen contractors. The bidding documents consist of blueprints of all mechanical requirements, equipment brochures and drawings and specifications of all custom equipment. Normally there is a time schedule and a penalty clause if the job is not completed on time.

A competent person must monitor the bidding process. Kitchen contractors might suggest equipment substitutions. The shop drawings of custom equipment must be submitted and signed off before it is constructed. In many cases field dimensions have to be taken.

Bids can vary between 5% to 10% and could save the operator a considerable amount of money.

The Banquet Kitchen

Restaurant kitchens are designed to produce a specific menu in individual portions at a constant speed. Banquet kitchens must be able to serve many people the same food at the same time. Banquet kitchens should be generic, because food and service requirements constantly change. A banquet kitchen must be capable of handling many different types of meals in varying quantities. Demands can range from box luncheons and simple breakfast buffets, to elaborate receptions and sit down dinners. Frequently one banquet kitchen handles food production for many different banquet rooms, some of them far away or even on different floors. The equipment should be selected with great care because it must be dependable, flexible and sturdy. Unfortunately banquet kitchen equipment gets abused.

Food Plating

Placing food on dishes or plates is a major segment of banquet food preparation. Obviously large table surfaces are needed to line up the plates and platters. Cold food is usually plated ahead, covered, and refrigerated.

> **New:**
> **Mobile plate trees are used to store plated cold food and can accommodate many plates on little floor space**.

The process of plating hot meals varies and there is not one single satisfactory method that can be applied in all situations. Smaller parties can be plated at the last moment; stacks of hot plates are put on heated tables and a number of cooks and helpers place the meal components on plates. Usually one person is needed for each component. The sauce is added last by the *Banquet Chef* who will give each plate a cursory inspection to make sure all components are placed on the right spot and the plate looks reasonably clean and tidy. A *Steward* often puts the covers on the plates and helps the *Servers* to put them on trays.

For larger groups this process could be too slow, even with a number of pick-up stations. To speed up the process other methods have been tried. Hospitals plate meals on trays using permanently installed conveyor belts. Conveyor belts have also been tried in banquet kitchens with mixed success. In a banquet kitchen the conveyor must be mobile because there is normally no room for a permanent installation. Some chefs just don't like it.

Frequently meals meant to be served hot are plated cold in advance and heated in special warming ovens, or they are plated hot and kept hot. Sauces and meat are usually added at the last moment.

> **New:**
> **There is wonderful equipment on the market to reconstitute or keep plated food hot. The equipment is equipped with timers, thermometers, and humidity sensors.**

Food for banquet rooms not adjacent to the banquet kitchen is taken in mobile cabinets to the closest satellite kitchen, pantry, or often to the next available hallway or empty banquet room. The availability of electrical outlets is crucial otherwise the food must be kept hot with canned heat.

> **New:**
> **Plastic film in large rolls can be used to completely wrap open trucks. This type of truck is nicknamed a Queen Mary.**

How to Select Equipment

Equipment is constantly improved and updated. When a new kitchen is built or when replacement equipment is needed for an existing kitchen it is difficult to choose the right equipment. The following should be helpful:

- Visiting trade shows and talking to manufacturers' representatives to make certain they are knowledgeable about the equipment they sell. Caution is advised if the sales people are not able to answer technical questions.

- Using professional chat-rooms on the Internet.

- Visiting locations where the equipment is installed and talking to the operator.

- Discussing the equipment with the in-house maintenance people.

- Finding out about options and additional accessories.

- Evaluating the basic models and finding out what they can do. Often gadgets are not necessary, adding only to the cost and maintenance expense.

- Inquiring in detail about warranties, service and who will perform the service locally.

- Considering if the new piece will need special installation, power, and other mechanical requirements. This is often crucial when the installation is inside office buildings.

- Shopping for price. List prices can be flexible.

Equipment and What It Can Do

This equipment list is not in any specific order, because some equipment will be more important for some operations than for others. This list is not intended to give specifications for each piece of equipment, or recommend brands. Some equipment is available for both gas and electric fuel, others for one type of fuel only. I have made comments when I liked a specific feature.

Stoves

In banquet kitchens, stoves are less important than in restaurant kitchens, because most food is prepared in bulk. However all banquet kitchens require stoves. There are four basic types of stoves on the market:

- Flat top stoves are most useful in banquet operations, because any size of pots or pans can be used. The center rings can be removed to allow direct access to the burners. Pots used on flat top stoves most be absolutely flat to get maximum heat conductivity. The stove is also called *French Top*.

- Even heat stoves are basically the same as flat top stoves except that there are no center rings that can be removed.

- Open burner stoves are available with four and six burners in standard size, and six or more burners in cafe size. For banquet use, the four-burner stove would be more practical than the six-burner stove, because larger pots can be used. These stoves provide fast heat for sautéing, and are indispensable when making omelets.

- Griddle stoves could be very useful. Small amounts of food, such as onions, potatoes, and bacon can be quickly sautéed on griddle stoves. They can be used to keep food hot. In places serving breakfast the griddle is needed to make pancakes and French toast.

- Chinese wok stoves have also become popular in some banquet operations. Wok stoves are gas fired and when the wok (kettle) is placed over the open flame it becomes very hot. Stir fry cooking is popular, and is an important component of many banquet menus. The wok stoves are also used for frying in Chinese kitchens but since they are not thermostatically equipped they could be a fire hazard.

Stoves in banquet kitchens should always be ordered with ovens underneath. There can never be too many ovens and having spare equipment is important. No oven can be placed in *Chinese Wok Stoves*.

Ovens are available as *Convection Ovens* and as regular ovens. *Convection Ovens* are equipped with an electric fan that circulates hot air, speeding up the cooking process. It is an important feature in bake ovens and in freestanding ovens. Because ovens in stoves are used mostly for roasting and for holding food, convection is less needed. In all *Convection Ovens* the fan motor will eventually burn out and is difficult to access in stoves unless the equipment is mobile.

A water spigot should be provided near all stoves, especially *Chinese Wok Stoves* to make filling pots, or for cleaning the wok kettles easily. The spigot should not be installed directly over the stove, since it would make the water too hot, and the gasket would burn out quickly. Water spigots should always be installed over spreader plates, which are metal plates of varying width between equipment. There are special pot fillers on metal hoses on the market.

Fryers

Deep fat fryers are indispensable in banquet kitchens. They are available in many sizes, and are sized by the amount of fat they hold. Fryers are available with and without automatic straining devices. Fryers cannot be installed next to an open flame appliance, such as an open burner stove, broiler, or grill. Spreader plates at least 8" wide must separate them. The spreader plates are useful for placing food to be fried, or for trays to receive the finished product.

Swiss Kettles/Tilting Frying Pans

Swiss Kettles are available electric or gas heated. In my opinion, electric frying pans are more dependable than gas heated pans, because the pilot light, which ignites the gas, could get wet when the equipment is cleaned and could go out. In addition the burners of gas fired pans are rather heavy, which make the equipment heavier to tilt.

Swiss Kettles are available in many sizes and have become the most versatile piece of heavy cooking equipment. They can be used for making soups, stocks, stews, and pot roast, sautéing meat, fish or vegetables and even for frying. They need a water spigot for easy cleaning and a deep floor trough that should be perpendicular to catch the runoff when the kettle is tilted.

Steamers

Steamers are just about indispensable in banquet kitchens and are available in many sizes. Steamers are used to cook vegetables, eggs, potatoes, rice and many other ingredients, even steamed desserts. The industry distinguishes between low and high-pressure steamers. Low-pressure steamers are very useful for last minute, nutritionally sound vegetable preparation.

Steamer ovens combine the browning capabilities of ovens with low pressure convection steam cooking. Meat cooked in these ovens stays moist and has little cooking loss. *Steamer Ovens* are also used for high moisture, low temperature cooking of pouch packaged food, referred to as *sous vide*. They are often called *Combi Ovens*.

Steamers can be self-generating using gas or electricity or can be connected to a steam source such as a steam generator in the kitchen or an outside source. Steam purchased from an outside source is not clean and a steam converter is needed. In large banquet kitchens the availability of steam to cook, heat and clean equipment is a great advantage.

Steam Kettles

Steam kettles are heated by steam injected into a jacket surrounding the kettle. They are available in many sizes, from 100-gallon floor models to 5-gallon table sized kettles. Steam kettles are very fast when connected to a strong outside steam source. All kettles should be equipped with a cold water faucet, and a deep trough for draining. Self-contained kettles can be gas or electrically heated.

Small kettles are often sold counter mounted in conjunction with a steamer. Built in steam boilers build up pressure relatively quickly and the small kettles can be brought to a boil very fast. Some manufacturers foolishly place the steam-regulating valve directly next to the kettle. If the kettle boils over there is no way to turn off the steam without the risk of burns.

Small table mounted electric kettles are often called *Truneon Kettles*. They are fast and are often installed in restaurant kitchens.

- Stationary kettles are equipped with a drain-off spout and are used for making stocks. After the stock is drained off the remaining bones or vegetables must be scooped out. In large operations, this type of kettle could be equipped with a basket connected to an overhead hoist to facilitate the removal of food.

- Tilting kettles with spouts can be tilted to remove the contents, and are also equipped with a drain off spigot. They are used for cooking vegetables and clear soups.

- Tilting kettles without spouts are used for making soups and sauces, and can be emptied by tilting. Because there is no strainer basket and faucet the inside surface is smooth.

Stock pot ranges, often called *Candy Stoves* are practical when there is no space or money to install kettles. They are basically low open burner stoves. Since they are low it is easier to lift a pot on top.

Ovens

There are many types of ovens, but in catering kitchens only some are of major importance. Bake ovens are not discussed.

- Deck ovens are used for both baking and roasting. They consist of horizontal ovens with usually one shelf in each oven. They are available in different heights. Their height could make the removing of heavy roasting pans dangerous.

- Rotating ovens have a number of rotating shelves and can be used for both baking and roasting. They come in different sizes and are high production ovens.

- Conveyor ovens are useful for fast continuous production, such as steaks for large parties.

- Convection ovens are probably the most popular ovens in banquet kitchens. They come as single and as double stack oven, and are equipped with fans, which circulate air to cook the product more evenly. They can be used for both roasting and baking.

- Combi ovens use any combination of convection steam and hot air. They can be used to bake, roast, oven-braise, poach, steam, rethermalize, wet roast, crust bake, proof, thaw, and warm. They come in many sizes ranging from small free standing models to roll in size. The manufacturers claim no flavor transfer from food to food, allowing for multiple dishes being cooked simultaneously.

- Roll-in ovens are constructed to allow racks loaded with food to be rolled directly into the oven. They can be used for baking and roasting, and are very useful in large banquet operations. Some roll-in ovens are equipped with timers, which turn the oven on and off. Roll-in ovens used for baking are provided with steam injectors and others have, in addition to heating elements, air blowers to cool the product when done. Ovens equipped with automatic thermostats keep the food at the desired temperature.

- Low temperature ovens. A number of models are on the market, all of them equipped with automatic timers. The principle is that the food is cooked at a very low temperature, so low that these ovens can be used without hoods. The meat stays moist, and shrinkage is very little. Meat can be put in the oven the night before, the automatic timer kicks in at the time set, and the meat is cooked the next day. These ovens also double as food heaters.

- Microwave ovens. No banquet kitchen should be without one or two microwave ovens. They are indispensable for quickly reheating a plate when a customer leaves the table, or for heating special request meals.

Most ovens are equipped with a choice of electronic gadgets and bells and whistles. These improvements are wonderful but more important is sturdy construction and availability of service and spare parts.

Broilers and Grills

Broilers have a heat source above the food. Grills have a heat source below the food. Gas or electric broilers are available.

- Double broilers have two broiling decks for high volume production.

Some broilers use infrared heating elements and can get very hot. These broilers are often used in steak houses.

- Broilers can be equipped with a roast oven below the broiling deck. These broilers have one single broiling deck but a small oven above called a finishing oven, which gets very hot. They are often installed in restaurant kitchens.

- Broilers with one single broiling deck and the finishing oven and no roast oven below. Instead of the oven are shelves.

Grills give attractive markings to steaks and vegetables. In banquet kitchens grills are generally used to mark, or pre-cook meat, fish or vegetables, which are then finished in the oven. Food cooked on charcoal grills will pick up flavor elements.

- Gas grills use lava stones, and the fat dripping on the hot stones imparts flavor to the meat. Propane gas grills are often used for outdoor barbecues.

- Electric grills come with different width grill rods. European grills consist of slanted, v-grooved heavy iron panels.

- Charcoal grills are seldom used in banquet kitchens. The intensity of the heat is difficult to regulate. Charcoal grills are occasionally used in restaurants. Operations specializing in outdoor barbecues normally use charcoal grills.

- A salamander is a cooking device with an overhead heat source. It is used to brown food. In banquet kitchens the broiler is usually used for this purpose. The cheese melter is a smaller version of a salamander.

- A rotisserie is a spit-roasting machine and is available in many sizes. It is seldom installed in banquet kitchens because the capacity of even large machines is seldom sufficient for banquet production.

Heating and Chilling

Keeping food hot and cold is a major challenge in banquet kitchens. Bacteria multiply rapidly in the danger zone from 40 degrees to 140 degrees. Banquet kitchens must be equipped to keep food out of the danger zone, before, during, and after preparation. After the food is prepared it can be chilled and kept cold until needed.

- *Bain-marie* is a French word for water bath. It is used to keep stocks and soups hot until service. The *Bain-marie* should accomodate large pots, but should not be too high so as to make lifting heavy pots in and out

as easy as possible. The best height is 20 inches, and the depth
16 inches. Gas or electric *Bain-maries* are available. The *Bain-marie*
should be equipped with a cold water source, a gate valve and with an
overflow drain. This way, it could be used as a temporary cooling tank.

- Food heaters can be stationary or mobile and are usually electrically heated. Some heaters can generate moist heat.

- Induction stoves generate heat through a magnetic field and get hot only when a pot made of a special alloy is placed on top. They are practical for buffet service or in banquet pantries without ventilation.

All refrigeration should be lockable and selectively keyed alike.

- Walk in coolers and freezers are usually pre-fabricated and can be installed in practically any configuration. It is important that refrigerators in banquet kitchens are flush with the kitchen floor. Food is normally placed on mobile carts and rolled into the refrigerator. Walk in freezers and refrigerators can be installed outdoors. A banquet operation can never have too much refrigeration equipment.

- Reach in refrigerators are necessary to store small material items.

- Mobile refrigerators are handy to transport food to other pantries and to roll close to the stoves when food is prepared.

- Quick-chill equipment has become indispensable in hospital kitchens and is slowly being installed in banquet kitchens. Most useful in banquet kitchens are blast chillers, which will chill food in hotel pans.

- Chill tanks are needed to quickly chill sauces and stocks. They are equipped with a refrigerator coil.

Sinks

Health departments require hand wash sinks in all food production areas. The sinks must be equipped with a soap dispenser. Other sinks essential in banquet kitchens are:

- Two compartment salad and vegetable sinks. Two compartments are needed when washing salads and vegetables. The process is to lift the product out of the water and place it the adjacent sink. Sand will sink to the bottom and stay behind. The sinks should have large draining boards with marine edges.

301

- Large defrost sinks. Most operations use frozen food and large sinks are needed when the food is unpacked. Often food must be rinsed after unpacking.

- Cook sinks at all stations.

- Pot-wash sink should have three compartments and be large enough to handle standard size sheet pans. The wash sink should be equipped with a heater. The draining boards should be large, and sloped toward the sinks.

Tables

There can never be too many tables in a banquet kitchen. There is always a need to put something down.

- Chef's tables are large tables in front of the stove where hot food is plated and picked up. It usually has one or more built in *Bain-marie* to keep sauces hot during pick up. Covers should be provided when the *Bain-marie* is not needed to increase useable space. Heated cabinets should be under the table to keep food, plates, and platters hot. The heat source could be steam or electricity. Overhead heaters should be over the full length of the chef's table to keep food hot while being dished out. There should be outlets above the table for plugging in slicing machines. The chef's table is usually custom made and should be about 4' wide.

- Worktables should be stainless steel and should have shelves for stability and to store equipment. Some tables should be mobile. Some tables should have outlets for plugging in slicers, mixers, and other kitchen machines. Some should have tool drawers. A number of tables should not have shelves underneath leaving room for garbage cans. Cutting boards should be used upon which to cut meat. Butcher shops require tables with hardwood tops for boning meats. Pastry shops require hardwood and stainless steel tables.

- Desk and bulletin board to process *BEOs* and make requisitions. If the space is enclosed it should be computer equipped. The bulletin board must be large enough to accommodate all menus.

Food Processing Equipment

Miscellaneous equipment needs vary depending on the menu, the type of raw material used, and how much support the banquet kitchen receives from other kitchens. Often the equipment listed is only available in the main kitchen and shared with other departments.

- An electric band saw is needed only when there is a butcher shop on premise. Since meat is purchased usually boned or portion cut, in-house butcher shops are being phased out.

- Meat slicers are available with manually operated or with automatic carriages, which can save time in large banquet operations. There should be many meat slicers on mobile stands.

- Meat grinders are indispensable in catering operations.

- The Buffalo chopper is used for making breadcrumbs and stuffing.

- Vertical cutters come in all sizes, and are standard equipment in most operations. Food processors are vertical cutters. *Cuisinart* and *Robotcoup* are brand names.

- Hand held electric mixers are available in many sizes and are very useful.

- Vacuum machine. Raw or cooked food can be vacuum packed to increase shelf life. A process called "sous vide" was developed in Europe and consists of vacuum packing food under strict sanitary conditions, and cooking with gentle heat. The products can be stored under refrigeration longer than non packaged products. The process reduces shrinkage and increases shelf life, but there is concern that the low heat cooking process does not kill all bacteria.

- Mixers come in all sizes, from floor models to table models. Banquet operations need mixers to make soups, dressing, stuffing, dough, and batters. Attachments are available to use the mixer as a meat grinder, a vegetable slicer, or grater.

Moving Food

In banquet operations as much equipment as possible should be on wheels. The requirements vary constantly and mobile equipment provides the flexibility to change the circulation pattern and workflow.

Food must be transported from the storeroom to the workstations and from there to refrigerators, heaters or to other banquet pantries. There should be hand trucks, flatbed trucks, and small table trucks. Cooks should be able to wheel ingredients directly to the stove.

All mobile equipment should have large wheels and rubber buffers to protect walls and equipment.

Cleaning Equipment

Sanitation is a major concern and responsibility. Dishwashing is a challenge because a large number of soiled dishes are generated at the same time and dumped on the soiled dish table. The soiled dish table can never be too big! Mobile soiled dish trucks are very practical because they can be wheeled to areas close to the banquet rooms and allow the *Servers* to rapidly bus the dishes.

The cleaning equipment often found in banquet kitchens is detailed here.

- Rack machines use racks, which are passed through one or more wash and rinse tanks. Rack machines can range in size from single tank manual machines to large conveyor driven installations. Racks can be purchased for glasses and plates in many different configurations. The disadvantage of rack machines is that many racks are needed in large operations.

- Conveyor or fly type machines use a belt equipped with plastic spikes to transport loose dishes through the machine. Glass and flatware racks can be placed on top of the belt. High volume operations prefer fly type machines because many pieces of the same size and shape are washed at the same time, and fly type machines can be loaded faster than rack machines. Fly type machines are high volume machines and require at least one person to load, and one person to unload.

- Pot washing machines are useful in large operations. In large machines, pots and pans and most mobile equipment can be washed.

- Hot water hose connections should be provided at many locations. A provision should be made at the loading dock to wash garbage cans and the garbage dumpster. A screen or air curtain will keep out flies.

- Slop sinks are needed to store and wash mops.

- Floor drains are needed in many locations to allow proper floor cleaning.

- Garbage disposal and recycling are important challenges to the operators. Compactors installed in the kitchen areas help reduce the garbage volume. Large banquet operations have garbage refrigerators to store wet garbage until pickup.

Miscellaneous Equipment

- Coffee urns must be available in different sizes to make it possible to brew coffee for smaller parties as close to service time as possible.

- Electric chain saws are popular for making ice carvings. It is very important that they are double grounded to avoid injury.

- Icemakers for making cubed and crushed ice. Banquet operations normally need both kinds; cubed ice for bar service, crushed ice for buffets and for chilling beverages.

Banquet Beverage Service

Banquet kitchens are normally equipped with a beverage storeroom, walk-in or reach-in refrigeration, and a service bar. The service bar must be outfitted with a Point of Sale System (POS) to handle cash bar transactions. Adjacent to the banquet kitchen there should be storage areas for mobile bars.

Layout of Banquet Kitchens

Special attention must be paid to traffic flow in the kitchen because many people could be working there at the same time. *Servers* from different banquet rooms should not have to cross each other when picking up food or bussing dishes. However, since these banquet activities rarely happen at *exactly* the same time, it is a lesser consideration than in a restaurant kitchen serving both a restaurant and banquet rooms.

Banquet houses using many ice carvings should provide an ice carving station. It should be away from the general traffic area, close to the freezer, and equipped with a floor drain and a grounded electric outlet, because many chefs use electric chain saws for carving ice. A simple frame about 20 inches high, built of cinder blocks and covered with a sturdy grill makes a solid base when carving ice.

Banquet kitchens require a lockable small dry storeroom.

There should be space to park mobile equipment when it is not in use. Soiled linen should be kept close to the loading dock. Garbage should also be kept close to the loading dock. Wet garbage should be refrigerated; dry garbage should be compacted. Next to the garbage room should be room to store items that are to be recycled, such as glass bottles, paper, empty containers and drums.

Installation

The walls of banquet kitchens should be tiled with glazed cinder blocks because they are sturdier than wall tiles. Wall tiles could become loose behind stoves because of heat. Wainscoting should not be used, because roaches can breed behind it. Ceilings should be as high as possible, to allow heat to rise. Floors should be slip proof quarry tiles. Sufficient floor drains should be provided, and the floor should be properly pitched. If the floor in walk in refrigerators is part of the kitchen floor, it must pitch away from the inside wall to prevent accumulation of water when the kitchen is cleaned.

Kettles should be hung on the wall when possible. Floor troughs should be installed perpendicular to the equipment in front of kettles and tilting frying pans so the water draining off will flow into the trough when the kettle is tilted. Water faucets should be installed next to kettles.

Summary

Banquet kitchens differ from restaurant kitchens, because they are used to preparing large amounts of food to be served at the same time. Some equipment is more likely to be used in banquet kitchens than in restaurant kitchens. Much equipment should be mobile, and it is important to provide roll in refrigeration, heaters, and roast ovens. The layout of banquet kitchens should provide for circulation space, and for storage of mobile equipment. Banquets take place intermittently, and when few or no functions are scheduled, food is often prepared ahead of time. For this reason, ample refrigeration and freezer space should be provided.

Kitchens should not be designed and built without an extensive study of present and future needs. This is best accomplished by a consultant, who will create a *Food Service Program.* Sanitation is a great concern in kitchen planning, specifically banquet kitchens because large amounts of food are often prepared ahead of time.

Discussion Questions

- Mention some limitations common to kitchen design.

- What should kitchen designers take into consideration when planning a banquet kitchen?

- List some stove types.

- List some oven types.

- What is Sous Vide?

- What is a Bain-Marie?

- What is the difference between a rack and a fly type dish washing machine?

- What are some principles of good traffic flow in banquet kitchens?

- Mention some installation concerns.

- List basic sanitation requirements.

Chapter Sixteen

BANQUET AND MEETING ROOM REQUIREMENTS

CONFERENCE CENTER HORS D'OEUVRES MENU
All items are sold in units of 50 pieces Buffet Style

Hot Selections

Grilled Baby Lamb Chops, Rosemary Butter
Beef Satay or Chicken Satay with appropriate Dips
Cornmeal fried Shrimp, Chutney Salsa
Small Egg Rolls, hot and mild Mustard Dip
Chicken Quesadillas, Guacamole
Bit-size Pizza with Cilantro Pesto
Deviled seared Sea Scallops
Crab Cakes

Cold Selections

Smoked Trout Terrine on toasted Brioche
Vegetarian California Sushi
Cocktail Shrimp with three Sauces
Peppered Melon and Prosciutto
Endive Leaves filled with Boursin Cheese
Peapods filled with Chive Cream Cheese
Smoked Salmon Canapés
Gravelax Canapés

From the Carving Station

Smoked boneless Pork Loin, Cranberry Relish
Roast Beef Tenderloin, Red Wine Pepper Sauce
Baked Honey glazed Ham, Cherry Preserve
Baked Salmon Sides, Caper Coulis
Marinated smoked Leg of Lamb

Vegetarian Choices

Grilled Vegetables with Olive Oil
Fried Swiss Cheese Sticks and Spinach Salad

Chapter Sixteen
Banquet and Meeting Room Requirements

Objectives

- To explain the importance of the conference business.

- To emphasize the economic importance of meeting business.

- To discuss the need and expectations of meeting planners.

- To evaluate the shortcomings of old space for meeting use.

- To learn about food and beverage service expectations.

Introduction

Meeting business is big business. Closely related to meeting business is the convention business and the trade show business. Most hotels find it increasingly difficult to fill their banquet space only with social business and their sleeping rooms only with business or pleasure travelers. Just about all hotels are booking meeting business and conventions.

Older luxury hotels were built for gracious travel and for holding glamorous social parties in mirrored ballrooms. Satisfying the meeting and convention requirements is often very difficult in these properties. In many older hotels, checking in and out large numbers of people at the same time is awkward, straining the capabilities of the front desk, baggage room, and elevators. One of the biggest problems is providing adequate meeting space. Banquet space built for social business lends itself poorly to meeting use.

The Difference Between Conferences and Conventions

Conferences and meetings are organized for learning, to disseminate information, to introduce new products and methods. The emphasis is on serious study.

Conventions can also have a learning purpose, but in many cases the emphasis is on fun and relaxation.

Note:
See Appendix D and E for Convention Resumés and BEOs.

CONFERENCE CENTER LUNCHEON BUFFET

Soups of the Day (choice of two)

****

**Cold Cut Board with Ham, Pastrami, Smoked Turkey, Leberwurst
Roast Beef Tenderloin
Gouda, Swiss and Maytag Blue Cheese**

**String Bean Salad, Red Bliss Potato Salad, Tortellini and Pesto Salad
No Mayo Chunk Tuna, Smoked Mackerel
Three Cabbage Cole Slaw, Mexican Corn Salad
Fruit Salad and Cottage Cheese   Yogurt and Granola
Mixed Green Salad, Low Calorie and Regular Dressings
Shrimp and Bean Sprout Wrap**

HOT SELECTIONS

**Hamburgers, Turkey Burgers and Vegetarian Burgers
French Fries, Home Fries and Steamed Potatoes**

**Grilled Chicken Breast with Basil Olive Oil
Grilled or steamed Catch of Yesterday**

****

**Braised Veal Shanks Cremolata
Rice Pilaf
Vegetarian Lasagna**

DESSERTS

**Fruit Salad   Seasonal Berries Apple Cobbler
Lemon Custard   Brownies
Ice Cream and Sherbets
Low Calorie Sherbets**

Conference Centers

Conference centers are an important segment of the hospitality industry and have become competitors to hotels. Conference centers can be company owned and operated only for their own employees, or they are for-profit businesses and are available for general use. Many universities, religious groups, and other non-profit organizations also offer conference facilities.

Conference Centers can be classified broadly into two groups:

- Day conference centers.

- Full service conference centers.

Day conference centers provide only meeting space and light meal service for the conference attendees. Full service conference centers have sleeping rooms and are operated like hotels. They provide dining rooms, athletic facilities, lounges, and bars. Both offer classrooms in different configurations, usually an amphitheater and many break out rooms. State of the art audiovisual installations are important.

Many conferences begin on Sunday evening and close on Friday afternoon making the facility available for public use on weekends if desired.

The Convention Business

Hotels also offer meeting and classroom facilities but in a more relaxing environment. In order to get a share of the conference business some hotels have added conference facilities or modified existing banquet space. Many seasonal hotels are marketed as conference and convention hotels during the off season.

There are many challenges that older hotels face in order to attract and handle conferences and meetings:

- Frequently banquet rooms are not the right size for the group. Many conferences are for 150 to 200 guests. Moveable walls to divide banquet rooms are hardly adequate, since they are seldom sound-proof.

- Insufficient number of break out rooms for 25 to 30 people.

- Room configuration can be a problem. Meetings require good sight lines to the speaker and to screens. In many older hotels, columns are in the way.

- Function rooms in older hotels are sometimes too ornate and do not project an atmosphere of learning. Even when the banquet rooms are not ornate, the lobbies and other public areas could be intimidating.

- Lighting can present problems. Ornate chandeliers do not give enough light to allow reading of printed material during a meeting or class.

- Large windows are difficult to black out when overhead projectors are used. The speaker should be able to control the light level and overhead projectors from the podium.

- Windows could be distracting. Windowless classrooms are preferred in North America, whereas Europeans like windows.

- The electrical installations, such as power outlets and strong circuits, may not be adequate.

- Lack of wall space. Conferences need wall space to post reports, graphs, and posters. Many hotel rooms do not have this type of space.

- The acoustics in many older banquet rooms are poor, or the technical installations are not up to date. Many speakers require podiums with microphones, and conferences may also require microphones on the floor. Older hotels do not generally have the necessary speakers and wall jacks.

Expectations of Auxiliary Areas

- Checkrooms are important if the guests are not staying on the property. If the coat room cannot be opened without incurring a large labor cost, coat racks should be provided in the function room.

- Committee tables are usually placed outside conference rooms, and telephones might still be needed to take messages. However, cell phones have fairly well eliminated the necessity of having telephone jacks in corridors.

- Toilet facilities should be able to handle a large crowd during breaks in the meetings.

- Meeting rooms should have built in sideboards to accomodate self-service coffee and soft drinks during the meeting. The refreshments should be replenished automatically during meeting breaks.

Frequent Complaints Made by Meeting Planners

- Meeting rooms too noisy.

- Meeting rooms hard to find, signage poor.

- Lines at checkroom long.

- Literature sent in before the convention hard to find.

- Breakfast late and set up was awkward causing lines delaying the start of the meetings.

- Orange juice not fresh.

- Snacks served during reception too salty causing more beverage consumption than budgeted.

- Sound system poor, microphone for guest speaker had to be replaced.

- Not enough *Banquet Servers* for the farewell dinner.

- Food for breaks boring, all week the same refreshments were served.

- The requested kosher meals took a long time to get served.

- One meeting room was not ready on time, attendees were left standing around.

- Hot main course on buffet luncheon ran out before everybody was served.

- Elevators not adequate to handle large groups.

- Fruits sent to VIP rooms hard, basically inedible.

Food Expectations

In *Conference Centers* breakfast and lunch are most likely self service from permanent buffet stations. Dinner appetizers and desserts are probably served from the buffet and the main course served at the table. Typically there are numerous choices, varying daily. If a conference lasts a number of days, it is a challenge for the chef to provide different meals every day, including breakfast.

Refreshment Breaks

- The area used for refreshment breaks should have windows when the classrooms are windowless. The attendees enjoy seeing daylight and looking out the window to unwind.

- The snack area should have stand up counters. After sitting at a meeting, people like to stand and walk around.

- It is essential that attendees can keep in touch with their offices during breaks. Telephones should be close by, and telephone jacks for computer connectivity enable conference attendees to receive and send email. Normally message boards are also provided.

- Restrooms should be close and adequate to handle the demand.

- It is very important that all food arrangements are very punctual. Most meetings operate with a tight schedule.

- The refreshments should be placed self-service buffets. Satellite buffets for beverages and snacks eliminate lines. Employees must be assigned to maintain the stations. In many conference centers the refreshment area is used by a number of groups and the break times vary. Coffee should be made available every day and replenished every hour.

- The food items should be interesting. Hot beverages are expected as well as juices, mineral waters, soft drinks, fruits, miniature pastries, cheeses, yoghurt, cookies, health drinks, and dry snacks. For the afternoon break a snack item is often served.

- The food selection and buffet setup should vary slightly every day to add interest without confusing the attendees. Depending on group size, cluster buffets and separate beverage stations are advisable to avoid queues.

Summary

The meeting and convention business is an important revenue source for most hotels. The sporadic social banquet business is not enough to justify the investment in space. Unfortunately, in many older hotels the banquet space is not automatically suitable as meeting space. There are many requirements that make meetings successful, and some banquet rooms cannot be adapted easily. For these reasons, some hotels have built specific conference and meeting spaces. Conference centers specialize in meetings. Day conference centers offer only meeting facilities, and provide food service for the conference attendees. Full conference centers operate like hotels, with the emphasis on providing an atmosphere of learning. Conference centers can be serious competition to hotels.

Discussion Questions

- Why is the conference business important to many hotels?

- Who competes for this business?

- Can banquet space be easily adapted for meeting use?

- List some difficulties that can be found in social banquet space.

- Mention meeting room expectations and needs.

- What other areas can contribute to the success of meetings?

- Elaborate on food expectations for meetings.

Appendix A

Samples of Corporate Menu Packages

Section 1: Breakfast

Selections of Breakfast Menus, and Menu Add - Ons.

BKF 1, CONTINENTAL BREAKFAST
Coffee, Tea, Decaffeinated Coffee
Orange Juice
Assorted Breakfast Breads and Bagels

$ XXX per person
$ XXX additional per person for Fresh Sliced Fruit Platter

BKF 2, HEALTHY CHOICE BREAKFAST
Coffee, Tea, Decaffeinated Coffee
Orange Juice
Low-fat Yogurt and Granola
Assorted Dry Cereals
Bran, Corn and Blueberry Muffins
Assorted Fruit Breads
Fresh Sliced Fruit Platter

$ XXX per person

BKF 3, FULL BREAKFAST
Coffee, Tea, Decaffeinated Coffee
Orange Juice
Assorted Breakfast Breads and Bagels
Scrambled Eggs
Bacon, Sausage
Toast, English Muffins
Fresh Sliced Fruit Platter

$ XXX per person

BREAKFAST ADD-ONS
Corned Beef Hash
Cheese Blintzes with Strawberry & Blueberry Sauce
Challah French Toast with Warm Maple Syrup
Hot Cereals: Oatmeal, Cream of Wheat or Farina
Sliced Smoked Nova Scotia Salmon with Cream Cheese
Turkey Bacon or Turkey Sausage
Belgian Waffles
Donuts
Hot Cross Buns
Granola Bars
Coffee Cake
Cinnamon Rolls

$ XXX per person

Section 2. Coffee Breaks

COFFEE BREAK
Coffee, Tea, Decaf
Assorted Sodas
Assorted Cookies

$XXX per person
$ XXX additional per person for Fresh Sliced Fruit Platter

COFFEE BREAK ADD-ONS

Biscotti - Almond and Fruit
Assorted Fruit Fritters
Scones with Devonshire Cream and assorted Jams
Tea Sandwiches
Miniature Pastries and Petits Fours
Brownies and Blondies
Ice Cream Bars or frozen Fruits
Assorted mixed Nuts
Bags of assorted Chips
(Popcorn, Pretzels, Potato Chips, Nachos, and Fritos)
Snapple Beverages
Assorted Miniature Candy Bars

$ XXX per person

Section 3
Luncheons

ITALIAN HOT AND COLD BUFFET LUNCH

Cold Selections

Baby Mozzarella, Cherry Tomato and Green Been Salad
Grilled Tuscan Vegetables
Endive, Radicchio, Romaine, Arugula with Goat Cheese & Walnuts

Hot Selections

Roast Basil Chicken with Wild Mushrooms
Penne with Prosciutto, Onions, Tomato and Ceci Ceci Peas
Foccacia Bread and Breadsticks

DESSERT

Chef's Choice Cake
Biscotti

Coffee, Tea, Decaffeinated Coffee, assorted Cold Beverages

$XX.XX per person

SANDWICH AND SALAD BUFFET LUNCH

Choice of three Salads

Tossed Garden Greens with Vinaigrette and Blue Cheese on the side
Cous Cous with Scallions and Sun Dried Cherries
Orzo with Sun Dried Tomatoes and Toasted Pine Nuts, Basil Vinaigrette
Grilled Vegetable Salad, with Honey Mustard Dressing
French Beans, Red Onion, and Roasted Peppers with Lemon Vinaigrette
Wheat Berry Salad with Raisins and Sun Dried Corn
Old Fashioned Dijon Potato Salad
Cabbage and Ramen Noodle Salad

Choice of four Sandwiches:

Chunk white Meat Tuna Salad
Country Cured Ham
Sliced Rare Roast Beef
Grilled Breast of Chicken Salad
Roast Turkey Breast

Served with Sliced Tomatoes, Pickles, Onions,
Mustard and Mayonnaise on assorted Sliced Breads

DESSERT

Fresh Fruit Platter
Chefs Choice Cake
Assorted Home Baked Cookies
Coffee, Tea, Decaffeinated Coffee, assorted Cold Beverages

$XX.XX per person

ELABORATE SANDWICH MENU

Choice of four Salads

Tossed Garden Greens with Vinaigrette and Blue Cheese on the side
Cous Cous with Scallions and Sun Dried Cherries
Orzo with Sun Dried Tomatoes and Toasted Pine Nuts, Basil Vinaigrette
Grilled Vegetable Salad, with Honey Mustard Dressing
French Beans, Red Onion, and Roasted Peppers with Lemon Vinaigrette
Wheat Berry Salad with Raisins and Sundried Corn
Old Fashioned Dijon Potato Salad
Cabbage and Ramen Noodle Salad

Choice of five Sandwiches

Grilled Breast of Chicken with Arugula, Tomato, Basil & Olive Oil
Shrimp Salad with Tarragon
Grilled Eggplant, Peppers, Zucchini and Mozzarella with Pesto
Rare Roast Beef with Horseradish Sauce
Honey Cured Ham with Gruyere and Honey Mustard
Chunk White Tuna with Roasted Onions and Tomato
Fresh Roast Turkey Breast with Cranberry Relish

DESSERT

Fresh Fruit Platter
Chef's Choice Cake
Assorted Home Baked Cookies
Coffee, Tea, Decaffeinated Coffee, assorted Cold Beverages
$XX.XX per person

LUNCH BUFFET

Make Your Own Deli Sandwich

SILVER PLATTER PRESENTATION OF SLICED
Grilled Chicken Breast
Rare Roast Beef, Fresh Roasted Turkey
Black Forest Ham

SILVER PLATTER PRESENTATION OF SLICED
Aged Vermont Cheddar, Jarlsberg
Havarti with Dill and Provolone Cheese
Served with a variety of Mustards, Mayonnaise,
Sliced Lettuce, Tomatoes, Onions, Olives and Pickles

Whole Grain Rolls, Pumpernickel Rolls, Brick Oven Rolls, and
Onion Sour Dough Rolls

SALADS
Seasonal Green Salad with Vinaigrette and Blue Cheese Dressing
Pasta Salad with Pesto
Green Cabbage & Ramen Noodles
Red Bliss Potato Salad

Sliced Fresh Seasonal Fruit
Chefs Choice Cake
Assorted Cookies

$XX.XX per person

Lunch Selections

FOR A HOT & COLD BUFFET
ADD THE FOLLOWING ITEMS TO THE COLD LUNCH BUFFET

Pan Seared Chicken Breast, Julienne of Leeks and Carrots
Rigatoni with Grilled Vegetables, Roasted Tomato Sauce
Penne with Tomato Vodka Sauce
Pan Seared Canadian Salmon with Lemon Buerre Blanc
Seasonal Vegetable and Starch

All Luncheon Buffets are served with
Coffee, Tea, Decaffeinated Coffee, and assorted Sodas

Please add an additional $XX.XX per person for each entree add-on

Section 4
Package Price Information

Package 1

Full Cocktail Reception

35 Persons and under
Two hour reception
Full Open Bar
Hot & Cold Hors d'Oeuvres
One Cold Display Item (see menu)
Labor Charge and Premise Charge included
Tax included

$XX.XX per person

Package 2

Full Cocktail Reception

35 - 75 persons
Two hour reception
Full Open Bar
Hot & Cold Hors d'Oeuvres
Two Cold Display Items (see menu)
Labor Charge and Premise Charge included
Tax included

$XX.XX per person

Package 3

Full Cocktail Reception

75 - 100 persons
Two hour reception
Full Open Bar
Hot & Cold Hors d'Oeuvres
Two Cold Display Items (see menu)
Labor Charge and Premise Charge included
Tax included

$XX.XX per person

Package 4

Full Cocktail Reception

Over 100 persons
Two hour reception
Full Open Bar
Hot & Cold Hors D'Oeuvres
Two Cold Display Items (see menu)
Labor Charge and Premise Charge included
Tax included

$ XX.XX per person

Package 5

Limited Reception

50 Persons and under
Two hour reception
Beer, Wine and Soda
Crudité with Assorted Dips
Cheese Board Garnished with Fresh Fruit and assorted Bread Display
Labor Charge and Premise Charge included
Tax included

$ XX.XX per person

Package 6

Limited Reception

50 Persons and above
Two hour reception
Beer, Wine and Soda
Crudite with assorted Dips
Cheese Board Garnished with Fresh Fruit and assorted Bread Display
Labor Charge and Premise Charge included
Tax included

$XX.XX per person

Package 7

Non-Alcoholic Reception

50 Persons and below
Two hour reception
Assorted Sodas, Juice and Water
Crudité with assorted Dips
Cheese Board Garnished with Fresh Fruit and assorted Bread Display
Labor Charge and Premise Charge included
Tax included

$XX.XX per person

Package 8

Non-Alcoholic Reception

50 Persons and above
Two hour reception
Assorted Sodas, Juice and Water
Crudité with assorted Dips
Cheese Board Garnished with Fresh Fruit and assorted Bread Display
Labor Charge and Premise Charge included
Tax included

$ XX.XX per person

Please Note

Optional stations will incur an additional per person cost depending on the
amount of people.

Rental items and flowers incur an additional cost.

All functions include house wines. Specialty wines will be priced accordingly.

324

Section 5
Hors d'Oeuvres and Reception Selections

HOT HORS D'OEUVRES

VEGETARIAN SELECTIONS

Roasted Peppers, Tomato and Parmesan
Black Bean Puff with Fresh Coriander
Vegetable Dim Sum (Steamed or Fried)
Three Cheese Pissaladiere
Spanaekopita
Spring Rolls with Spicy Dipping Sauce
Mozzarella, Tomato & Basil on Bruschetta
Parmesan Artichoke Hearts
Goat Cheese Pizza
Assorted Miniature Quiche

SEAFOOD SELECTIONS

Coconut Shrimp served with Sweet and Sour Sauce
Swordfish Kebobs served with Pepper & Teriyaki Sauce
Brochettes of Shrimp & Scallops in a Lemon & Butter Sauce
Mini Crab Cakes served with a Remoulade Sauce
Mushrooms stuffed with Crabmeat
Seafood Strudel
Scallops wrapped with Bacon
Crabmeat Dim Sum (Steamed or Fried)

POULTRY SELECTIONS

Chicken Sate with Peanut Sauce
Sesame Chicken with a Sweet and Sour Sauce
Buffalo Style Chicken Wings served with Blue Cheese, Carrots, & Celery
Herb Roasted Chicken Tenderloins
Ginger Teriyaki Chicken Brochettes
Chicken and Mushrooms in Phyllo

LAMB, BEEF AND PORK

Miniature Reuben Sandwiches
Skewered Beef Teriyaki with Snow Peas & Water Chestnuts
Cocktail Meatballs with Sweet & Sour Sauce or Swedish Style
Empanaditas with Salsa
Miniature Frankfurters in a Blanket
Hot Mustard Pork Tenderloin
Cajun Marinated Steak on Skewer served with Barbecue Sauce

COLD HORS D'OEUVRES

Roasted Yukon Gold Potato with Sun Dried Tomato and Cream Cheese
Smoked Turkey with Cranberry Relish Tartelettes
Endive leaves filled with Chicken and Wild Mushrooms
Smoked Salmon and Dill, Tartar on Pumpernickel
Seasonal Melon & Prosciutto
Shrimp Mousse on Vinegared Rice and Pickled Ginger
Regular Mozzarella, Tomato & Fresh Basil Kebobs
Orange Sesame Beef in Cucumber
Asparagus rolled with Prosciutto di Parma
Chicken with Figs & Prosciutto in Tartelette Shell
Herbed Goat Cheese & Tomato Crostini
Tenderloin of Beef on Tuscany Toast with Horseradish
Chicken Guacamole on grilled Polenta Cakes
Fruit Kebobs

COLD DISPLAYS
All served with appropriate Garnish

Crudite with assorted Dips
Antipasto Display (assorted Meats, Cheese & Vegetables)
Cheese Board Garnished with Fresh Fruit and assorted Bread Display
Smoked Nova Scotia Salmon with appropriate Condiments
Poached Salmon with Sauce Verte
Japanese Handrolls
Iced Shrimp Display served with Lemons and a Cocktail Sauce
Caviar with appropriate Condiments

PASTA STATION (Choice of Sauce)
An Additional $ XX.XX per person

Tortellini with Cheese
Penne   Capellini
Rigatoni   Agnolotti

SAUCE SELECTIONS

Marinara
Filetto de Pomodore (Prosciutto and Fresh Basil)
Wild Mushrooms and Herbs in a light Veloute
A la Vodka
Herb Primavera
Fresh Tomato with Sausage and Parsley

CARVING STATION

Roast Turkey Breast with appropriate Condiments
Peppercorn Seared Beef Tenderloin
House Cured Gravlax
Barbecued Pork Loin
Marinated Boneless Breast of Capon
Barbecued Brisket of Beef
$ X.XX per person additional

ORIENTAL STATION

Peking Duck with Crepes, Cucumber & Scallions
Pad Thai Noodle or Bean Thread Noodle with Shrimp or Chicken
Crispy Noodles
Fortune Cookies
$ X.XX per person additional

Section 6: Reception and Dinner Packages

Reception & Dinner

20 Persons and under

Reception includes:
Hot & Cold Hors D'Oeuvres to be passed and open bar
45 minutes
Four Course Sit Down Dinner
Red and White House wines
Labor Charge and Premise Charge included
Tax included
Price based on selected main course

$XX.XX to $XX.XX per person

Reception & Dinner

20 - 40 persons

Arrangements the same as above
Price based on selected main course

$XX.XX to $XX.XX per person

Reception & Dinner

40 - 60 persons

Arrangements the same as above
Price based on selected main course

$XX.XX to $XX.XX per person

Reception & Dinner

60 - 80 persons

Arrangements the same as above
Price based on selected main course

$XX.XX to $XX.XX per person

Reception & Dinner

80 - 100 persons

Arrangements the same as above
Price based on selected main course

Please see menus to follow

Please Note: Rental items, Flowers, and Specialty wines will be charged additionally.

Section 7
Dinner Suggestions

Package A1

Appetizer
Lobster and Chanterelle Strudel with Lobster Beurre Blanc.

Salad
Mesclun Salad with Raspberry Vinaigrette

Entree
Grilled Filet Mignon served with Frizzled Leeks and Red Wine Demi Glace
or
Grilled Sirloin Steak
Chef's Choice Vegetable & Starch

Dessert
Assorted Sorbet Medley
Assorted Cookies
Coffee, Tea, Decaffeinated Coffee

Package A2

Appetizer
Penne Pasta, with Vodka and Tomato Cream

Salad
Arugula and Endives served with Lemon Vinaigrette

Entree
Grilled Swordfish with Fresh Herbs and Air Dried Tomatoes
Roasted Shallot Sauce
Asparagus
Potatoes Dauphine

Dessert
Tuile with Assorted Mixed Berries & Creme à l'Anglaise
assorted Cookies
Coffee, Tea, Decaffeinated Coffee

330

Package A3

Appetizer
Grilled Portabello Mushrooms with Field Lettuce with Balsamic Vinaigrette
Warm Crusted Goat Cheese

Entree
Fillet Turbot or Red Snapper served with Five-Spice Napa Cabbage
Cous Cous with seasonal Herbs
Asparagus, Orange Hollandaise Sauce

Dessert
Frozen Coffee and Praline Tranche
Bourbon Sauce
Assorted Cookies
Coffee, Tea, Decaffeinated Coffee

Package A4

Appetizer
Parma Prosciutto with shaved Parmesan Cheese
Marinated Mozzarella and crisp Lettuce
Basil Vinaigrette

Entree
North Atlantic Salmon in a crisp Potato Crust
Balsamic Vinegar Reduction
Basmati Rice
Melange of Baby Vegetables

Dessert
Crème Brulée
Assorted Cookies
Coffee, Tea, Decaffeinated Coffee

Package A5

Appetizer
Citrus Marinated Grilled Sea Scallops with Julienne of Vegetables

Salad
Lamb's Lettuce with grilled Porcini Mushroom and Asparagus

Entree
Roast Rack of Lamb with Rosemary
Dauphinoise Potatoes
Sautéed Spinach and Eggplants

Dessert
Chocolate Velvet Mousse Cake
Assorted Cookies
Coffee, Tea, Decaffeinated Coffee

Package A6

Appetizer
Buck Wheat Blini with Smoked Salmon and Salmon Caviar

Salad
Grilled Zucchini and Roasted Peppers
Chardonnay Vinaigrette

Entree
Grilled Veal Chop or Veal Medallions with Wild Mushroom Ragout
Haricots Verts and Vegetable Medley
Roasted Shallot Mashed Potatoes

Dessert
Warm Apple Strudel with Cinnamon Ice Cream
Assorted Cookies
Coffee, Tea, Decaffeinated Coffee

Package A7

Appetizer
Fresh Mozzarella, Vine ripened Tomatoes and Seasonal Greens
Drizzled Extra Virgin Olive Oil with Cracked Black Pepper

Entree
Boneless Chicken Piccata and Shrimp
sautéed with Lemon and White Wine
Sugar Snap Peas, Pilaff Rice Starch

Dessert
California Fruit Tart served with Angelica Zabaglione Sauce
Assorted Cookies
Coffee, Tea, Decaffeinated Coffee

Package A8

Appetizer
Warm Hazelnut Crusted Brie Cheese
Frisée and Radicchio Lettuces

Entree
Sea Bass Fillet with Artichoke Ragout
Parsley Sauce and Tomato Coulis
Jasmine Rice
Seasonal Vegetables

Dessert
Alsacian Apple Tart with Fresh Raspberries
Vanilla Sauce
Assorted Cookies
Coffee, Tea, Decaffeinated Coffee

Package A9

Appetizer
Penne Pasta with Gulf Shrimp, Roasted Tomatoes and Herbs

Salad
Traditional Caesar Salad

Entree
Grilled Chicken Breast stuffed with Leeks and Mushrooms
Natural Chicken Jus
Root Vegetable Medley
Roasted Fingerling Potatoes

Dessert
Bitter and Sweet Chocolate Terrine
Custard Sauce with Grand Marnier
Assorted Cookies
Coffee, Tea, Decaffeinated Coffee

Section 9
Buffet Dinner Prices and Choices

B1, Buffet Dinner

For 20 Persons and under

Choice from accompanying menu:
Cold salad, three entrees, vegetable and starch
Cakes, cookies and fresh sliced fruit
Assorted hot & cold beverages
Red and white house wines

$XX.XX to XX,XX per person
Tax, Labor Charge, and Premise Charge included

B2, Buffet Dinner
For 20 - 40 persons

Selection as above

$XX.XX to XX.XXper person

B3, Buffet Dinner
For 40 - 60 persons

Selection as above

$ XX.XX to XX.XX per person

B4, Buffet Dinner
For 60 - 80 persons

Selection as above

$XX.XX to XX.XX per person

B5, Buffet Dinner
For 80 - l00 persons

Selection as above

$XX.XX to XX.XX per person

Buffet
MENU # 1

California Mesclune Salad with Champagne Vinaigrette
****

Boneless Breast of Chicken with Sage and Brown Chicken Jus
and
Red Snapper with Fennel and Tomato

Four Cheese Agnolotti with Sun Dried Tomato Basil & Olive Oil
Saffron Rice
****

Bread Display with Butter
****

Assorted Cakes and Cookies
Sliced Fruit Display
Regular and Decaffeinated Coffee
Select Teas

Buffet
MENU #2

Caesar Salad with Croutons and Parmesan Cheese
****

Roast Turkey Breast
and
Grilled Salmon with Grain Mustard Sauce
Ratatouille
Roasted Shallot Mashed Potatoes
****

Bread Display with Butter
****

Assorted Cakes and Cookies
Sliced Fruit Display
Regular and Decaffeinated Coffee
Select Teas

Buffet

MENU #3

Bibb, Endive and Watercress with Raspberry Vinaigrette
****

Grilled Herb Chicken Breast with Coriander & Turmeric
Roasted Shallot Sauce
and
Penne with Roasted Eggplant, Tomatoes and Zucchini

Roasted Red Bliss Potatoes
Grilled Asparagus, Carrots with Dill and Parsley with Orange Butter
****

Bread Display with Butter
****

Assorted Cakes and Cookies
Sliced Fruit Display
Regular and Decaffeinated Coffee
Select Teas

Appendix B

Luxury Hotel
Banquet Event Sheets (BEOs)

Sample of a fairly typical hotel meeting arrangement. The banquet salesperson used the silly cliché *Freshly squeezed* in connection with juices. I have yet to find a chef who will squeeze cranberries and tomatoes. The coffee break menus are the bare minimum and are usually much better in conference centers.

Elegant Corporate Meeting and Luncheon

Luftwasser & Jenkins, Inc.
PA: Nasdaq Research
Continental Breakfast, Meeting
Breakout, Coffee Break
Approximately 175 guests
Ms. Denise Krakauer in charge

Wednesday, November 20, 2005
Continental Breakfast 7:00 AM to
8:00 AM Park Avenue Room
Meeting 8:00 to 5:00 PM Ballroom
Breakout 8:00 AM to 5:00 PM B Room
Coffee Break 9:15 AM Garden Foyer
Lunch 12:00 to 2:00 PM Trianon Room
Coffee Break 3:00 to 3:25 PM Rotunda

Note: Have available 75 Wall Street Journals, 30 New York Times and 40 Financial Times. Charge $ XX and add to the account.

At 7:00 AM in the Park Avenue Room
Continental Breakfast

Selection of freshly squeezed Orange, Grapefruit and Cranberry Juice
Assortment of Homemade Muffins: Corn, Blueberry, Carrot, and Raspberry
Jelly, Jams, Marmalade
Gâteau Bretonne, Raisin Bread, Lemon Pound Cake
Assorted Yoghurt, Granola
Baskets of whole Fruits
Assorted Bagels, Cream Cheese, Sliced Smoked Salmon
Doughnuts
Coffee, Cream, Decaffeinated Coffee

$ XX per person

At 9:15 AM in the Garden Foyer
Morning Break

Coffee, Selection of Teas, Decaffeinated Coffee
Assorted Soft drinks and Mineral Waters

$ XX per person

At 12:00 PM in the Trianon Room
Lunch
Pre-set on all tables Thermal pots of coffee, Iced Tea, Mineral Waters, Rolls, Butter,
Coffee Cups and Saucers, Cream and Sugar

Grilled peppered Shrimp with White Bean Salad, Lemon Mustard Sauce

Petit Filet Mignon, Sauce Bordelaise
Sautéed baby Artichokes and Tomatoes, Puréed Potatoes with Herbs

Have 1 vegetarian **and** 3 Kosher Meals available
*****
Chocolate Cake, Espresso Sauce
Petits Fours

$ XX per person

At 3:00 in the Rotunda
Afternoon Break

Coffee, Assortment of Teas, Decaffeinated Coffee
Assorted Soft Drinks and Mineral Waters
Assorted Cookies

$ XX per person

Extra Items and Arrangements: See separate sheet

Wedding Event Sheet

In Honor of Ms. Barbara Johns &
Mr. Ludwig Schleser
Wedding Reception and Dinner Dance

Approximately 175 Guests
Mr. Frederick Johns in charge

Saturday, June 24, 2005
Photos: 6:30 PM in the Gazebo
Reception 7:30 PM – 8:30 PM
Garden Foyer
Dinner Dance 8:30 PM- 1:30 AM
Petite Ballroom

China: Showplate supplied by Green Leaf Florist

Reception at 7:30 PM in the Garden Foyer

Hors d'Oeuvres and Canapés
Passed Butler style
(Please make sure all are bite-size)

HOT

Miniature Veal Burgers with Mustard Bèarnaise
Miniature Spring Rolls
Miniature Roasted Shallot Tartines with Goat Cheese
Miniature Peking Duck Pancakes with Hoisin Sauce

****

Crêpes with Beluga Caviar
New Potatoes with Caviar and Sour Cream
Roasted Vegetables on Rosemary Focaccia
Bows of Cocktail Shrimp with Dipping Sauces

****

Dinner At 7:30 PM in the Petite Ballroom

Selection of assorted Breads and Rolls
Parmesan Cheese Toast

****

Cold Medallions of Lobster with red and yellow Pear Tomatoes
Served over Mediterranean Vegetables
Plated, very decorative
(Lobster slightly smaller in size than at the tasting)

****

Entrees Choices:

Sliced Chauteaubriand
Haricots verts tied with Leek Ribbon
Baby Carrots with Stems
Rosemary Mashed Potatoes in Potato Basket

– or –

Herb crusted Chilean Sea Bass
Served over Julienne of Vegetables

****

Vegetarian Entrees available upon request

Raspberry, Lemon and Passion Fruit Sorbets
Served in Pastry Basket
Decorated with Raspberries, Blueberries and Raspberry Coulis
Topped with Caramel Cage
(Decorative Plate)

****

Wedding Cake
(Supplied by XYC)
(Serve after dessert at approximately 11:30 PM)

****

Petits Fours and Cookies
Chocolate covered Orange Peels and Candied Orange Peels
Almond Macaroons and Chocolate Truffles
(Use special tiered Silver Stands)

****

Coffee, Tea, Brewed Decaffeinated Coffee
Offered at the tables

****

**$ XXX.XX per person for food and beverages
Wine and Champagne charged as consumed.
20% service charge will be added to the total bill of which 15% is paid to hourly
employees and 5% to sales and supervisory personnel.**

Extra Items and Arrangements:

Set Up:

By Diagram

Beverages:

During the reception we will have 4 complete bars set up for the service of the following: Dewars, Johnnie Walker Black, Seagreams VO, Jack Daniels, Old Grand Dad, Ketel One, Belvedere, Absolute Vodka, Bombay Sapphire Gin, Single Malts - McAllen 18 year, Longmorn Glenlivet Scotch, Dry Sherry, Fruit Juices, Mineral Water, Coke, Diet Coke, 7 Up, Heineken Beer, Samuel Adams Beer, Far Niente, Grgich Hills Cabernet Sauvignon, Perrier Jouet Fleur de Champagne.

Martinis to be available.
4 Bartenders – included
Pass Champagne, White Wine and Mineral water during the reception.

During dinner offer San Pelligrino and Vitell water to all guests.

Selection of Wines & Champagnes charged as consumed:
White Wine: Far Niente Chardonnay 1998 @ $ XXX per bottle.
Red Wine: Grgich Hills Cabernet Sauvignon, 1994 @ $ XXX per bottle.
Champagne: Perrier Jouet Fleur de Champagne 1995 @ $ XXX per bottle.

After-dinner cordials and single malt Scotches to be offered.

The legal age for the sale of alcoholic beverages is 21. Please be advised that alcoholic beverages will not be served to persons under the legal age. Proof of age will be requested when necessary.

Linen:	Reception: Hotel to provide ivory floor length cloths. Dinner Linen by: Green Leaf Florist.
Flowers:	By: Green leaf Florist.
Candles:	By: Honeybee.
Amplifications:	Microphone for ceremony.
Photography/Video:	By: Andy Snapshot.
Music:	By: George Upbeat.
Check Room:	Fully staffed, included. No Tipping Sign displayed.
Lounges:	Fully staffed, included.
Electrician:	Available.
Service notes:	White tie and tails required.

Arrangements by: Frederic de Cavalero Ingnazio. 6/1/2001. BEO 0017783

Accepted:

Date:

Event Order Sheet Sample
for
Commercial Dinner and Reception

Makemoney.com
Certificate Department
Reception, Dinner
Approximately 50 guests
Ms Leslie Jones in charge
China: Lennox

Monday, October 39, 2003
Reception: 6:00 PM – 6:45 PM Salon
Dinner: 6:45 PM – 9:15 PM Rose Room

Hors d'Oeuvres and Canapés
Served in the Salon

Passed butler style

Hot

Assorted Dim Sum with Soy Dipping Sauce
Baby Artichoke Beignets
Phyllo Bundles of Lobster and Shiitake Mushrooms
Coconut Fried Shrimp

****

Cold

Baby Mozzarella with Sun Dried Tomatoes
Endives filled with Boursin Cheese and Orange Zest
Roulade of Chicken with Herb Cheese on Corn Bread
Rillettes of Duck and Shiitake on Herb Brioche

****

Dinner at 6:45 PM in the Rose Room

Parmesan Cheese Toast (passed)
Selection of assorted Breads and Rolls

Herb Goat Cheese and Tomato Tart
Arugula Salad

****

Tournedos of Veal with Calvados Reduction
Sautéed Spinach and Leeks, Wild Rice with Pine Nuts and Currants

****

Individual hot Apple Charlotte with Cinnamon Whipped Cream
Calvados Sauce, fried Apple Skins

****

Petits Fours and Cookies

Coffee, Tea, Brewed Decaffeinated Coffee

$ XXXXX per person for Food and Bar
20% gratuity will be added to the total bill of which 15% is paid to hourly person-
nel and 5% to sales and supervisory employees.

Extra Items and Arrangements:

Set –Up: By Diagram.

Beverages: During the reception we will have 1 complete
                            bar set up for the service of the following
                            items: Dewars, Johnny Walker Black,
                            Seagrams VO, Jack Daniels, Old Grand Dad,
                            Ketel One, Asolut Vodka, Bombay Sapphire
                            Gin, Dry Sherry, Fruit Juices, Mineral water,
                            Coke, Diet Coke, 7-Up, Heineken Beer,
                            Samuel Adams Beer, Canyon Road
                            Chardonnay, Cambria Pinot Noir.

                            1 Bartender at $ XXX.

                            Selection of Wines:
                            White Wine: Frog's Leap Chardonnay @ $ XX
                            per bottle.
                            Red Wine: Markham Merlot @ $ XXX per
                            bottle.

Linen: Ivory with Ivory Napkins.

Flowers: Rosebud Florist to provide centerpieces @
                            $XXXX per arrangement for each dinner table.

Candles: Hotel to provide 5 votive candles for each table
                            complimentary.

China: Lennox Rose pattern.

Amplification: Podium and Microphone in the Rose Room.

Audio Visual: By: Clearview Company to be charged directly to client.

Checkroom: $ X per person added to the account based on guarantee or number of guests attending, whichever is greater. No Tipping Sign displayed.

Lounges: Attendant not required.

Electrician: None.

Service Notes: None.

Arrangements by: Melissa Smart booked 3/29/2000, code 666XyZ – BEO 0006453

Accepted: **Date:**

Note: The extra items and arrangements are explicit and leave no room for error.

The menu is not well balanced. Herb cheese, Shiitake mushrooms, and Calvados are used twice on the same menu. This should not happen in a luxury hotel unless requested by the client.

Appendix C

Sample of a Typical Convention Resume
in a Resort Hotel

Page

Section 1

Convention Resumé,
Program and General Information

The Tall Timber Resort

ARMAR CORP RESEARCH GROUP
JULY 9-12, 2002
ARMC0 Convention Resume

In Charge of Arrangements: Attendance: 56 Persons

ARMAR CORP RESEARCH GROUP, WRITERS FORUM
MR. SAMUEL L. ADABEI, PRESIDENT
300 PARK AVENUE SUITE 1100
ALLENTOWN, CA 90097
PH   # (604) 555 - 0331
FAX # (604) 555 - 4274
Tall Timber Resort Coordinators:
Conference: Julius Precise
Reservation: Brenda Keyless
Sales: Mary Helpful
SPECIAL NOTE: See comments in Audio/Visual Section

In House Client Contact: Mr. Samuel Adabei

The following 2002 Modified American Plan rates per person to apply:

	Double	Single
Minimum	$ 247.00	$ 461.00
Intermediate	$ 279.00	$ 524.00
Superior	$ 304.00	$ 574.00
One-bedroom Suite	$ 390.00	$ 750.00
Lakeside Villa	$ 352.00	$ 670.00

GROUP BIOGRAPHY

This is a meeting of the individuals charged with overseeing the management of the food writer's division of the ARMAR CORPORATION. This is a return visit for the group.

The Tall Timber Resort

Armco Convention Resumé

VIPS:

Mr. Francisco Muñez, Chairman
Mr. Rod M. Steiger
Ms. Claudia Del Giocomo
Mr. Frederic Overland, Jr.

MEAL PLAN

The above group is to be registered on the Modified American Plan, which includes breakfast in the Main Dining Room or Evergreen Cafe and dinner in the Main Dining Room or Clubhouse Grill. Guests using Truffle's restaurant for dinner will be charged $ 40.00 additional.

GENERAL ACCOUNT

The Tall Timber Resort billing coordinator - Ms. Rosie Counter, Ext. 9258

A master or General Account is to be established to which certain charges are to be billed. 90% of the total bill is due upon receipt of the invoice and the remaining 10% can be retained should there be any questionable items. This will provide an opportunity to check all items in detail prior to making final payment. To avoid a finance charge, balance is payable within 30 days from the billing date. Account balances not paid within 30 days will accrue at an annual interest rate of 18%. This account, at the conclusion of the meeting, is to be billed to Mr. SAMUEL ADABEI at the above address.

SERVICE CHARGE

The Tall Timber Resort pays certain employees service fees in lieu of the normal gratuities. This includes room maids, servers, bus boys, roll girls and dining room captains. A daily service charge of $22.00 per person is added to each account for service provided under the Modified American Plan. For all à la carte food and beverage service, 17.5% will be added to the check.

To award an individual for superior service, a guest may leave cash or indicate "special gratuity" on the check while noting the amount. This will be added to the guest's room account.

The Tall Timber Resort
Armco Convention Resumé

ARRIVALS/DEPARTURES

All attendees are individually responsible for making any necessary transportation arrangements.

LATE ARRIVALS/EARLY DEPARTURES

Please note late arrival or early departure causes forfeiture of deposit, unless cancellations or changes are made 15 days in advance of scheduled arrival date.

AUDIO VISUAL

All audio visual equipment is to be billed to the individual presenter who is making the request. No A/V charges are to go to the General Account.

EMERGENCY PROCEDURE

In the event of an emergency (accident) relating to a member of this group, please notify Mr. SAMUEL ADABEI, Group Contact.

BANQUET POLICIES

For all receptions and hospitality functions scheduled in public areas, **The Tall Timber Resort** service personnel are required. In these cases, a $10.00 per person setup charge will apply for each two-hour period. The setup charge covers the cost of bar service, ice, glasses, mixers (soda, tonic water, mineral water, cola, lemon-lime, ginger-ale, orange juice, bloody mary mix), peanuts, pretzels and potato chips. Liquor, wine, and beer will be charged as consumed at prevailing hotel prices. A final attendance figure for morning and lunch functions must be specified 24 hours in advance. Attendance figures for evening functions must be specified by 3:00 PM the day before.

If an event is scheduled outdoors and there is a threat of inclement weather, please inform your *Conference Service Manager* as to your desire to relocate to an alternate location at least three hours prior to the event. If a decision has not been made, your *Conference Service Manager* will make a decision that is best for your guests. A service charge of 17.5% and state sales tax of 6% will be added to all food and beverage charges. For any function at a location outside the main building a $200.00 catering fee will apply.

The Tall Timber Resort

The Tall Timber Resort
Armco Convention Resumé

HOURS FOR MEAL SERVICE:

6:30 -10:00 AM	Breakfast Buffet	Evergreen Cafe
7:30 -10:00 AM	Breakfast	Main Dining Room
10:00 -11:00 AM	À la Carte Breakfast	Evergreen Cafe

No reservations required.

11:30 AM - 2:00 PM	À la Carte luncheon	Clubhouse Grill
11:30 AM - 5:00 PM	À la Carte luncheon	Evergreen Cafe
11:30 AM - 4:30 PM	À la Carte luncheon	Outdoor Pool

No reservations required.

5:30 - 7:30 PM	Dinner	Evergreen Cafe
6:30 - 9:00 PM	Dinner	Main Dining Room
6:30 - 9:30 PM	Dinner	Clubhouse Grill
7:00 - 9:30 PM	À la Carte dinner	Truffle's Restaurant

Reservations required. Please call the Dining Room Manager's office before 5:00 PM on ext. 8267.

ALL TALL TIMBERS DINING OUTLETS ARE NON-SMOKING.

Room service is open 24 hours. Please order breakfast prior to midnight the day before.

ROOM SERVICE HOURS:

7:00 AM -11:00 AM	Breakfast	Included in Modified American Plan
11: 00 AM -12:OO Noon	Breakfast	À la Carte
12:00 Noon - 7:00 PM	Luncheon	À la Carte
6:45PM - 9:30 PM	Dinner included in Modified American Plan	
9:30 PM - 12:00 AM	Late Supper	À la Carte
12:00 AM - 6:30 AM	Late Night	À la Carte

A Room Service charge of $3.45 per person in the hotel and $4.45 in Lakeside Villas will apply to all Room Service food orders.

The Tall Timber Resort
Armco Convention Resumé

INDIVIDUAL BILLING SCHEDULE

Below indicates the individual billing instructions for the attendees' room accounts:

.... All charges listed below to be billed to the individual account

.... All charges listed below to be billed to the general account

.... Only charges marked below to be billed to the general account

ROOM
    Room & Tax
    Service Charge
    ABC Membership
    Spouse Rate/Service Charge
    Children's Rate/Service Charge
    Early Arrivals/Late Departures

FOOD
    A la Carte Lunches
    Room Service
    Mini Bar Refreshments
    A la Carte Dinner (Truffle's Restaurant)

BEVERAGES
    All Beverage Charges
    Golf Course Beverages

TRANSPORTATION (Ground)
    Transportation In
    Transportation Out

MISCELLANEOUS
    All Business Center Charges
    Computer Usage
    Laundry
    Long Distance Telephone Calls
    Shop Purchases

The Tall Timber Resort
Armco Convention Resumé

THE TALL TIMBER RESORT SPORTS
- All Golf Charges
- Green Fees
- Carts
- Lessons
- Rental Clubs
- All Tennis Charges
- Court Fees
- Lessons
- Rental Rackets
- Bowling
- Croquet
- Fishing
- Children's Program

SPA/SALON
- All Spa Charges
- Spa Exercise Room
- All Salon Charges
- Manicure/Pedicure/Facial

RECREATIONAL VENDORS
- Outdoor Adventures
- Nature Hike

Section 2. Comprehensive Daily Events Program

The Tall Timber Resort
Armco Convention Resumé

D A I L Y   E V E N T S
WEDNESDAY, JULY 09

12:08 PM. 4:30 PM. Golf Tee Time   16 Guests **- The Tall Timber Resort** course
BEO# 100143

6:30 PM. 8:00 PM. Reception   55 Guests - West View Lounge & Terrace
BEO# 100146

8:00 PM. 9:00 PM.
Delivery/Room Service   4 Guests - Room Deliveries
BEO# 100145

8:00 PM. 10:00 PM. Dinner   55 Guests - Main Dining Room
BEO# 100147

D A I L Y   E V E N T S
THURSDAY, JULY 10

7:00 AM. 7:30 AM. Delivery/Bellstand   5 Orders - Rose Room
BEO# 110996

8:00 AM. 12:00 PM. Meeting   25 Guests - Rose Room
BEO# 100149

10:01 AM. 2:30 PM. Golf Tee Time   8 Guests - Blue Mountain Course
BEO# 104884

12:34 PM. 5:00 PM. Golf Tee Time   20 Guests - Blue Mountain Course
BEO# 100150

6:30 PM. 8:00 PM. Reception   65 Guests - Jade Room
BEO# 100151

8:00 PM. 10:00 PM. Dinner   65 Guests - Main Dining Room
BEO# 100152

The Tall Timber Resort
Armco Convention Resumé

DAILY EVENTS
FRIDAY, JULY 11

8:00 AM. 12:00 PM. Meeting   25 Guests - Rose Room
BEO# 100153

10:01 AM. 2:30 PM. Golf Tee Time   8 Guests Running - Brook Course
BEO# 104887

12:34 PM. 5:00 PM. Golf Tee Time   20 Guests Running - Brook Course
BEO# 100155

6:30 PM. 8:00 PM. Reception   45 Guests - Greenhouse Patio
BEO# 100156

8:00 PM. 10:00 PM. Dinner   45 Guests - Main Dining Room
BEO# 100157

DAILY EVENTS
SATURDAY, JULY 12

8:00 AM. 12:00 PM. Meeting   12 Guests - Rose Room
BEO# 100158

Appendix D

**Comprehensive Convention Package
with Daily Event Sheets (BEOs)
including recreational activities**

The Tall Timber Resort

Resumé and Banquet Event Order Distribution

ARMAR CORP. Group Wednesday July 09 to Saturday July 12, 2002

Full Resumé:

General Manager (2)
Resident Manager (2)
Front Office (4)
Accounting (2)
Bell Staff (1)
Security (2)
Convention Service (4)
Business Center (1)

Full Resumé and all BEOs:

Food and Beverage Director (2)
Housekeeping (2)
Chef's Office (6)
Purchasing (1)
Beverage Service (2)
Dining Room Manager (4)
Golf Pro (4)
Bellstand (2)
Room Service (2)
Housemen (3)
Banquet Service (3)
Sunflower Decorators (2)
Computer Room (2)

The Tall Timbers Resort
Individual Banquet Event Order

BEO# 100143
As of: 6/13/2002
Contact: Mr. Samuel Adabei
The Tall Timber Contact: Julius Precise
Location:
Code: ARMCO
Billing: Individual Responsibility

Date: Wed. July 9, 2002
Group: Armar Corp.
Time: 12:08 P M - 4:30 PM
The Tall Timber Resort Course
Function: Golf Tee Time
Count: 16 Golfers

Food And Beverage:
   All Food & Beverage Charges (Beverage Carts & Halfway Houses) are individual responsibility.

RECREATION:

Golf Tee Times:
   The following Tee Times have been reserved directly through the Central Starting Office, ext. 8001.

Four (4) tee times - 12:08, 12:17, 12:26, 12:35pm - The Tall Timber Resort Course

   From this date until 30 days prior to your arrival, you may cancel up to 20% of your starting times without penalty. A $200 per-starting-time fee will be billed if more than 20% of your times are cancelled.

   From 30 days to 7 days prior to your arrival, you may cancel an additional 10% of your starting times without penalty. A $300 per-starting-time fee will be billed if more than 10% of your times are cancelled.

   Less than 7 days prior to your arrival, you will be billed $400 for any cancelled or unused starting times, less one gratis time per day.

   To be certain clubs will be loaded on golf cart prior to play, it is imperative that Central Starting Office receive first & last names of players & rental club requirements by 6:00 PM the day prior by calling (793) 778 1770, Fax (793) 778 1771.

The Tall Timber Resort
Individual Banquet Event Order

BEO# 100146
As of: 9/13/2001
Contact: Mr. Samuel Adabei
The Tall Timber Contact: Julius Precise
Cocktail Reception

Date: Wed. July 9, 2002
Group: ARMAR CORP.
Time: 6:30 PM - 8:00 PM
Location: West View
Lounge and Terrace

Code: ARMCO
Billing: Writers Forum

Count: 55 Guests

BANQUET SET UP:

The reception to be set in the West View Lounge according to diagram with group flowing onto terrace (weather permitting).

FOOD:

Cold Canapes passed Butler Style:

Puff Pastry Roll with Seafood Louis
Endive Leaves with Oven Roasted Tomatoes and Basil Cheese
Pinwheel of Garden Vegetables with Blue Cheese and Garlic Dip
Smoked Colorado Brook Trout with Horseradish Cream

2 Bowls of Jumbo 50 Gulf Shrimp with Cocktail and Louis Sauces
$ 126.00 per Bowl

Hot Hors d'Oeuvres passed Butler Style:

Maryland Crab Cakes, Light Remoulade Sauce
Pork Egg Roll with Hot Mustard Sauce
Skewered Chicken Tenderloin with Raspberry Salsa

CHARGES:

Food Reception at $ 25.00 per person for up to a 2-hour period.
Beverages charged as consumed as per hotel liquor price list.
17.5% Service Charge and 6% State Sales Tax will be added to the account.

The Tall Timber Resort
Individual Banquet Event Order

Continuation of BEO# 100146

Date: Wednesday July 9, 2002

MUSIC:

None Required.

FLOWERS/DECOR:

One Buffet Table Arrangement per Sunflowers Decorators at $ 60.00 each

ACCOUNTING:

Kindly charge: Writers Forum
Mr. Lou Spender
555 Park Avenue
Newark, NJ 08805
(908) 777 8675
Fax (908) 777 8504

The Tall Timber Resort
Individual Banquet Event Order

BEO# 100145
As of: 1/24/2002
Contact: Mr. Samuel Adabei
The Tall Timber Contact: Julius Precise
Location:
Code: ARMCO
Function:
Billing: Mr. Matt Grande Jr.

Date: Wednesday July 9. 2002
Group: ARMAR CORP.

Guest Rooms

Delivery/Room Service
Count: 4

FOOD AND BEVERAGE:

The following items are required for delivery:

4 (four) each **The Tall Timber Resort** logo baskets featuring a full bottle of **The Tall Timber Resort** pinot noir, apples, grapes, cheddar cheese, flat bread, spiced pecans, and **TheTall Timber Resort** chocolate bar.

$ 60.00 per basket

Plus 17.5% service charge and 6% State Sales Tax

NOTE:
(4) note cards (supplied by computer room).

Please deliver one logo basket and one note card to each of the following rooms:

      Mr. and Mrs. Franz Wielander
      Mr. ans Mrs. Gregory Peck
      Mr. and Mrs. Paul Herkheimer
      Mr. and Mrs. Jonathan Rostov

COMPUTER ROOM:

Please create four (4) small Pink Rose note cards to read as follows:

Compliments of:
Dick, Dixie, Matt & Barbara

Charge of $1.00 per note card to apply.

364

The Tall Timber Resort
Individual Banquet Event Order

BEO#100147
As of: 6/13/2002
Contact: Mr. Samuel Adabei
The Tall Timber Contact: Julius Precise
Event:
Code: ARMCO
Billing: Room account

Date: Wednesday July 9, 2000
Group: ARMAR CORP.
Time: 7:30 PM
Location: Main Dining Room
Function: Dinner
Count: 55 customers

DINING ROOM MANAGER:

Dinner reservations have been made by the conference office. Please call the Dining Room Manager's office, ext. 8236 if any changes or special requests are necessary.

The group requests adjacent tables of 10.

Please note that a few of these attendees will be non-registered guests. A rate of $70.00 per person, plus service charge and tax to apply. Room Captain to ask group contact, Mr. Samuel Adabei to identify these people.

SOMMELIER:

Please note that all beverages are individual responsibility.

Note: All **The Tall Timber Resort** dining outlets are non-smoking.

The Tall Timbers Resort
Individual Banquet Event Order

BEO#110996
As of: 6/13/2002
Contact: Mr. Samuel Adabei
The Tall Timber Contact: Julius Precise
Event:
Code: ARMCO
Billing: Mr. Samuel Adabei

Date: Thursday July 10, 2002
Group: ARMAR CORP.
Time: 7:00 AM - 7:30 AM
Location: Rose Room
Function: Delivery/Bellstand
Count: 5 Customers

FOOD AND BEVERAGE:

The following items are required for delivery:

5 (five) each **The Tall Timber Resort** logo baskets featuring a full bottle of **The Tall Timber Resort** pinot noir, apples, grapes, cheddar cheese, flat bread, spiced pecans and **The Tall Timber Resort** chocolate bar.

$ 60.00 per basket

Plus 17.5% service charge and 6% State Sales Tax

5 (five) Note Cards (supplied by computer room)

Please deliver all five (5) logo baskets and note cards to the Rose Room and place them on the table against the north wall.

COMPUTER ROOM:

Please create five (5) small Dusty Rose note cards to read as follows:

Compliments of:
Dick, Dixie, Matt & Barbara

Charge of $1.00 per note card to apply.

366

The Tall Timber Resort
Individual Banquet Event Order

BEO # 100149
As of: 6/13/2002
Contact: Mr. Samuel Adabei
The Tall Timber Contact: Julius Precise
Event:
Code: ARMCO
Billing: General account

Date: Thursday July 10, 2002
Group: ARMAR CORP.
Time: 8:00 AM - 12:00 Noon
Location: Rose Room
Function: Meeting
Count: 25 Customers

MEETING SET UP & AUDIO VISUAL REQUIREMENTS:

Room to be set according to diagram in a hollow square with 3' of space per person.
Two (2) skirted 6' tables are to be set against the south side wall. So far group made
no Audio Visual equipment request.

If any of the presenters request Audio Visual equipment, the charge is not to be billed
to the general account and should be an individual responsibility.

Coffee Service for 20 at 7:30 AM
Set buffet table on north wall according to diagram.

Menu
Coffee   Decaffeinated Coffee   Tea
Assorted Soft Drinks
Fruit Juices
The Tall Timber Resort Sparkling Water
Assorted Breakfast Pastries

Refresh at 9:30 AM and 11:00 AM, Remove at 12:00 noon.

$ 8.00 per person plus 17.5% service charge and 6% State Sales Tax .

The Tall Timber Resort
Individual Banquet Event Order

BEO #104884
As of: 6/13/2002
Contact: Mr. Samuel Adabei
The Tall Timber Contact: Julius Precise
Event:
Code: ARMCO
Billing: Individual responsibility

Date: Thursday July 10, 2002
Group: ARMAR CORP.
Time: 10:01 AM - 2:30 PM
Location: Blue Mountain Course
Function: Golf tee time
Count: 8 Customers

FOOD AND BEVERAGE:

All food & beverage charges (Halfway Houses & Beverage Carts) are an individual responsibilities.

RECREATION:

Golf tee times.

The following tee times have been reserved directly through the Starting Office, ext. 8001.

Two (2) tee times - 10:01 and 10:10am - Blue Mountain Course.

From this date until 30 days prior to your arrival,
you may cancel up to 20% of your starting times without penalty. A $200 per-starting-time fee will be billed if more than 20% of your times are cancelled.

From 30 days to 7 days prior to your arrival, you may cancel an additional 10% of your starting times without penalty. A $300 per-starting-time fee will be billed if more than 10% of your times are cancelled.

Less than 7 days prior to your arrival, you will be billed $400 for any cancelled or un-used starting times, less one gratis time per day.

To be certain clubs will be loaded on golf cart prior to play, it is imperative that central starting times receive first & last names of players & rental club requirements by 6:00 pm the day prior by calling (793) 778 1770, Fax (793) 778 1771.

368

The Tall Timbers Resort
Individual Banquet Event Order

BEO # 100150
As of 6/13/202
Contact: Mr. Samuel Adabei
The Tall Timber Contact: Julius Precise
Event:
Code: ARMCO
Billing: Individual responsibility

Date: Thursday, July 10, 2002
Group: ARMAR CORP.
Time: 12:34 PM - 5:00 PM
Location: Blue Mountain Course
Function: Golf tee time
Count: 20 Customers

FOOD AND BEVERAGE:

All food & beverage charges (Halfway Houses & Beverage Carts) are an individual responsibility.

RECREATION:

Golf tee times.

The following tee times have been reserved directly through the Starting Office, ext. 8001.

Five (5) Tee Times - 12:34, 12:43, 12:51, 1:00, 1:08 PM Blue Mountain Course.

From this date until 30 days prior to your arrival,
you may cancel up to 20% of your starting times without penalty. A $200 per-starting-time fee will be billed if more than 20% of your times are cancelled.

From 30 days to 7 days prior to your arrival, you may cancel an additional 10% of your starting times without penalty. A $300 per-starting-time fee will be billed if more than 10% of your times are cancelled.

Less than 7 days prior to your arrival, you will be billed $400 for any cancelled or un-used starting times, less one gratis time per day.

To be certain clubs will be loaded on golf cart prior to play, it is imperative that central starting times receive first & last names of players & rental club requirements by 6:00 pm the day prior by calling (793) 778 1770, Fax (793) 778 1771.

The Tall Timber Resort
Individual Banquet Event Order

BEO # 100151
As of: 7/24/2002
Contact: Mr. Samuel Adabei
The Tall Timber Contact: Julius Precise
Event:
Code: ARMCO
Billing: General Account

Date: Thursday July 10, 2002
Group: ARMAR CORP.
Time: 6:30 PM to 8:00 PM
Location: Jade Room
Function: Reception
Count: 65 Customers

BANQUET SET UP:

Set room with small cocktail tables Vanderbilt style.

FOOD:

Cold Canapés passed Butler Style:

Curried Chicken in Phyllo Cup with Toasted Coconut
Sliced Smoked Salmon with assorted Condiments and Party Rye
International Cheese Board with an Array of Fresh Fruit
Bruschetta with Oven Roasted Tomatoes & Eggplant

Hot: Hors d'Oeuvres passed Butler Style:

Warm Crab Meat Tartelettes
Sea Scallops wrapped with Bacon
Marinated Beef Fajita Kabobs

Also Include:

Two Iced Bowls of 50 Jumbo Gulf Shrimp

The Tall Timber Resort
Individual Banquet Event Order

BEO # 100156
As of: 7/24/2002
Contact: Mr. Samuel Adabei
The Tall Timber Contact: Julius Precise
Event:

Code: ARMCO
Billing: General Account

Date: Friday July 11, 2000
Group: ARMAR CORP.
Time: 6:00 PM -7:00 PM
Location: Greenhouse Patio
Alternate location: Silver Room
Function: Farewell Reception
Count: 45 Customers

ROOM SET UP:

Cocktail reception set up with cocktail tables Vanderbilt style. Two 8' skirted buffet tables in center of room.

FOOD:

Cold Canapés Buffet:

Platters of assorted smoked Seafood featuring Shrimp, Salmon, Scallops, and Trout with Horseradish Cream.
Smoked Pork Loin, Pepper, Onion and Corn Relish.
Baskets of assorted Breads including Pumpernickel, Seven-Grain and Sesame Lavash.

One Ice Centerpiece in the shape of a Book, surrounded by 150 Jumbo Shrimp.

Hot Hors d'Oeuvres Buffet:

Skewered Beef with Spicy Dipping Sauce
Marinated Vegetable Kabobs
Coconut crusted Chicken Tenderloins with Pineapple Salsa
Seared Sea Scallops on a Bed of Red Onion Marmalade
Brie Cheese with caramelized Pecans

Food charges $ 45.00 per person. $ 250.00 for ice piece and shrimp.
17.5% service charge and 6% State Sales Tax to be added.

BEVERAGES:

Open bar, premium brands only. Charge as consumed at hotel liquor price list.
17.5% service charge and 6% State Sales Tax to be added.

MUSIC: None.

371

The Tall Timber Resort
Individual Banquet Event Order

BEO #100157
As of: 7/24/2002
Contact: Mr. Samuel Adabei
The Tall Timber Contact: Julius Precise
Event:
Code: ARMCO
Billing: Room Account

Friday, July 11, 2002
Date: Friday July 11, 2000
Group: ARMAR CORP.
Time: 7:30 PM - 9:00 PM
Location: Clubhouse Grill
Function: Farewell Dinner
Count: 65 Customers

DINING ROOM MANAGER:

Dinner reservations have been made by the conference office. Please call the Dining Room Manager's office, ext. 8236 if any changes or special requests are necessary.

SEATING:

Open seating at adjacent tables.

SOMMELIER:

Please present one glass Moet Chandon brut, bin # 3004 when guests arrive. Open bar throughout the evening.

Charge General account.

The Tall Timber Resort
Individual Banquet Event Order

BEO #100158
As of: 7/24/2002
Contact: Mr. Samuel Adabei
The Tall Timber Contact: Julius Precise
Event:
Code: ARMCO
Billing: General Account

Date: Saturday, July 12, 2002
Group: ARMAR CORP.
Time: 8:00 AM to 10:00 AM
Location: Rose Room
Function: Ex.Committee Meeting
Count:12 Customers

ROOM SET UP:

As per diagram one oval conference table with 12 boardroom chairs, note pads, **The Tall Timber Resort** mineral water, and candies on table.

COFFEE SERVICE:

Provide on Sideboard Buffet at 7:30 AM

Menu

Carafes with assorted Juices

Smoked Salmon with Cream Cheese and toasted Bagels

Assorted Breakfast Pastries

Coffee   Decaffeinated Coffee   Tea

Charge $ 25.00 per person. 17.5% service charge and 6% State Sales Tax to be added.

Index of Menus

Subject Index

Recommended Books from C.H.I.P.S.

__	The Banquet Business	79.95
__	Exceptional Events	79.95
__	Food Equipment Facts	39.95
__	Larousse Gastronomique	60.00
__	Manual of Equipment & Design for the Foodservice Industry	79.95
__	Menuspell© Menu Terms Diskette	39.95
__	The Meat Buyers Guide	49.95
__	Repertoire de la Cuisine	17.95

For more information or to order please visit our website
www.chipsbooks.com

Prices subject to change

C.H.I.P.S. • 10777 Mazoch Road • Weimar • Texas • 78962 • Tel. 979 263 5683 • Fax 979 263 5685